THE NORTH AMERICAN AUTO INDUSTRY UNDER NAFTA

EDITED BY

SIDNEY WEINTRAUB AND

CHRISTOPHER SANDS

THE CSIS PRESS

Center for Strategic
and International Studies
Washington, D.C.

Significant Issues Series, Volume XX, Number 5
© 1998 by The Center for Strategic and International Studies
Washington, DC 20006
Printed on recycled paper in the United States of America

01   00   99   98   4   3   2   1

Library of Congress Cataloging-in-Publication Data

The North American auto industry under NAFTA / Sidney Weintraub
   and Christopher Sands, editors.
       p. cm. — (Significant issues series, ISSN 0736-7136 ; v. 20, no. 5)
   Includes bibliographical references and index.
   ISBN 0-89206-337-8 (alk. paper)
       1. Tariff on automobiles—North America.   2. Automobile industry
   and trade—North America.   3. Automobile industry and trade—
   United States.   4. Automobile industry and trade—Canada.
   5. Automobile industry and trade—Mexico.   6. Free trade—
   North America.   7. Canada. Treaties, etc. 1992 Oct. 7.   I. Weintraub,
   Sidney, 1922– .   II. Sands, Christopher.   III. Series.
   HF2651.A8N76   1998
   338.4'76292'097--dc21
                                                                98-42162
                                                                CIP

Cover design by Robert L. Wiser
Archetype Press, Washington DC

Contents

6

**Incomes and Productivity in the Auto Industry in
North America   221**

Sidney Weintraub

7

**The North American Auto Industry:
Where Do We Go from Here?   241**

Sidney Weintraub and Christopher Sands

Tables and Figures

Preface

The North American Free Trade Agreement was debated in the U.S. Congress and across the United States in late 1993. Despite its approval, NAFTA remains controversial in some quarters to this day. Nevertheless, now approaching five years of existence, NAFTA is a fact of life in North America and, therefore, has consequences.

In 1994, in *NAFTA: What Comes Next?* (Praeger/CSIS), Sidney Weintraub called for a follow-on strategy to build on the agreement and to manage the pressures it was sure to create. The challenge, as he saw it, was to consider the appropriate balance between efforts at "widening" the group of countries participating in liberalized trade through hemispheric trade negotiation and "deepening" the economic integration that would take place among the three NAFTA countries. Since then, analysts and scholars have paid close attention to the potential for a Free Trade Area of the Americas (FTAA). Less has been done to assess the process of economic integration within North America.

The issue is not trivial. Since NAFTA, Mexico has surpassed Japan to become the second largest trading partner of the United States, after Canada. Exports to Canada and Mexico account for one-third of total U.S. exports. Canada and Mexico each send more than 80 percent of their exports to the United States. Significantly, that trade is increasingly intra-industry in nature—that is, trade between companies on different sides of the border working together to manufacture a single product. Canada and Mexico are becoming more than U.S. trading partners—they are increasingly coproducers.

Nowhere is this phenomenon more visible than in the North American auto industry, which, for some time, has been the most integrated manufacturing sector in the region. The auto industry now accounts for 40 percent of North American trade. Automotive products are the largest component of all three bilateral trade relationships—and in each direction in all three cases.

With this in mind, the Center for Strategic and International Studies launched a detailed study of the North American auto industry. Our broad aim was to respond to two questions. First, how well is NAFTA working for the auto sector and what lessons can be drawn from this experience for future trade negotiations? And, second, what are the implications of an integrated industry for governments and the industry in North America in terms of policy, consultation, coordination, and harmonization? In addition, we wished to learn something about the larger phenomenon of continental economic integration from the experience of this key sector.

We discussed our ideas with many people who early on in the project offered advice and encouragement. In particular, we are grateful to David Cole and Michael Flynn of the Office for the Study of Automotive Transportation at the University of Michigan Transportation Research Institute; Marina Whitman of the University of Michigan; and James Womack, who codirected the International Motor Vehicle Project at the Massachusetts Institute of Technology.

In 1996, our research proposal won the support of key industry leaders. General Motors chairman, chief executive officer, and president Jack Smith joined with Joseph Gorman, chairman and CEO of the important automotive supplier TRW, Inc., to cochair the CSIS Task Force on Policy and the Competitiveness of the North American Auto Industry, which would sponsor the CSIS study. Ford Motor Company chairman, president, and CEO Alex Trotman and Chrysler Corporation chairman and CEO Bob Eaton agreed to join the Task Force. The other members of the Task Force, in addition to these four, are Curtis H. Barnette of Bethlehem Steel; Southwood J. Morcott of Dana Corporation; Stephen Hardis of Eaton Corporation; John B. Yasinsky of GenCorp, Inc.; Samir Gibara of Goodyear Tire and Rubber Company; Frank Macher of ITT Industries, Inc.; James H. Keyes of Johnson Controls, Inc.; Victor A. Rice of LucasVarity; Kenneth L. Way of Lear Corporation; Lee Gardner of MascoTech Inc.; Larry D. Yost of Meritor, Inc.; Raymond LeBoeuf of PPG Industries, Inc.; and Thomas E. Evans of Tenneco Automotive. We are grateful for the support of these individuals and their companies, but their support should not be construed as an endorsement of all the contents of this volume, responsibility for which rests with the authors themselves.

The Task Force cochairmen, Mr. Smith and Mr. Gorman, made an additional important contribution to the initiative by involving two of their top executives in the planning phase of the project. Special thanks are due to Harry Pearce, GM's vice chairman, and Bill Lawrence, TRW's executive vice president for planning and development, each of whom sat down with Chris Sands early on to work through the project plan and operationalize key details.

The research presented here was informed by the constructive comments of many other thoughtful people within the sponsor group, who saw chapter drafts and provided the authors with a private-sector perspective on the work. They helped to shape the initial research agenda, focused on the effects of NAFTA, and suggested additional topics for further inquiry. We are indebted to these individuals for their gracious contributions of time and insight. Specifically, we want to thank Stephen Donches of Bethlehem Steel; W. Van Bussmann of Chrysler Corporation; Edward McNeal of Dana Corporation; John Hushen and James P. Meil at Eaton Corporation; Martin Zimmerman, William Kelly, and Rod Seib at Ford Motor Company; Marc Watson and Eric Schwartz at GenCorp, Inc.; George Peapples, Mustafa Mohatarem, and Jeanne Dangerfield Pryce at General Motors Corporation; Isabel Jasinowski at Goodyear Tire and Rubber Company; James Mallak at ITT Industries; Stacy Fox at Johnson Controls, Inc.; Timothy Williams at LucasVarity; Leslie Touma at Lear Corporation; Henry Thiele and Neil DeKoker at MascoTech, Inc.; Raymond Garcia of Rockwell International and Jerry Rush of Meritor Automotive (formerly Rockwell Automotive); Blaine Boswell and John Reichenbach at PPG Industries, Inc.; Theodore Austell of Tenneco Automotive; and James Christy, Dennis Haggerty, and Michael Schilling at TRW.

A number of other persons played key roles in developing this project. Former deputy secretary of state Clifton Wharton provided advice from his vantage as a member of the Ford Motor Company Board of Directors. Homer Neal, a member of the CSIS Board of Trustees and physics professor at the University of Michigan, and Marvin Parnes, assistant vice president for research at the University of Michigan, spent considerable time with us in getting the project off the ground, and Dr. Neal continues to advise as we proceed. Gordon P. Street Jr., of North American Royalties (which owns Wheland Foundry, an automotive supplier based in Chattanooga, Tennessee) was gracious with his time and candid advice to us throughout the first phase of the project. Donald Beall of Rockwell International and Dana Mead of Tenneco lent their support to the project at key points. Heinz

Prechter of ASC, Inc. offered his valuable insights as we developed the initial research agenda.

At CSIS, Ambassador Anne Armstrong, chairman of the CSIS Board of Trustees and a longtime member of the General Motors Board of Directors, offered advice, invaluable introductions, and warm encouragement. Ambassador David Abshire, CSIS cofounder, president, and CEO, gave generously of his time and helped us recruit the participation of industry leaders.

Like all large initiatives, this one began as a small idea. For 14 months, it was a concept that developed over coffee in Washington and evolved in further discussions in Detroit, Ann Arbor, and East Lansing. Georges Fauriol, senior fellow and director of the Americas Program at CSIS, was involved in discussing the substantive issues with us from the beginning, and his strategic counsel and support continue to help us to realize our goals for this project.

This book has come together over many months thanks to the hard work of many people to whom we are very grateful. We want to thank our authors, who have delivered multiple drafts and responded to comments and constructive criticism from all quarters. We benefit from having the assistant director of the Americas Program at CSIS, Joyce Hoebing, on our team. Her management skill, budget expertise, editing experience, and generally sound advice have been a great asset to the project. We appreciate the hard work of the CSIS publications department, especially Roberta Howard, Mary Marik, and Jim Dunton.

Finally, with so many people involved, it must be acknowledged that this book and this project would not have come together without the assistance of a number of talented interns at CSIS, Mason Barlow, Siddarth Sudhir, and Diana Wiss, who at different times provided research and administrative support to the project. They worked with our authors, assisted with our own research, and helped to make the project possible through their impressive energy and talent.

SIDNEY WEINTRAUB
CHRISTOPHER SANDS
Washington, DC

1

The North American Auto Industry since NAFTA: Introduction

Sidney Weintraub and Christopher Sands

The North American Free Trade Agreement (NAFTA), which entered into effect on January 1, 1994, was the culmination of a series of bold decisions taken by the governments of the United States, Mexico, and Canada to foster the integration of their economies. The United States and Canada had entered into a free trade agreement starting in 1989, and their bilateral trade was already substantial prior to NAFTA. So was U.S.-Mexico trade, but at a much lower level. NAFTA not only removed many trade barriers, but also institutionalized the integration of economic activity in North America that had begun much earlier, particularly in the automotive industry.

The auto industry is at the heart of NAFTA. Motor vehicles and their parts are the most traded items between the United States and Canada, between the United States and Mexico, and between Mexico and Canada. If any single sector can provide a measure of NAFTA's performance, it is the auto industry.

U.S. firms invested in Mexico and Canada to manufacture automobiles there in the first two decades of the twentieth century. The auto industries in the three countries were therefore linked by common ownership, and this meant that technology, the organization of production, and even systems for marketing and distribution were comparable from the beginning, particularly between Canada and the United States. Industrial and trade policies in Canada and Mexico were designed to promote national economic development and led manufacturers to structure their investments in these countries to form miniature industries sufficient to supply only local demand. This policy was replaced in Canada after the 1965 Canada-United States Automotive Products Trade Agreement, or Auto Pact, that allowed greater numbers of imported vehicles and components from the United States. The integration of Mexico into this arrangement was completed by NAFTA.

Mexico unilaterally structured its domestic auto industry with the promulgation of a series of automotive decrees (the first of which was issued in 1962, the last in 1990). These decrees divided the market into segments, awarding rights to manufacturers to build classes of vehicles based on size. Only the Mexican domestic market, however, was circumscribed by the automotive decrees. Manufacture for export was encouraged by the Mexican government, and considerable investment was made in *maquiladora* (in-bond manufacturing) plants, typically owned by U.S. firms, which used Mexican labor to produce and finish products that were then sent to the United States for incorporation in the final assembly process.

NAFTA revised the rules for trade in automotive goods with both Canada and Mexico, creating a phased movement to a single regime with a consolidated set of rules to govern that trade. The 1989 Canada-U.S. Free Trade Agreement (CUFTA) revisions to the Auto Pact were brought into the North American agreement; and the rule of origin that operated for U.S.-Canada trade in the auto sector was changed to count Mexican content as North American and to raise the level of content required for eligibility for NAFTA tariff treatment. Mexico, for its part, agreed to phase out the application of the automotive decree system, and *maquiladora* rules were altered to permit these plants to serve the Mexican domestic market. A more detailed consideration of the effect of NAFTA on each of the three countries' domestic segments of the industry is included in separate chapters in this volume, but from this short review the significance of NAFTA for the integration of production in this sector may already be perceived.

Countries enter into economic integration arrangements, whether free-trade areas or customs unions, so as to take maximum advantage of specialization and economies of scale. There obviously are political motives as well; one such example was the desire of the founders of the European Community to reduce the hostility between France and Germany that had led to successive wars between them. What follows focuses on the economic aspects of NAFTA, or, more precisely, the automotive aspects of that agreement.

When the products produced in any one country face no competition in a second country, there is no compelling reason to seek out economic integration between the two. In such a case, there is little reason for protection in the importing country in the first place. It makes little sense for the United States to impose protective barriers against, say, coffee imports from Mexico because there is no U.S. coffee production to protect. Similarly, Mexico would have no reason to impose import barriers against wide-bodied U.S. aircraft because these are not produced in Mexico.

When the products produced across national boundaries are similar, however, a basis for national protection exists. Yet, as the United States learned under the Articles of Confederation, protection by the initial 13 states was inefficient. The U.S. Constitution instead established what today would be called a customs union precisely to permit unfettered movement of goods and services. Today, few products are produced completely in any one U.S. state, but rather parts, designs, and components move freely across state lines. This intra-industry trade, based on production in many localities, is taken for granted within the United States. A U.S. automobile is produced not just in Michigan, but in Ohio and many other locations as well. This type of trade encourages different specialties to develop in a variety of locations. An automobile, after all, is made up of thousands of components, and there is ample scope for specific concentrations in many locations.

The idea of NAFTA, and CUFTA before that, is to expand the scope of this specialization to all of North America. In the case of the United States and Canada, this was preceded by the aforementioned Auto Pact. U.S.-Canada two-way trade in motor vehicles and parts has exploded since then, from $73 *million* in 1964 to $88.4 *billion* in 1997. (All dollar figures in this volume are U.S. dollars, unless otherwise specified.) NAFTA expands this regionalization south to Mexico.

The purpose of specialization is to increase competitiveness, without which the U.S. auto industry could not survive, even in its home market. The U.S. market is large, but rates of growth in the auto industry are rising faster in emerging countries than in the United States. To be competitive, plants of a sufficient size generally are necessary in order to achieve economies of scale; and this, in turn, requires specialization. The North American scope of this specialization is made possible in the assembly of cars and trucks by the fact that the Big Three auto producers (Chrysler, Ford, and General Motors, or GM) operate in all three countries. The nature of this production and trade is set forth in much detail in the various chapters of this publication. So, too, is the production of parts necessary for this assembly and for after-market replacement parts.

Table 1.1
**Real Gross Domestic Product (GDP) of the
North American Economies, 1992–1997**
(annual percentage change)

Country	1992	1993	1994	1995	1996	1997
Canada	0.9	2.5	3.9	2.2	1.2	3.8
Mexico	3.6	2.0	4.5	-6.2	5.2	7.0
United States	2.7	2.3	3.5	2.0	2.8	3.8

Source: International Monetary Fund 1998.

It is still early to pass final judgment on the success of NAFTA overall. But it is fair to say that the auto industry is becoming more efficient in North America because the assemblers and the many parts producers have been able to organize more efficiently thanks to integration encouraged by NAFTA. In fact, the health of the North American auto industry overall has been quite good in the years since NAFTA.

The Health of the North American Auto Industry

The health of the North American auto industry owes much to the strength of the U.S. economy. All three countries experienced growth in real gross domestic product (GDP) in 1994, after which growth rates slowed, and in Mexico's case plummeted, in 1995 (see table 1.1). For Mexico, this depression was directly related to the devaluation of the peso in December 1994, followed by full-blown restructuring in 1995. The Mexican economy recovered rapidly in 1996 and 1997. In Canada, the slowdown in growth after 1994 has been persistent. The U.S. growth rate has been similar to Canada's during the past several years.

Retail sales of both passenger cars and light trucks in the United States have outperformed the 1992 level in every year since (see table 1.2). Canadian passenger car sales gained in 1994, but then fell in 1995 and 1996. Light-truck sales have been more robust in Canada, growing almost every year since 1992. Domestic sales of passenger cars and light trucks fell sharply in Mexico in 1995 as a result of the economic decline, recovered somewhat in 1996 as the economy rebounded, and were robust in 1997.

As shown in table 1.3, production levels in Canada and Mexico did not fluctuate as sharply. This is in part because U.S. demand remained strong enough to absorb vehicles produced there, and trade barriers had been liberalized sufficiently to allow manufacturers to ship products from Canada and Mexico to the U.S. market.

For 1997 to date, retail sales of passenger vehicles and light trucks have been strong in both Canada and Mexico. This rebound is prolonging what has been a healthy period for the auto industry in North America.

The Auto Industry in the United States

In the United States, the persistently strong economy has boosted both sales and profits for manufacturers, which in turn has allowed them to reorganize worldwide operations, amass capital, and expand their operations overseas. In critical emerging markets such as Eastern Europe, Russia, Latin America, China, and Southeast Asia, the U.S.-headquartered assemblers and Tier One suppliers are establishing market share.

A sense of the strength of the U.S. industry was conveyed by the Office of the U.S. Trade Representative in the summer of 1997, when it reported to Congress that

- U.S. employment in the automotive industry [since NAFTA] grew by 14.1 percent overall, with an increase of 16.1 percent in the auto parts sector and of 10.1 percent in the motor vehicle assembly sector

- U.S. productivity in the automotive industry grew by 7 percent between 1993 and 1995

- hourly earnings for production workers grew by 5.6 percent between 1993 and 1996 (Office of the United States Trade Representative 1997, 46).

In chapter 2 of this volume, American University professor Jonathan Doh concludes that the U.S. segment of the North American auto industry has benefited from NAFTA based on an examination of preliminary data that show growth in total trade (both imports and exports), healthy output and capacity utilization (suggesting no underemployment of U.S. production capabilities in favor of lower-cost Mexican facilities), and continued growth in auto industry investment in the United States (indicating the continued competitiveness of the U.S. industry and the U.S. workforce).

Table 1.2
Passenger Car and Light Truck Sales in North America, 1992–1997

Passenger Car Sales	1992	1993	1994	1995	1996	1997
Canada	797,922	739,051	748,697	671,818	660,765	739,926
Mexico	445,311	398,744	415,650	115,091	200,561	303,577
United States	8,210,627	8,519,573	8,991,347	8,635,557	8,529,124	8,289,413
Total	9,453,860	9,657,368	10,155,694	9,422,466	9,390,450	9,332,916
Light Truck Sales*						
Canada	412,226	431,837	483,548	465,176	518,939	654,310
Mexico	258,870	204,323	212,078	68,715	133,361	184,882
United States	4,674,589	5,398,491	6,097,787	6,130,411	6,611,099	6,871,093
Total	5,345,685	6,034,651	6,793,413	6,664,302	7,263,399	7,710,285

Source: Automotive News 1998 Market Data Book 1998.
* Canada figures include some heavy trucks; Mexico figures include tractor trailers and buses.

Table 1.3
Passenger Car and Light Truck Production in North America, 1992–1997

Passenger Car Production	1992	1993	1994	1995	1996	1997
Canada	1,034,197	1,348,350	1,211,428	1,338,517	1,288,676	1,375,814
Mexico	778,413	835,079	839,939	698,028	797,680	854,809
United States	5,659,323	5,988,534	6,609,523	6,326,700	6,055,939	5,922,205
Total	7,471,933	8,171,963	8,660,890	8,363,245	8,142,295	8,152,828
Light Truck Production						
Canada	935,505	890,517	1,069,244	1,091,803	1,109,034	1,205,828
Mexico	274,994	219,901	240,818	231,866	413,615	483,193
United States	4,116,642	4,901,548	5,707,176	5,577,515	5,658,812	6,129,982
Total	5,327,141	6,011,966	7,039,797	6,861,954	7,181,461	7,819,003

Source: Automotive News 1998 Market Data Book 1998.

Doh carefully analyzes the impact of the peso devaluation on the North American auto industry and finds that the Mexican devaluation had an adverse effect on the industry, but that the damage done to the growth of the Mexican domestic consumer market for new vehicles was at least partially offset by the fact that NAFTA permitted output intended for Mexico to be redirected to satisfy strong demand in the United States and Canada. This diversion of Mexican output to the U.S. market prevented larger assembly losses and represents a key element of flexibility in the post-NAFTA environment.

Doh also notes that despite the phased elimination of Mexican protectionism embodied in Mexico's automotive decree system, rationalization of production has generated significant cost reductions within the Mexican segment of the industry, which have benefited U.S. manufacturers. As indicated above, the domestic automotive market in Mexico has recovered, as Mexico's economy recovered, and in the first nine months of 1997, wholesale sales nationally from domestic production increased to 224,744 units from 151,418 in the same period of 1996; domestic sales from imports over the same nine-month period rose from 55,060 in 1996 to 82,989 in 1997. Export sales from Mexico over this period remained more or less constant (Grupo Financiero Bancomer 1997, 49–64).

The U.S. automotive parts industry has faced growing imports from Canada and, in particular, from Mexico since NAFTA. Doh observes that this growth in imports has taken place while total exports of U.S.-originated parts and components to the other two NAFTA countries have remained flat or fallen. Doh also notes, however, that U.S. parts have achieved higher export sales to non-NAFTA markets since 1994, suggesting that trade substitution, rather than trade destruction, may be taking place.

The U.S. tariff on light trucks has protected automakers headquartered in the United States from foreign competition in this highly profitable market segment. In addition, consumer preferences for trucks, minivans and sport-utility vehicles have resulted in a lower average fuel economy rating for the mix of vehicles purchased in the United States in each of the last five years. Should fuel prices rise suddenly, the current model mix could prove vulnerable to a sudden change in consumer preferences, forcing a reallocation of production among models that would be a costly shock to the Big Three—but which, due to the truck tariff, would have a smaller impact on the operations of Asian and European companies.

The Auto Industry in Canada

In chapter 3, Queen's University professors Pradeep Kumar and John Holmes point out that the proximity of Canadian manufacturing facilities (for both assembly and supply) to the main concentration of automotive plants in the United States has proved to be a decisive advantage within the current system of lean production favored by firms in the auto industry. Inventory and logistics management on a "just-in-time" basis and the industry's dependency on land transportation for the shipment of components and even finished vehicles make location a key element in the determination of sourcing and production. In effect, the flexibility gained by having a facility nearby can compete against other elements of cost, such as lower wages, as companies assign production within the integrated North American industry.

Mexico is shipping more automotive goods (parts and finished vehicles) to Canada since NAFTA, but Kumar and Holmes believe this is part of the growth in total trade and has no adverse effect on the Canadian share of the North American industry.

As we consider the medium term for the Canadian segment of the industry, the aggressive use of trade policy by the Canadian federal government to leverage investment in the auto sector from foreign-owned assemblers and suppliers may be significant. Unilateral tariff elimination by Canada has benefited Asian assemblers by permitting them to source some components competitively from across the Pacific. Additionally, recent Canadian interest in pursuing trade liberalization with Brazil and other countries in the MERCOSUR trading group could result in an agreement that would make Canada a preferred location for investment by manufacturers of certain automotive components who wish to supply customers in both North and South America from a single facility.

The Auto Industry in Mexico

In chapter 4, Mexican economist and economic consultant Rogelio Ramírez de la O considers the impact of NAFTA on Mexico's segment of the continental auto sector. Ramírez identifies macroeconomic stability as the major necessity for the growth of Mexican auto suppliers. Mexico's automotive components industry has become stronger over the years and now employs more Mexicans than do the major assemblers. From 1987 to 1994, Ramírez observes, employment in the parts industry trebled.

The auto industry is Mexico's largest exporter, generating more foreign exchange revenue than oil or tourism. While employment in the Mexican segment of the North American auto industry is positively related to growth in domestic sales, it is also closely linked to export sales to the United States and, to a modest extent, to Canada. According to Ramírez, the strong performance of the U.S. economy has been the main contributor to the growth in Mexican automotive exports. His study finds that Mexican exports of auto-related products grew 6.6 times the rate of growth of the U.S. GDP in the period since 1990.

The relationship between wages and productivity is changing in the auto sector in Mexico. Ramírez demonstrates that productivity improved more quickly than wages in the 1980s, but more recent evidence suggests that wages are gradually becoming more responsive to productivity gains, although there is not yet a firm relationship between the two. Auto industry employment is also growing now that the crisis of 1995 is over, despite the growth in wages. This result is based on preliminary data and may not be sustained in the future; nevertheless, it is an important observation that merits further investigation.

The future of the domestic market for automotive products in Mexico depends on the country's overall economic growth and distribution of income. The expectation of overall growth and the establishment of a middle class was the lure that attracted the auto companies to Mexico in the first instance when the market was highly protected and regulated. This limited imports from outside. NAFTA has changed part of the equation and will do so increasingly as import liberalization is fully phased in. For some aspects of the industry, the attraction of low wages is significant but should not be overstated. The auto assemblers have not, on the whole, opted for a production strategy of high labor usage and low use of capital, but rather have been constructing state-of-the art plants. The lure of a growing domestic market remains strong.

NAFTA, however, has permitted the establishment of a more sophisticated strategy of specialization. This takes the form not only of setting up specialized plants that can serve the domestic Mexican market as well as the North American market, but also of concentrating the production of different models in the three countries of North America. Looked at broadly, the development has been to focus primarily on sport utility vehicles in Canada; large and medium-sized cars, sport utility vehicles, and light trucks in the United States; and smaller cars in Mexico. This Mexican specialization was implicit in the NAFTA agreement under which the U.S. producers could meet their CAFE (U.S. corporate average fuel economy) requirements from Mexican production.

The strategy relies heavily on differentiated production. It is worth repeating, however, that the success of this strategy is predicated on a growing domestic market in Mexico for automotive products—a market that is expected to grow more rapidly there than in either Canada or the United States, where the demand is based largely on consumer replacement of existing vehicles.

Environmental Regulation and the Auto Industry

The preliminary evidence presented by John Kirton of the University of Toronto in chapter 5 shows a trend in the automotive sector in the three NAFTA countries toward "upward" convergence, that is, to higher levels of environmental protection. Growing public pressure is fueling the movement toward tougher standards in Canada and the United States and increasingly in Mexico; and the process of integration and rationalization in the auto industry is exerting pressure for harmonization of production methods and standards.

Despite these positive developments, Kirton warns that the proliferation of standards at the subnational level in the United States and Canada fragments the market and thereby counters and slows progress toward standards harmonization among the three countries. In addition, NAFTA established two bodies that are particularly relevant in the automotive sector—a tri-national Committee on Standards-Related Measures, which embodies a Land Transportation Subcommittee, and a North American Automotive Standards Council—and charged each to put together a work plan for the harmonization of emission standards by January 1997. Neither group has yet produced such a plan. Kirton also notes that Mexico has not been an active participant in discussions between officials in the United States and Canada on the diffusion of technology for pollution measurement, control, and prevention.

Kirton's analysis leads to recommendations for improving environmental policy coordination in North America. Specifically, Kirton recommends that each country make serious efforts to curtail the establishment of subnational standards and that Mexico take steps to integrate itself into the tri-national consultative bodies working on environmental matters. He proposes further legitimation of the post-NAFTA process of environmental policy harmonization through a focus on science and technological cooperation—in effect, a deliberate depoliticization of the harmonization process.

Incomes and Productivity

Automotive assemblers and suppliers in all three countries have improved productivity in the 1990s, in part through new capital investments and the application of technology but also through upgrading worker training and skills, particularly in Mexico. In chapter 6, Sidney Weintraub offers a preliminary assessment of the trends in both areas since NAFTA came into effect. The evidence, though limited, suggests that Mexican incomes have not kept up with improvements in productivity, due largely to the economic crisis and devaluation in 1994-1995. Weintraub finds no evidence of erosion in incomes in the United States or Canada, while the productivity of facilities in both countries continues to improve overall. But policymakers and others using either factor as a NAFTA yardstick face a serious problem, and that is the lack of data. Weintraub notes that in many important sectors of the economy the three countries do not record or distribute comparable figures, which creates an unnecessary handicap for decisionmakers in and out of the three governments.

Researching the North American Auto Industry: NAFTA and Beyond

We began at CSIS to look carefully at this sector in the context of continental economic integration because the auto industry is central to North American economic relations. In addition, the situation that exists today is still relatively new. The United States and Canada have long had free trade in this sector, whereas Mexico, until NAFTA, had a highly protected industry. The substantive and policy implications of this new arrangement are not yet fully clear. How will policymakers pursue their policy objectives without doing coincidental damage to the complex web of relationships necessary to the rationalized design, production, and marketing of vehicles on a continental scale? How does policy made in one of the three countries affect the competitiveness of an industry so critical to all three? The closing chapter of this volume, chapter 7, looks ahead to the future and to the questions that these analyses raised in our minds about the implications of integration for policymakers (and automakers) in North America.

Bibliography

Automotive News 1998 Market Data Book. 1998. Detroit, Mich.: Crain Communications, Inc.

Competitiveness of the North American Auto Industry. 1992. Report of the U.S.-Canada Automotive Select Panel. June.

Grupo Financiero Bancomer. 1997. *Economic Report*. November-December.

Holmes, John. 1996. Restructuring in a Continental Production System. In *Canada and the Global Economy*, edited by John N. H. Britton. Montreal: McGill-Queen's University Press.

International Monetary Fund (IMF). 1998. *World Economic Outlook*. (Washington, D.C.: IMF. May.

Office of the United States Trade Representative. 1997. *Study on the Operation and Effect of the North American Free Trade Agreement*. Washington, D.C.: Government Printing Office.

———. *Potential Impact on the U.S. Economy and Selected Industries of the North American Free Trade Agreement*. 1993. Washington, D.C.: Government Printing Office.

Stokes, Bruce. 1995. The Automotive Sector. In *The Future of the U.S.-E.U.-Japan Triad: How Dominant? How Interdependent? How Divergent?* edited by John Yochelson. Washington, D.C.: Center for Strategic and International Studies.

Strauss, William A. 1997. Auto Industry Cruises On. In *Chicago Fed Letter*. No. 121. Chicago: Federal Reserve Bank of Chicago. September.

Taylor, Glen. 1993. Strategic Manpower Policies and International Competitiveness: The Case of Mexico. In *Driving Continentally: National Policies and the North American Auto Industry*, edited by Maureen Appel Molot. Ottawa: Carleton University Press.

United States International Trade Commission. 1996. *Production Sharing: Use of U.S. Components and Materials in Foreign*

Assembly Operations. Washington, D.C.: Government Printing Office. May.

Weintraub, Sidney. 1997. *NAFTA at Three: A Progress Report*. Washington, D.C.: Center for Strategic and International Studies.

Womack, James P. 1991. A Positive Sum Solution: Free Trade in the North American Motor Vehicle Sector. In *Strategic Sectors in Mexican-U.S. Free Trade*, edited by M. Delal Baer and Guy F. Erb. Washington, D.C.: Center for Strategic and International Studies.

2

The Impact of NAFTA on the Auto Industry in the United States

Jonathan P. Doh

The North American Free Trade Agreement, entered into force on January 1, 1994, has resulted in significant changes in the North American economic landscape. It has drawn the economies of the region closer together and fostered an environment in which industries have been forced to adjust and adapt to new competitive conditions. The automotive industry, which constitutes more than 40 percent of North American trade, has a particularly important stake in NAFTA because of its large share of intra-North American trade and its importance to the individual economies of the United States, Canada, and Mexico. This chapter presents basic economic and trade data on trends in the North American automotive industry and preliminary analyses of the causes and consequences of those trends.

The chapter is also designed to stimulate further research in areas related to NAFTA and auto trade and concludes with suggestions for such inquiry, especially in the areas of intra-industry integration, productivity, and future treatment of automotive products under NAFTA accession and negotiations on a Free Trade Area of the Americas. A statistical appendix explains the various data sets used in the chapter and references other data sets in use by other organizations.

Key NAFTA Provisions Affecting Automotive Trade

NAFTA contains important provisions affecting automotive trade, including the elimination of tariffs on cars and trucks, rules of origin that specify which products will qualify for preferential tariff treatment, and a work program to harmonize automotive standards.[1] The most important provisions are contained in annex 300-A to chapter 3 of the agreement (U.S. Government 1994). This annex specifies the process and schedule for the reduction and elimination of the national value-added and trade-balancing requirements of Mexico's *Decreto para el Fomento y Modernización de la Industria Automotriz* ("Auto Decree").

Tariffs and Import Restrictions

Under NAFTA, Mexico reduced its 20 percent duty on automobiles to 10 percent upon entry into force of the agreement. The remaining tariff of 10 percent will be phased out over a period of 5 years for light trucks and 10 years for cars, making the tariff 8 percent in 1995, 6 percent in 1996, 4 percent in 1997, 2 percent in 1998, and 0 percent in 1999. Tariffs on 75 percent of auto parts (now at 10–20 percent) are eliminated within 5 years. The remaining tariffs on auto parts are eliminated in 10 years.

For imports from Mexico to the United States, the 2.5 percent tariff on automobiles and the tariff on parts (averaging 3.1 percent) were eliminated on January 1, 1994, and the tariff on light trucks was cut from 25 percent to 10 percent when the agreement entered into force, with the remaining tariff reduced by a quarter each year until 1998 (1995: 7.5 percent, 1996: 5 percent, 1997: 2.5 percent, 1998: 0 percent), when it will be eliminated. (Most automotive products traded between the United States and Canada were already duty free as a result of the tariff elimination schedule under the U.S.-Canada Free Trade Agreement, or CUFTA.)[2]

Changes to Mexico's Automotive Decree

NAFTA requires Mexico to make substantial changes to its Auto Decree, phasing out many of the most restrictive provisions of the decree with respect to North American automotive trade. Although the 1989 Auto Decree, which was the fifth in a series of auto decrees put in place beginning in 1962, substantially liberalized Mexican rules governing the automotive industry, it was nonetheless a significant impediment to U.S. exports of parts and vehicles to Mexico and to the ability of the North American automotive industry to rationalize and restructure. In particular, the national value-added and trade-balancing requirements forced producers to build small, inefficient plants with short productions runs if they wanted to sell vehicles in Mexico, because the requirements severely impeded exports from the United States to Mexico, making investment in Mexico the only viable mode of entry.

NAFTA requires that all provisions of the Auto Decree be brought into conformity with the agreement by 2004. During the transition period, the trade balancing requirement, which had mandated that assemblers maintain a positive trade balance of two units for every one unit of value in new vehicles, will be reduced as a result of two separate but related procedures. First, in calculating the trade balance, the assembler will be required to include only a percentage of the imported parts and components in vehicles sold in Mexico, rather than the entire amount. For 1994, the percentage was 80 percent; it will be reduced to 55 percent in 2003, after which it will be eliminated. At the same time, the limitation on annual imports of new vehicles as a share of vehicles sold in Mexico will be reduced and then eliminated. In 1994, the percentage was 80 percent, so that the extended trade balance was divided by 0.8 instead of 2. The 36 percent national value-added requirement dropped to 34 percent from 1994 to 1998 and then drops one percentage point each year until 2004, when it is eliminated. The national value-added requirement for the auto parts industry and "national suppliers" is reduced from 30 percent to 20 percent. A *maquiladora* can now qualify as a national supplier, provided that it is not owned by the assembler that it is supplying.

Other Provisions

The ownership restrictions on enterprises of the auto parts industry are eliminated for investors of Canada and the United States and their Mexican subsidiaries by 1999. The restriction on the sale of *maquiladora* production into the Mexican market is eliminated over seven years, with up to 60 percent of production permitted to be sold from *maquiladora* into the Mexican market the first year, growing to 85 percent in the sixth year, with the restrictions removed in the seventh.

Mexico is required to immediately eliminate the Auto Decree that covers large trucks and buses. Until 1999, however, Mexico may restrict the number of vehicles imported by assemblers to 50 percent of the number produced in Mexico and require the assembler to satisfy a 40 percent national value-added requirement. Mexico is also required to eliminate the import ban on used cars by 2009.

Rules of Origin

NAFTA rules of origin build on and enhance the rules contained in the 1989 U.S.-Canada Free Trade Agreement. Like CUFTA, the rules of origin pertaining to automotive products under NAFTA emphasize "substantial transformation" as the general criterion that qualifies a product for designation as originating in North America. Also like CUFTA, NAFTA employs a value content rule to determine origination. For passenger vehicles, light trucks, and their engines and transmissions, NAFTA imposes a requirement of 62.5 percent North American content, calculated on a "net cost" basis. For all other vehicles and parts, the threshold is 60 percent. Although both of these requirements are higher than the 50 percent content requirement in CUFTA, the NAFTA rules are broader and more inclusive than the CUFTA rules and are not directly analogous to the previous requirements. In particular, NAFTA resolves two specific problems encountered in the administration and enforcement of CUFTA rules, which together have the effect of expanding the scope of the rules' coverage.

First, NAFTA allows manufacturers to "trace" content back from final assembly, allowing for more accurate inclusion of the specific content of intermediate components and parts. Under CUFTA, these components were either "rolled up" (the entire value was counted toward the content requirement, even if the products barely originated) or "rolled back" (none of the value could be counted, even if the product barely missed the threshold). Second, NAFTA clearly states that "non-mortgage interest" is creditable toward the content requirement. Under CUFTA, "mortgage interest" could be included in the content calculation; however, the agreement was silent on non-mortgage interest, for example, interest paid on leased equipment. This issue was the subject of a CUFTA dispute settlement panel that generated considerable concern, especially in Canada.

CAFE Standards

NAFTA allows assemblers producing in Mexico before model year 1992 to count Mexican value added toward the corporate average fuel economy (CAFE) standards after 1997, provided that the vehicle is imported for sale into the United States and meets the 75 percent North American-content requirement. For manufacturers that initiated production of vehicles in Mexico after the 1991 model year, NAFTA provides for Mexican value added to be counted toward CAFE requirements either in the first model year after 1994 or from the date that the manufacturer initiated production.

North American Automotive Trade Post-NAFTA

This section discusses and presents tabular and graphic information on trade in passenger vehicles, trucks, and automotive parts
during the period 1992–1996. This period was chosen because it
captures trade flows during the two-year period preceding
NAFTA's implementation (1992–1993), the three-year period
following implementation (1994–1996), and the relevant years
before, during, and after the economic consequences of Mexico's
peso devaluation. (See the appendix for an explanation of the
statistics used.)

One objective of regional economic integration is to promote
specialization and increased inter- and intra-industry trade. One
simple way to measure this integration is to compare increases
in trade within the integration region with trade between the
region and the rest of the world. The tables in this section show
absolute levels of U.S. trade with the world, Canada, and Mexico; with NAFTA (Canada and Mexico); and with non-NAFTA
countries (trade with the world excluding Canada and Mexico).
The tables also show growth in trade with the world, Canada,
Mexico, NAFTA, and non-NAFTA countries as one way to measure the relative impact of economic integration within the
region as compared to integration with the rest of the world.
This phenomenon can be seen in the generally rising shares of
NAFTA trade as a percentage of U.S. trade with the world.

Overall Motor Vehicle Trade

Overall, North American motor vehicle trade, which includes
passenger vehicles, trucks, buses, used vehicles, chassis with
engines, and sport-utility vehicles (but not snowmobiles and
golf carts), increased throughout the period.

Exports.   From 1992 through 1996, U.S. motor vehicle exports to the world rose from $18.8 billion to $24.4 billion, or
nearly 30 percent (table 2.1). By comparison, exports to Canada
rose from $8.3 billion to $12.3 billion, or nearly 50 percent, and
exports to Mexico grew from $278 million to nearly $1.3 billion,
an increase of more than 350 percent. Overall, exports to North
America outpaced exports to the rest of the world by a significant margin, growing from $8.6 billion to $13.6 billion, a gain of
more than 58 percent, while exports to the rest of the world grew

Table 2.1
U.S. Motor Vehicle Exports to Canada, Mexico, and World,
1992–1996
(millions of $)

	1992	1993	1994	1995	1996	% Change 1992–1996
World	18,791	19,367	22,038	22,864	24,404	29.87%
Non-NAFTA[a]	10,214	9,918	9,932	10,911	10,820	5.93%
NAFTA[b]	8,577	9,449	12,106	11,953	13,584	58.38%
Mexico	278	195	683	394	1,265	355.04%
Canada	8,299	9,254	11,423	11,559	12,319	48.44%
NAFTA % of total exports	45.64%	48.79%	54.93%	52.28%	55.66%	

Source: U.S. Department of Commerce Office of Automotive Affairs as derived from Bureau of the Census Database using the Office of Automotive Affairs Product Dictionary (see appendix).
[a] U.S. exports to the world excluding Mexico and Canada.
[b] U.S. exports to Canada and Mexico.

from about $10.2 billion to $10.8 billion, a gain of just 6 percent, increasing the percentage of U.S. exports to North America as a share of total exports from about 46 percent to about 56 percent.

Imports. For 1992–1996, U.S. motor vehicle imports from the world rose from $57.1 billion to $79.7 billion, or nearly 40 percent (table 2.2). By comparison, imports from Canada rose from $22.5 billion to $33.7 billion, or nearly 50 percent, and imports from Mexico grew from $3.1 billion to $11.3 billion, an increase of more than 260 percent. Overall, imports from North America outpaced imports from the rest of the world by a significant margin: imports from Canada and Mexico grew from $25.7 billion to $45 billion, more than 75 percent, while imports from the rest of the world grew by about 10 percent, from $31.4 billion to $34.7 billion, increasing the percentage of U.S. imports from North America as a share of total imports from about 45 percent to 56 percent.

Table 2.2
U.S. Motor Vehicle Imports from Canada, Mexico, and
World, 1992–1996
(millions of $)

	1992	1993	1994	1995	1996	% Change 1992–1996
World	57,086	62,992	72,596	76,685	79,750	39.70%
Non-NAFTA[a]	31,434	32,496	36,850	35,485	34,731	10.49%
NAFTA[b]	25,652	30,496	35,746	41,200	45,019	75.50%
Mexico	3,109	3,727	4,787	7,829	11,305	263.62%
Canada	22,543	26,769	30,959	33,371	33,714	49.55%
NAFTA % of total exports	44.94%	48.41%	49.24%	53.73%	56.45%	

Source: U.S. Department of Commerce Office of Automotive Affairs as derived from Bureau of the Census Database using the Office of Automotive Affairs Product Dictionary (see appendix).
[a] U.S. imports from the world excluding Mexico and Canada.
[b] U.S. imports from Canada and Mexico.

Passenger Vehicles

Two-way trade in passenger vehicles, an important share of overall motor vehicle trade, was up sharply throughout the period.

Exports. U.S. exports of new passenger vehicles to the world rose from about $12.7 billion in 1992 to $15.2 billion in 1996, an increase of about 20 percent (table 2.3). Sales of new vehicles to Mexico grew from about $80 million to $835 million, an increase of over 940 percent, while sales of new vehicles to Canada rose from about $6 billion to $7.8 billion, an increase of about 30 percent. Overall, U.S. sales of new vehicles to Canada and Mexico combined grew from just over $6 billion to $8.6 billion, a rise of 42 percent, while sales to the rest of the world remained flat at about $6.6 billion in both 1992 and 1996, increasing the percentage of U.S. world exports received by Canada and Mexico from 48 percent to about 57 percent.

Table 2.3
U.S. New Passenger Vehicle Exports to Canada, Mexico,
and World, 1992–1996
(millions of $)

	1992	1993	1994	1995	1996	% Change 1992–1996
World	12,659	13,084	15,251	14,965	15,218	20.21%
Non-NAFTA[a]	6,587	6,582	7,148	7,412	6,585	-0.03%
NAFTA[b]	6,072	6,502	8,103	7,553	8,633	42.18%
Mexico	80	90	569	290	835	943.75%
Canada	5,992	6,412	7,534	7,263	7,798	30.14%
NAFTA % of total exports	47.97%	49.69%	53.13%	50.47%	56.73%	

Source: U.S. Department of Commerce Office of Automotive Affairs as derived from Bureau of the Census Database using the Office of Automotive Affairs Product Dictionary (see appendix).
[a] U.S. exports to the world excluding Mexico and Canada.
[b] U.S. exports to Canada and Mexico.

Imports.   Table 2.4 shows a similar story with respect to new passenger vehicle imports. Imports of new passenger vehicles globally were up 43 percent, growing from $46.7 billion to nearly $67 billion. Imports from Canada grew more than 75 percent, rising from $14.4 billion to $25.3 billion, while imports from Mexico were up over 200 percent, from $2.6 billion in 1992 to $7.9 billion in 1996. Imports from Canada and Mexico combined increased 95 percent from $17 billion in 1992 to 33.2 billion in 1996 while imports from the rest of the world rose just 13 percent from about $30 billion to about $33.8 billion, increasing the share of U.S. imports from Mexico and Canada as a percentage of global imports from 36 percent to almost 50 percent.

Units.   Overall, new passenger vehicle exports to the world, in units, grew from 901,839 in 1992 to 1,024,721 in 1996. U.S. passenger vehicle exports to Canada grew from 465,437 units in 1992 to 508,363 in 1996 (figure 2.1). Exports to Mexico grew from 4,270 units in 1992 to more than 51,000 units in 1996, more than a twelvefold increase (figure 2.2). Overall new passenger vehicle imports (units) grew from 3,615,467 in 1992 to 4,064,447 in 1996;

Table 2.4
U.S. New Passenger Vehicle Imports from Canada, Mexico, and World, 1992–1996
(millions of $)

	1992	1993	1994	1995	1996	% Change 1992–1996
World	46,729	52,208	61,367	64,526	66,916	43.20%
Non-NAFTA[a]	29,736	30,857	34,908	34,073	33,761	13.54%
NAFTA[b]	16,993	21,351	26,459	30,453	33,155	95.11%
Mexico	2,591	3,084	3,943	5,815	7,899	204.86%
Canada	14,402	18,267	22,516	24,638	25,256	75.36%
NAFTA % of total exports	36.37%	40.90%	43.12%	47.19%	49.55%	

Source: U.S. Department of Commerce Office of Automotive Affairs as derived from Bureau of the Census Database using the Office of Automotive Affairs Product Dictionary (see appendix).
[a] U.S. imports from the world excluding Mexico and Canada.
[b] U.S. imports from Canada and Mexico.

imports from Mexico grew from 266,149 to 550,622 units and from Canada, from 1,200,358 to 1,688,123 units (figures 2.3 and 2.4).

Trucks

Two-way trade in trucks was up sharply throughout the period, especially exports to and imports from Mexico.

Exports. U.S. exports of new passenger trucks to the world rose from about $3.3 billion in 1992 to $6.2 billion in 1996, an increase of about 90 percent (table 2.5). Sales of trucks to Mexico increased by more than 300 percent, growing from a small base of $87 million to more than $360 million. Sales of trucks to Canada were up more than 100 percent, rising from $1.9 billion in 1992 to nearly $3.8 billion in 1996. Overall, U.S. sales of trucks to Canada and Mexico combined were up more than 110 percent, growing from just under $2 billion to more than $4.1 billion, while sales to the rest of the world grew a more modest 57 percent, from $1.3 billion to just over $2 billion, increasing the percentage of total trade received by Canada and Mexico from 60 percent to 67 percent.

Figure 2.1
U.S. Exports of New Passenger Vehicles to Canada, 1992–1996
(units)

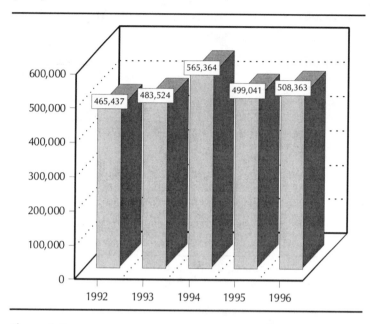

Figure 2.2
U.S. Exports of New Passenger Vehicles to Mexico, 1992–1996
(units)

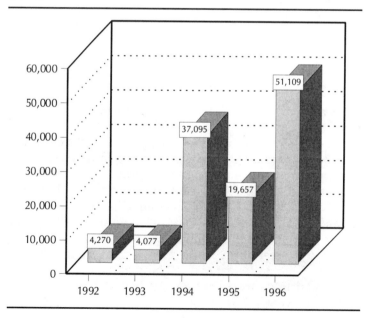

Figure 2.3
U.S. Imports of New Passenger Vehicles from Mexico, 1992–1996
(units)

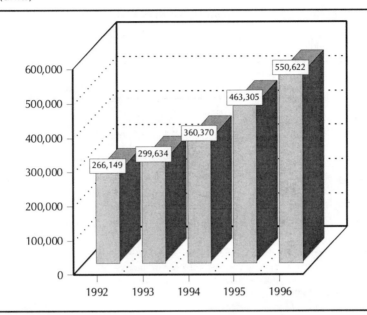

Figure 2.4
U.S. Imports of New Passenger Vehicles from Canada, 1992–1996
(units)

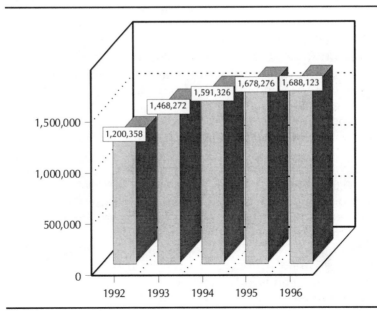

Table 2.5
U.S. New Truck Exports to Canada, Mexico, and World,
1992–1996
(millions of $)

	1992	1993	1994	1995	1996	% Change 1992–1996
World	3,273	3,741	4,680	5,198	6,193	89.21%
Non-NAFTA[a]	1,300	1,275	1,171	1,393	2,036	56.62%
NAFTA[b]	1,973	2,466	3,509	3,805	4,157	110.69%
Mexico	87	24	48	57	361	314.94%
Canada	1,886	2,442	3,461	3,748	3,796	101.27%
NAFTA % of total exports	60.28%	65.92%	74.98%	73.20%	67.12%	

Source: U.S. Department of Commerce Office of Automotive Affairs as derived from Bureau of the Census Database using the Office of Automotive Affairs Product Dictionary (see appendix).
[a] U.S. exports to world excluding Mexico and Canada.
[b] U.S. exports to Canada and Mexico.

Imports.   Table 2.6 shows an even more dramatic shift in import patterns for trucks. Imports of trucks globally were up 18 percent from $9.7 billion to $11.4 billion, while imports from Canada actually declined marginally from $7.7 billion to $7.6 billion. Imports from Mexico, on the other hand, shot up more than 590 percent, from $442 million to more than $3 billion. Non-NAFTA imports declined by half, from $1.6 billion to $800 million, while NAFTA imports grew from $8.1 billion to $10.6 billion, a rise of more than 30 percent, increasing the U.S. share of truck imports from Mexico and Canada as a percentage of global imports from 84 percent to almost 93 percent.

Units.   Overall, new truck exports to the world increased from 166,682 units in 1992 to 318,734 units in 1996. Exports to Canada of new trucks increased from 118,769 units in 1992 to 192,131 units in 1996 (figure 2.5). Exports to Mexico increased from 4,506 units in 1992 to 31,589 in 1996 (figure 2.6). Global imports of trucks actually decreased from 757,936 to 657,336 units in 1996. Imports from Canada declined from 532,213 units in 1992 to 403,300 units in 1996, while imports from Mexico grew from 24,424 units to 200,954 units (figures 2.7 and 2.8).

Table 2.6
U.S. New Truck Imports from Canada, Mexico, and World,
1992–1996
(millions of $)

	1992	1993	1994	1995	1996	% Change 1992–1996
World	9,688	9,997	10,180	11,079	11,432	18.00%
Non-NAFTA[a]	1,572	1,463	1,779	1,234	803	-48.92%
NAFTA[b]	8,116	8,534	8,401	9,845	10,629	30.96%
Mexico	442	543	643	1,773	3,055	591.18%
Canada	7,674	7,991	7,758	8,072	7,574	-1.30%
NAFTA % of total exports	83.77%	85.37%	82.52%	88.86%	92.98%	

Source: U.S. Department of Commerce Office of Automotive Affairs as derived from Bureau of the Census Database using the Office of Automotive Affairs Product Dictionary (see appendix).
[a] U.S. imports from the world excluding Canada and Mexico.
[b] U.S. imports from Canada and Mexico.

Parts

Trade in automotive parts presents a very different picture than trade in vehicles and trucks: U.S. exports to the world increased much faster than to North America throughout the period, while U.S. imports from Canada and Mexico grew more quickly than imports from elsewhere.

Exports. From 1992 through 1996, U.S. exports of automotive parts rose about 43 percent worldwide, from about $28.5 billion to more than $40.8 billion (table 2.7). Exports of parts to Mexico grew only about 8 percent from just over $6.5 billion to about $7 billion. Exports to Canada grew more quickly, up from $15.3 billion to almost $22.1 billion or about 45 percent. Exports to Mexico and Canada combined grew about 34 percent, up from $21.8 billion in 1992 to $29.1 billion in 1996. Sales to the rest of the world, however, grew nearly 75 percent, up from $6.7 billion in 1992 to $11.7 billion in 1996, causing a reduction in the share of U.S. world exports received by Canada and Mexico from about 77 percent to about 71 percent.

Figure 2.5
U.S. Exports of New Trucks to Canada, 1992–1996
(units)

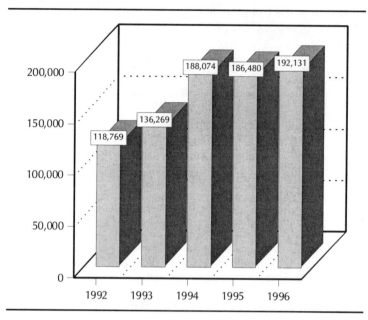

Figure 2.6
U.S. Exports of New Trucks to Mexico, 1992–1996
(units)

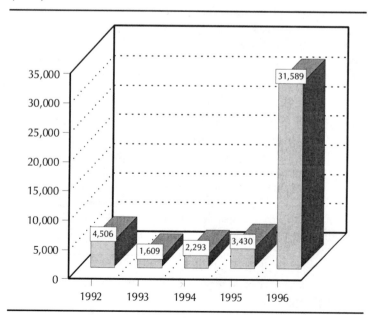

Figure 2.7
U.S. Imports of New Trucks from Canada, 1992–1996
(units)

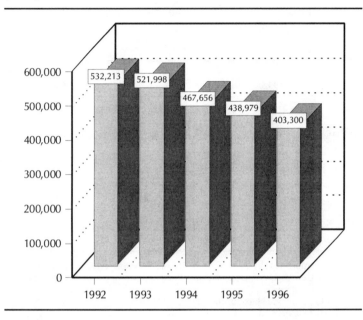

Figure 2.8
U.S. Imports of New Trucks from Mexico, 1992–1996
(units)

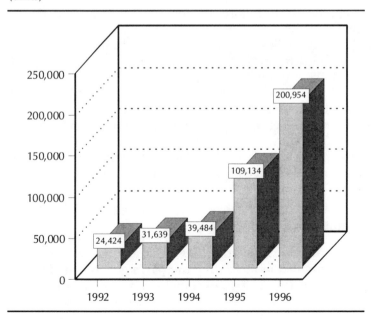

Table 2.7
U.S. Automotive Parts Exports to Canada, Mexico, and World,
1992–1996
(millions of $)

	1992	1993	1994	1995	1996	% Change 1992–1996
World	28,483	33,457	37,131	39,144	40,809	43.27%
Non-NAFTA[a]	6,687	7,858	9,374	11,306	11,677	74.62%
NAFTA[b]	21,796	25,599	27,757	27,838	29,132	33.66%
Mexico	6,514	7,317	7,662	6,019	7,058	8.35%
Canada	15,282	18,282	20,095	21,819	22,074	44.44%
NAFTA % of total exports	76.52%	76.51%	74.75%	71.12%	71.39%	

Source: U.S. Department of Commerce Office of Automotive Affairs as derived from Bureau of the Census Database using the Office of Automotive Affairs Product Dictionary (see appendix).
[a] U.S. exports to the world excluding Canada and Mexico.
[b] U.S. exports to Canada and Mexico.

Imports. U.S. imports of automotive parts rose about 44 percent worldwide through the period, up from $33.5 billion in 1992 to $48.3 billion in 1996 (table 2.8). Imports from Mexico were up 88 percent, rising from $6.2 billion in 1992 to $11.6 billion in 1996. Imports from Canada grew 40 percent, rising from just under $9 billion in 1992 to $12.6 billion in 1996. Imports of parts from non-NAFTA countries were up 31 percent over the period, increasing from $18.3 billion to $24.1 billion, while imports from Mexico and Canada were up nearly 60 percent, rising from $15.2 billion to $24.3 billion, increasing the share of U.S. world imports received from Canada and Mexico from 45 percent to 50 percent.

Explanation of Trade Trends

A review of automotive trade flows during the period 1992–1996 reveals a number of interesting trends. In general, the growth of trade as measured by U.S. exports to and imports from Canada and Mexico has been faster than the growth of trade with the

Table 2.8
U.S. Automotive Parts Imports from Canada, Mexico, and World,
1992–1996
(millions of $)

	1992	1993	1994	1995	1996	% Change 1992–1996
World	33,525	38,306	44,854	46,355	48,346	44.21%
Non-NAFTA[a]	18,327	20,652	23,873	24,715	24,092	31.46%
NAFTA[b]	15,198	17,654	20,981	21,640	24,254	59.59%
Mexico	6,203	7,354	9,702	10,501	11,645	87.73%
Canada	8,996	10,301	11,279	11,139	12,609	40.16%
NAFTA % of total exports	45.33%	46.09%	46.78%	46.68%	50.17%	

Source: U.S. Department of Commerce Office of Automotive Affairs as derived from Bureau of the Census Database using the Office of Automotive Affairs Product Dictionary (see appendix).
[a] U.S. imports from the world excluding Canada and Mexico.
[b] U.S. imports from Canada and Mexico.

rest of the world, as measured by U.S. imports from and exports to the rest of the world. The one exception is trade in auto parts, where imports from North America grew faster than imports from the rest of the world, while exports to North America grew more slowly.

In reviewing this data, three interrelated phenomena stand out as the likely sources of impact on the volume and composition of trade: (1) the provisions of NAFTA itself, especially those pertaining to the elimination of the Mexican Auto Decree; (2) the Mexican peso devaluation and resulting economic recession; and (3) domestic demand in the United States resulting from the robust and sustained economic recovery that began in 1992 and continued throughout the period. This section presents a short discussion of each of these drivers of North American automotive trade to provide an overall picture of how they have affected the economic patterns of trade and production in the North American automotive industry. The section concludes with a listing of production and investment announcements, primarily by automobile assemblers, during the period.

NAFTA

In reviewing the impact of NAFTA on automobile trade in North America during the period 1992–1996, it is apparent that the reduction of tariff and nontariff barriers to trade, especially the phased elimination of Mexico's Auto Decree, had a discernable impact on trade flows in finished passenger vehicles and trucks in North America. In particular, the reduction of NAFTA's trade-balancing requirement, from $2 of production and export for every $1 of imports into Mexico to $.80 of production and export for every $1 of imports into Mexico, appears to have liberalized finished assembly production to allow for significantly more vehicles exported from the United States to Mexico, albeit on top of a relatively small base. This can be seen in the dramatic increase in the value of U.S. exports of finished passenger vehicles and trucks to Mexico, with vehicle exports up more than ninefold and truck exports up more than 300 percent over the period.

Not surprisingly, the reduction of the burdens placed on U.S. manufacturers by these requirements had the effect of freeing previously restricted automotive trade, and this can be seen in the dramatic increase in U.S. vehicle sales to Mexico from 1994 over 1993 and again in 1996 over other years. In 1992, the United States exported $80 million of new vehicles to Mexico. In 1993, this figure grew to $90 million; in 1994, the first year of NAFTA's implementation, sales reached $569 million. In 1995, when the peso devaluation and resulting economic recession was wrenching Mexico's economy, sales fell to $289 million. But they recovered in 1996 to $835 million, nearly ten times the 1993 figure and nearly a third more than in 1994. Truck sales also increased dramatically, growing more than 300 percent during the period.

U.S. exports to Canada of passenger vehicles also grew, although beginning from a much higher base. As mentioned earlier, trade between the United States and Canada in passenger vehicles was largely free at the onset of NAFTA negotiations as a result of the 1965 Auto Pact and the U.S.-Canada Free Trade Agreement. Trade between the United States and Mexico, however, was severely restricted by Mexico's Auto Decree that placed specific requirements on the United States and other foreign automotive assemblers and parts manufacturers seeking to sell in Mexico.

Rationalization of automotive production also appears to play a role; however, this rationalization appears to be occurring

Table 2.9
U.S. Exports to and Imports from Mexico:
New Passenger Vehicles
(value, units, and value/unit)

	1992	1996	% Change 1992–1996
Export value ($ millions)	80	835	943.75%
Export unit	4,270	51,000	1,094.38%
Export value/unit ($)	18,735	16,373	-12.61%
Import value ($ millions)	2,541	7,899	210.86%
Import unit	266,149	550,622	106.88%
Import value/unit ($)	9,547	14,346	50.26%

Source: U.S. Department of Commerce Office of Automotive Affairs as derived from Bureau of the Census Database using the Office of Automotive Affairs Product Dictionary (see appendix).

Table 2.10
U.S. Exports to and Imports from Mexico: Trucks
(value, units, and value/unit)

	1992	1996	% Change 1992–1996
Export value ($ millions)	87	361	314.94%
Export unit	4,506	31,589	601.04%
Export value/unit ($)	19,308	11,428	-40.81%
Import value ($ millions)	442	3,055	591.18%
Import unit	24,424	200,954	722.77%
Import value/unit ($)	18,097	15,202	0

Source: U.S. Department of Commerce Office of Automotive Affairs as derived from Bureau of the Census Database using the Office of Automotive Affairs Product Dictionary (see appendix).

as much within specific sectors of the automotive industry as between them. Tables 2.9 and 2.10 show the changes in export and import value, units shipped, and the relative value per unit for both cars and trucks for 1992 and 1996. Interestingly, there appears to be a convergence in the relative value of cars and trucks exported to and imported from Mexico. The average value of new vehicles exported to Mexico declined from nearly $19,000 to $16,000 from 1992 to 1996, while the average value of imports from Mexico increased from just under $10,000 to more than $14,000. Similarly, the average value of exports of trucks to Mexico decreased from $19,300 to $11,400 while the average import value also decreased, from $18,100 to $15,200. On the basis of this somewhat crude calculation, it appears as if convergence is occurring in the value and sophistication of vehicles sold between the United States and Mexico, a somewhat unexpected development given the relative factor endowments of the two countries.

Mexican Peso Devaluation and Economic Recession

On December 20, 1994, the Bank of Mexico, in conjunction with the Mexican Ministry of Finance and Public Credit, decided to allow the narrow band within which the Mexican peso had floated against the U.S. dollar to widen by 13 percent.[3] The next day, the domestic and international investment community began to sell pesos at an unprecedented pace, forcing the Mexican government to let the peso float freely and, in so doing, dramatically changing the economic landscape in Mexico for years to come.

The immediate macroeconomic impact of the devaluation was hyperinflation, skyrocketing interest rates, and a massive withdrawal of funds from both the equity markets and general economy, which, in turn, caused the government to impose harsh austerity measures. Inflation reached 80 percent for the month of April 1995. Rates on government *cetes* (the equivalent of U.S. Treasury bills) rose to more than 40 percent, and consumer interest rates jumped to 82 percent. Mexico's stock exchange, the Bolsa, dropped by 53 percent in the first three months of the crisis.

The Mexican government quickly announced an emergency plan to control wage and price increases and to accelerate privatization of certain state-owned industries. The initial plan, however, was met with skepticism from the business community. The U.S. announcement in early January of a package of loan guarantees, in conjunction with the International Monetary Fund, helped to restore confidence.

The implications of the radical change in economic performance in 1995 were profound: employment, purchasing, industrial output, consumption, and individual firm-level profitability all dropped dramatically. The combination of high interest rates, a contracting economy, spiraling inflation, and general economic instability created massive changes in production and sales expectations.

Automotive production contracted sharply during the first six months of the year, with sales of new vehicles off more than 75 percent over 1994 levels. These trends can be seen in the significant falloff in U.S. exports of passenger vehicles and trucks to Mexico in 1995. From 1994 to 1995, exports of passenger vehicles to Mexico fell by nearly half, from $569 million to $290 million. Impressively, however, sales recovered in 1996 to $835 million, nearly ten times the 1993 figure and nearly a third more than in 1994. Interestingly, truck sales did not experience a fall from 1994 to 1995 but actually grew, from $48 million to $57 million, perhaps because trucks were still in relatively high demand as Mexico began the process of recovery because of infrastructure and construction, and as a result of already-committed investment. By 1996, truck sales were up significantly, reaching $361 million for the year.

U.S. Market Conditions

The third factor that has had a significant influence on trade flows in the automotive industry in North America throughout this period is the prolonged and stable economic recovery in the United States, which has stimulated increased sales, production, and employment in the automotive industry. This demand for U.S.- and North American-produced trucks in both domestic and international markets had a particularly stimulative effect on industry trends.

Table 2.11 shows major automotive indicators by value from 1991 through 1995. The table illustrates the steady overall economic growth experienced by the United States throughout the period, as demonstrated in the cumulative 22 percent increase in GDP over the five years. The table also shows similar increases in passenger vehicle output, final sales, and personal consumption. Net truck output and sales increased at about four times the rate of passenger vehicle output and in 1995 nearly eclipsed it, as measured by total sales.

Table 2.12 shows automotive indicators by units, which demonstrated fairly slow growth of 5.6 percent over the period. The table also shows, however, the increasing substitution of

Table 2.11
Major U.S. Automotive Indicators by Value, 1991–1995
(millions of 1995 $)

	1991	1992	1993	1994	1995	Net % Change 1991–1995
GDP (U.S.)	5,916.7	6,244.4	6,550.2	6,931.4	7,245.8	22.46%
Net auto output[a]	109.3	121.6	131.0	143.6	134.8	23.33%
Final sales	109.4	122.1	129.2	141.8	133.8	22.30%
Personal consumption	107.3	117.6	127.3	137.4	137.3	27.96%
New	75.3	82.1	86.5	91.3	84.6	12.35%
Net used	32.0	35.5	40.8	46.1	52.7	64.69%
Net truck output[a]	67.6	83.7	97.2	121.2	127.6	88.76%
Final sales	69.3	82.4	97.6	118.0	125.5	81.10%
Personal consumption	38.8	45.8	51.6	57.1	56.9	46.65%
New	75.3	82.1	86.5	91.3	84.6	12.35%
Net used	32.0	35.5	40.8	46.1	52.7	64.69%

Source: Survey of Current Business as reported by the U.S. Department of Commerce Office of Automotive Affairs and derived from Bureau of the Census Database using the Office of Automotive Affairs Product Dictionary (see appendix).
[a] Combined value of new and used.

domestic production for imported production, with domestic sales increasing by 19 percent to 89 percent of overall sales by unit, and imports falling by 26 percent to just over 10 percent of total sales. This phenomenon demonstrates the increased competitiveness of U.S.-based automotive producers as well as more assembly in the United States by Japanese companies, resulting in purchases of U.S.-made cars in substitution for imports. Truck production by unit grew more than 40 percent over the period.

Table 2.12
Major U.S. Automotive Indicators by Units, 1991–1995
(thousands)

	1991	1992	1993	1994	1995	% Change 1991– 1995[a]
U.S. automotive sales[a]	8,175.0	8,214.4	8,517.7	8,990.4	8,636.2	5.64%
Produced in the United States	6,136.9	6,276.6	6,734.0	7,255.2	7,728.8	25.94%
% produced in the United States	75.07%	76.41%	79.06%	80.70%	89.49%	19.21%
Produced abroad	2,038.1	1,937.8	1,783.7	1,735.2	1,507.4	-26.04%
% produced abroad	24.93%	23.59%	20.94%	19.30%	10.51%	-57.86%
Average expenditure per car[b]	16,083	17,137	17,678	18,657	18,360	14.16%
Trucks	45,788	53,580	60,516	65,598	64,726	41.36%

Source: National Income and Product Accounts (NIPA) Table 1.1, Gross Domestic Product; and Supplementary Tables 8.3, Auto Output, and 8.5, Truck Output, as reported in the Commerce Department's monthly publication *Survey of Current Business* as reported in U.S. Department of Commerce Office of Automotive Affairs and derived from Bureau of the Census Database using the Office of Automotive Affairs Product Dictionary (see appendix).

[a] Not seasonally adjusted.
[b] In 1995 dollars.

Table 2.13 provides figures on employment in the automotive industry throughout the period 1991–1995. Overall U.S. employment grew by 5.6 percent over the period, while employment in manufacturing grew by just .34 percent. By comparison, employment in the motor vehicle and equipment industry grew by 22.7 percent. Wages grew by 14 percent in the automotive industry, while wages in overall manufacturing grew by 10.6 percent. Employment in parts and accessories grew by about 21 percent, and wages in this category grew by 18.8 percent.

In sum, one of the major factors in explaining the post-NAFTA changes in trade and investment flows in North America, especially increased imports of parts and vehicles from Mexico, is the steady demand and relatively robust growth in

Table 2.13
Employment and Wages in the Automotive Industry, 1991–1995
(employment in thousands)

	1991	1992	1993	1994	1995	% Change 1991–1995[a]
Average annual total U.S. employment[a]	8,175.0	8,214.4	8,517.7	8,990.4	8,636.2	5.64%
Motor vehicle and equipment, all employment	788.8	812.5	836.6	909.3	968.0	22.72%
Average hourly earnings[b]	$15.23	$15.45	$16.10	$17.02	$17.36	13.99%
Parts/accessories employment	398.0	417.0	430.0	467.0	483.0	21.36%
Average hourly earnings[b]	$13.62	$14.22	$14.74	$15.96	$16.18	18.80%
Overall manufacturing employment	18,406	18,104	18,075	18,321	18,468	0.34%
Average hourly earnings[b]	$11.18	$11.46	$11.74	$12.07	$12.37	10.64%

Source: U.S. Department of Labor, Bureau of Labor Statistics, as derived from Bureau of the Census Database using the Office of Automotive Affairs Product Dictionary (see appendix).

[a] Not seasonably adjusted.
[b] In 1995 dollars.

the industry, as measured by sales, exports, and employment, creating constraints and limits to domestic production and increasing demand, especially from Mexico.

Major Production and Investment Announcements Post-NAFTA

The following list of production, investment, and sales announcements from major motor vehicle producers, assemblers, and parts manufacturers provides a representative indication of firm-specific activities in the first two years of NAFTA:

1994

- In February 1994 just one month after NAFTA's implementation, Blue Bird Corporation of Fort Valley, Georgia, said it would begin production in March 1995 at its 3,000-unit bus plant in Monterrey, Mexico. The plant will produce 51-seat urban buses, the 18-seat Micro Bird, and full-sized transit buses. The Fort Valley Georgia-based school bus maker had previously announced that it would open a commercial bus plant in Mexico by the end of 1994 (*Atlanta Constitution*, February 4, 1994, C8).

1995

- In February 1995, Chrysler Corporation reopened its plant in South St. Louis, Missouri, using it to produce its new minivan model. The plant, previously used for automobile production, was closed in 1991. Chrysler said it expects to employ 3,500 full-time workers at the re-opened plant (*St. Louis Dispatch*, January 5, 1995, C1).
- In May 1995, General Motors Corporation announced that its assembly plant in Arlington Texas, which had been building large cars, would begin making C/K light trucks after the 1996 model year. Similar vehicles are also produced in Mexico (*Wall Street Journal*, May 17, 1995, B4).
- In August 1995, Chrysler said it planned to spend $1 billion to build a new plant in Kokomo, Indiana, to make truck transmissions, expanding a program to upgrade engines and transmissions. The new plant is part of a previously announced $1.3 billion spending program to bring out a series of new Chrysler engines. The plant will be fully operational in 1999 (*New York Times*, August 8, 1995, D19).
- In November 1995, Chrysler announced a $350 million investment to build a newly designed V-6 engine at its Kenosha, Wisconsin, plant. Production began in 1997 for use in several best-selling vehicle lines, starting with the 1998 model year (*Chicago Tribune*, January 6, 1995, 1).

1996

- In April 1996, General Motors announced plans to invest $280 million in Mexico during 1996 to complete the construction of a new plant in Silao. GM also added a new, locally produced model for the Mexican market, similar to another compact Chevy already sold in Mexico (*Wall Street Journal*, April 22, 1996, A8).

- In April of 1996, PACCAR, Inc., headquartered in Bellevue, Washington, bought out its Mexican partner. PACCAR, which is the parent company of Peterbilt Motors Co. and Kenworth Truck Co., recently shifted production from its Canadian plant to plants in the United States and Mexico. Its Mexican operation makes and markets Kenworth medium- and heavy-duty trucks for the Mexican market. With the transfer of Canadian production to Mexico, the plant now exports to the United States, Canada, and other countries (*Los Angeles Times*, April 11, 1996, D1).

- In October 1996, in a move to push into the Latin American truck market, the board of Navistar International Corporation, the Chicago-based truck and diesel-engine manufacturer, approved a plan to build a $167 million truck-assembly plant in Mexico. The plant will supply heavy- and medium-duty trucks to Mexico and Latin America. In November 1996 Navistar announced it had selected a site near Escobedo, Mexico, for its new manufacturing facility. The plant will build trucks for Mexico and the Latin American market (*Wall Street Journal*, November 27, 1996, B4).

NAFTA Implementation

This section discusses issues that have arisen in the course of NAFTA implementation that have required or may require some adjustment or action on the part of automobile producers or their representative governments.

Modifications to Mexican Maquiladora and Automotive Decrees

On October 23, 1996, the Mexican government published a decree amending the 1989 *Maquiladora* Decree and its 1993 revisions. The new law gives the Mexican government the power to deny registration of new *maquiladoras* (Article 5) or to cancel existing *maquiladoras* (Article 30) that might negatively affect the non-*maquiladora* industry in Mexico. Article 7 states that the application and execution of the *maquiladora* program will depend on the commitments assumed by the government of Mexico in its international treaties.

NAFTA stipulates that the level of sales permitted into the Mexican domestic market by a particular *maquiladora*—a percentage of the value of its previous year's exports—be incrementally increased from 1994 to 2000. As of January 1, 2001, all restrictions on domestic sales will disappear. The proportion of a *maquiladora*'s production that may be sold into the domestic market from 1994 to 2000 is as follows: 55 percent (1994), 60 percent (1995), 65 percent (1996), 70 percent (1997), 75 percent (1998), 80 percent (1999), 85 percent (2000), and 100 percent (2001).

NAFTA also requires Mexico to grant "national supplier" status to an independent *maquiladora* that requests such status, provided the *maquiladora* otherwise meets the requirements under the Auto Decree. On January 20, 1997, the Mexican government published new restrictions on the national supplier status by prohibiting arrangements such as trusts, contracts, pyramid schemes, and other governance systems that allow assemblers to act as the majority owner of the national supplier. The decree grandfathered existing arrangements.

Notification under the GATT TRIMs Agreement

In early 1994, Mexico notified the World Trade Organization (WTO), as required, that it had identified the Auto Decree as a measure inconsistent with the agreement on trade-related investment measures (TRIMs). Under the WTO TRIMs agreement, measures inconsistent with the non-discrimination, most-favored-nation, and national treatment obligations of the agreement must be removed upon entry into force of the 1994 GATT agreement. A country may request a waiver to allow for a transition period according to the following schedule: 2 years in the case of a developed country, 5 years in the case of a developing country, and 10 years in the case of a least-developed country. Mexico identified itself as a developing country for these purposes, and, as such, the discriminatory provisions of the Auto Decree must be removed for all GATT members by January 1, 1999. (Identification under the TRIMs notifications procedures does not prejudice a country from requesting a different level-of-development designation for other WTO provisions.)

Implementation of Rules of Origin and Marking Rules

On September 1, 1994, the government of Mexico implemented new certification-of-origin requirements for non-NAFTA goods subject to anti-dumping (AD) or countervailing duty (CVD) orders. The requirements, intended to prevent circumvention of Mexican AD/CVD orders and published as a decree in Mexico's *Diario Official*, compel Mexican importers to file a certificate of origin for all imported goods that may be subject to Mexican AD or CVD orders. If a certificate is not filed, it is because the goods originate from a country against which an AD or CVD order is directed, and AD or CVD duties are applied. Although these measures apply mainly to textiles, apparel, and footwear, one automotive product, lubricants, was also subject to the procedures. Many exporters complained that the procedures were onerous and unfair because of the difficulty in getting the certificates "authenticized" and the "guilty until proven innocent" approach to enforcement.

Regarding general rules of origin and rules for marking, as mentioned earlier, two difficulties that had arisen under CUFTA were largely resolved by NAFTA; hence additional problems have been few. The overall complexity of the rules, however, continues to involve substantial costs and time, especially record-keeping requirements that make inventory management systems more difficult to administer. These difficulties would likely increase if and when NAFTA is expanded to include other countries.

Standards

NAFTA recognizes the importance of standards to the health and safety of the populations of the three countries, but also the potential that standards-related measures can pose barriers to trade. NAFTA therefore established a committee to work toward minimizing the trade-restricting potential of standards and to promote harmonization, compatibility, and conformity assessment procedures for standards recognition and certification. In the automotive area, NAFTA establishes an automotive standards council that is designed to promote compatibility and mutual recognition of standards, testing, and labeling practices. Since NAFTA's implementation, several problems have arisen in the standards area, although these issues have largely been resolved through NAFTA's institutional arrangements.

First, a problem arose with respect to recognition by Mexican authorities of the U.S. standard on tires. Although the Mexican standard is quite similar to the U.S. standard, Mexico was not obligated to recognize U.S. conformity assessment standards (nor to conduct tests to verify compliance with standards) until January 1, 1998. As such, tires made in the United States had to be tested at specially designated laboratories in Mexico, which were operated by what the U.S. tire producers viewed as competitors. An agreement was reached under which each country designated a series of tire labs within its own borders that were recognized for their technical capabilities to conduct tests and ensure the reliability and uniformity of test results in accordance with applicable international guidelines.

Tire producers had also been subject to a requirement that they label each tire in Spanish and that the label be molded into the tire (as opposed to being applied with an adhesive). This requirement effectively compelled U.S. tire manufacturers to produce a separate line for the Mexican market, which they deemed cost-prohibitive. Mexico did publish a revised standard in September 1996 that allowed information in Spanish to be affixed using paper-tread labels.

Finally, U.S. automotive parts suppliers have, to date, been required to adhere to NOM-50, the Mexican standard pertaining to consumer goods, which requires several pieces of information to be affixed to products in Spanish. The labels can be affixed either pre- or post-entry, but if companies elect the latter option, they must have the labels inspected in Mexico by an authorized verification entity. A February 24, 1997, notice listed the specific products that would be subject to NOM-50 when it went into effect on March 1, 1997. The list included several auto parts. Although the notice exempted companies that use products "to render services to third parties," this service-provider exemption was not immediately granted to auto part producers even though in Mexico their goods were generally sold to professional mechanics and service providers; this was because in most cases the importer of record was not the service provider but an intermediary.

Consequences of NAFTA for the Industry

This chapter has provided a brief discussion of some of the most significant developments in the United States and North American automotive industry in the past five years. Although preliminary, it suggests that the U.S. and North American automotive industries have benefitted from the integration and rationalization brought about by the North American Free Trade Agreement, as well as the strong economic growth in the United States.

- NAFTA has had a generally positive impact on the U.S. automotive industry as measured by exports and imports, production, and overall investment activity. In particular, the removal of Mexican restrictions on automotive imports associated with Mexico's Auto Decree has resulted in significant increases in U.S. exports of passenger vehicles and trucks and has allowed efficient rationalization to occur, which is critical to the future competitiveness of the U.S. automotive industry. These aggregate indicators are supported by the many announcements by U.S. automotive companies of increased investment and production plans throughout North America.
- Parts trade presents a somewhat different picture. U.S. imports from NAFTA partners (especially Mexico) grew quite rapidly throughout the period, although parts exports to Canada and Mexico have remained flat or fallen; exports to the rest of the world have increased rapidly.
- The peso devaluation and the ensuing economic depression in Mexico severely dampened the positive impact of NAFTA during 1995. U.S. exports to Mexico became much more expensive for Mexicans in relative terms, and final demand in Mexico was significantly curtailed because of the fiscal and monetary tightening necessary to stem price inflation and stabilize the currency.
- Fortunately, demand conditions in the United States and Canada throughout this period were strong, limiting the potential negative impact of Mexico's economic difficulties on production and sales of U.S.-made vehicles and parts. In fact, the difficulty in meeting demand from U.S. plants was somewhat mitigated by imports of U.S. nameplate vehicles from Mexico, helping manufacturers to avoid distribution bottlenecks.
- Overall, implementation of NAFTA's automotive provisions has been relatively smooth. In general, provisions relating to rules of origin, standards, and Mexico's modifications to its automotive regime to make it conform to both NAFTA and other WTO obligations have been accomplished with little difficulty. Some problems have arisen, however. One is in the area of "tracing" content under NAFTA's rules of origin pertaining to autos. A second has to do with determining the definition of "national suppliers" under NAFTA, which permits preferential treatment for designated suppliers in Mexico.

Additional research questions and avenues of inquiry remain that should be examined in order to gain a deeper and more complete understanding of the forces shaping the North American automotive industry. These might include the following:

- Intra-industry trade: What are the long-term trends in intra-industry trade and how has NAFTA affected this trade?
- Supplier relationships: How has NAFTA and integration affected the relationships between suppliers and assemblers?
- Productivity: How has NAFTA and integration affected the productivity of the North American automotive industry in comparison to European, Asian, and other competitors?
- Jobs and wages: What are the long-term prospects for employment and wages in the North American automobile industry?
- Rules of origin: Are NAFTA's rules of origin accomplishing their stated objective? Are the rules overly complex, and will this complexity increase as NAFTA is expanded? Can the rules be streamlined and/or simplified?

The North American Free Trade Agreement is a useful starting point for fostering continued integration of the automotive industry in North America. It provides a benchmark for negotiations toward expanding NAFTA membership as well as achieving a Free Trade Area of the Americas.

Appendix
Statistics Used in Chapter 2

Motor Vehicle Export Data

These data are a subset of the official statistics published by the U.S. Department of Commerce, Bureau of the Census, using certain Harmonized System of tariff classification (HS) numbers selected by the department's Office of Automotive Affairs (OAA). The categories selected are primarily of vehicles designed for the on-road transport of persons or commercial cargo. Military and construction vehicles are excluded where possible. The "Total Motor Vehicles" tables include the "New Passenger Vehicles" tables (cars, minivans, sport-utility vehicles, and multipurpose passenger vehicles), plus the "New Trucks" tables (pickups, commercial straight-trucks, and tractors), in addition to used vehicles, buses, chassis with engines, and "Special Purpose Vehicles not elsewhere classified."

Tables 2.1–2.8 provide trade values in current year U.S. dollars as determined and reported by the U.S. Customs Service. Figures 2.1–2.8 report unit exports and imports. Data reported are international trade shipment transactions, not retail market sales. Some imported products may be re-exported without entering the U.S. retail market. Some imports may not be sold on the retail market in the same calendar year in which they enter the United States. Some U.S. exports may be reshipped by the receiver to other countries. The import reporting category used here, "General Imports," excludes vehicles completed in U.S. Foreign Trade Zones. U.S. trade data include transactions by original manufacturers and other entities, including individuals. Federal law prohibits the Census Bureau from disclosing the identity of any exporter or importer.

AAMA Data

The American Automobile Manufacturers Association reports North American (U.S. and Canadian) production and export as one combined figure, that is, production and export in Canada and the United States is considered as representative of total output. As mentioned earlier, as a result of the 1965 U.S.-Canada Auto Pact and the 1989 U.S.-Canada Free Trade Agreement, the U.S. and Canadian motor vehicle industries are largely integrated. From the vantage of the AAMA, this integration makes differentiating between U.S. and Canadian production unnecessary.

Parts Data

Parts data are compiled by the U.S. Department of Commerce Office of Automotive Affairs and represent production composed of HS codes whose descriptions state that they are for motor vehicle use (passenger vehicles and light- , medium- , and heavy-duty trucks) as well as those categories that the OAA has determined are principally for automotive end use, even if they fall in HS categories not specifically designated as automotive-related.

Notes

The author would like to thank Paul Dacher, Doug Karmin, and Laurie Goldman of the NAFTA Office, as well as staff of the Office of Automotive Affairs, U.S. Department of Commerce, for helpful assistance and to acknowledge extensive use of data and other information from both offices. The views expressed and any errors are those of the author.

1. For a summary of NAFTA's provisions affecting automotive trade, see Hufbauer 1993.

2. For a summary of NAFTA's automotive provisions from a Canadian perspective and the history of automotive trade liberalization between the United States and Canada, see Johnson 1993.

3. For a summary of the events leading to the peso devaluation and the impact on U.S.-Mexico bilateral trade, see Weintraub 1994 and Doh 1996.

Bibliography

Doh, J. 1996. "Managing Credit Risk during a Financial Storm: The Case of Mexico 1994–1996." *Financial and Credit Management Review* 2 (Spring 1996).

Hufbauer, Gary C., and Jeffrey J. Schott. 1993. *NAFTA: An Assessment,* pp. 27–33. Washington, D.C.: Institute for International Economics.

Johnson, John R. 1993. "NAFTA and Trade in Automotive Goods," pp. 87–129 in *Assessing NAFTA: A Trilateral Analysis.* Edited by Steven Globerman and Michael Walker. Vancouver, B.C.: The Fraser Institute.

U.S. Government. 1994. *North American Free Trade: Implementing Bill, Statement of Administrative Action, and Required Support Statement.* Washington, D.C.: Government Printing Office.

Weintraub, Sidney. 1994. *NAFTA: What Comes Next?* Westport, Conn.: Praeger/CSIS.

3

The Impact of NAFTA on the Auto Industry in Mexico

Rogelio Ramírez de la O

The vehicle assembly industry has created only 20,000 jobs in Mexico since 1970 while the automotive parts industry has created close to 100,000, most of them in the in-bond *maquiladora*. Although this is not an impressive achievement, the largest part of the increase took place after the government resolved to liberalize its trade regime, a liberalization that was consolidated by the North American Free Trade Agreement (NAFTA). This industry—representing 7.4 percent of gross domestic product (GDP), 14 percent of manufacturing output, and 9 percent of employment—looms large in any discussion of Mexico's industrial development or international trade. Its exports of $15 billion made up almost one-quarter of all exports of manufactures, which were $67 billion in 1996. For this reason this industry was key for the NAFTA negotiations and, therefore, for the appraisal of its effects. This chapter addresses such effects and focuses on labor, in particular employment, productivity, and wages.

NAFTA has been in force only since 1994, and many of its expected effects were blurred by the economic crisis that hit Mexico in December 1994. In 1995 a radical stabilization program depressed domestic demand and domestic sales plummeted; this explains why some of the effects of NAFTA, particularly on employment, were not evident although the effects on exports and imports were.

In 1996 the economy began to recover and with it domestic sales and employment. The industry, however, has not reattained its 1994 levels.

To appraise the effects of NAFTA, one must understand the changing policy regimes as well as the nature of the global auto industry. Mexico has experienced three distinct domestic policy regimes during the past 35 years: (1) an import-substitution phase; (2) a transition phase in which the aim was to increase exports; and (3) a gradually opening trade regime that began in the late 1980s. NAFTA came to limit the protectionist features of the first two regimes as they evolved during the 1990s and reinforced the competitive features of a global industry that needs unrestricted free trade to be efficient.

But in removing restrictions, NAFTA allowed for a long phaseout period. In particular, it transformed national-content into regional-content restrictions and provided a 10-year phaseout of restrictions contained in the 1989 automotive industry decree. By doing so, it validated a regime that over the previous decades had been aimed, somewhat in contradiction, at promoting domestic industrialization by forcing the inclusion of Mexican components while encouraging exports. The long phaseout of protection has, therefore, allowed Mexican industry to adapt to a more efficient and demanding model of operation without facing the threat of closures from competitive pressures. It thus put a lid on import growth of both autos and parts while it reassured exporters on access to the U.S. market. The largest marginal growth in employment consequently has been in the parts *maquiladora* industry, where exports rise steadily. Employment in the auto industry has not risen although, because of growing exports, it did not fall in 1995 as it should have fallen with its much lower domestic sales. Employment in the non-*maquiladora* parts industry was protected by NAFTA (through the long phaseout of protection) although firms have been forced gradually to become more efficient.

In this analysis the distinction made by the government between vehicle assembly (known in Mexico as "terminal" industry) and auto parts is maintained. We refer to the former as the assembly or auto industry and to the latter as the parts industry.

This chapter consists of six sections. The first section describes the background of the Mexican auto industry and discusses the government changes. The second looks at the state of affairs at the start of NAFTA. The third section examines the relevant sections of NAFTA and their implications. The fourth examines trends in activity and employment. In the fifth, some estimations of domestic sales and exports, employment, and wages are performed.

The sixth and final section presents conclusions, formulates some policy recommendations, and discusses salient issues that merit further investigation.

Evolution of the Auto Industry in Mexico

The auto industry plays an important role in the Mexican economy not only because it produces an important consumer durable but also because its performance is an indicator of welfare and modernization. The use of vehicles replaces less efficient means of transportation, which helps to explain that, over the long run, the stock of vehicles has increased despite many interruptions to the process of economic growth in Mexico.

First Regime: Import Substitution and Local Development

Similar to other countries that embarked on industrialization policies through import substitution, Mexico in the early 1930s put in place a policy to force auto manufacturers to develop local production and increase the local content of vehicles. This policy reflected in part the government's long-held intention to rely on automobile production for promoting industrialization and employment while it protected the balance of payments.

In 1962 the government issued the first in a series of unilateral automotive decrees. This first decree required that every vehicle produced include an engine and a transmission manufactured in Mexico and a vehicle composition of at least 60 percent local content; these requirements gave rise to the local engine and transmission industries. In 1969 a new decree required that an increasing share of each assembly firm's imports be offset by exports. With this legislation, the government expected to provide an impetus to industrialization as well as increase exports to finance at least part of the growth in imports.

One result of this policy was that producers established large plants to manufacture engines, which led Mexico to become a prominent producer of transmissions and, later, engines and, eventually as these industries became more efficient, an exporter of these parts.

A decree in 1972 gave final form to this strategy that now focused not only on national content but also on protection of the balance of payments because it linked the domestic sales of producers, which were limited by a quota system, to their foreign-trade balance. Thus assembly firms that wished to maintain their shares of the domestic market found it necessary to develop local suppliers, dedicating resources to improve the quality and prices of local components.

Because components produced locally were not of competitive price or quality, these policies made the assembly and parts industries highly dependent on trade protection. Price controls on automobiles were applied to set a lid on costs and inefficiencies, but such prices were regularly much higher than the equivalent international prices. Although the local market grew quickly, it never acquired the size to justify large-scale production; producers were always too many for the size of the market and the many car models tended to reduce the scale of production in each model.

The government also encouraged local investment in auto assembly firms and itself even went as far as investing in automobile and truck production. Thus Chrysler had a local private partner, while the government participated in Renault and VAM (a joint venture with American Motors to assemble Rambler vehicles) and fully owned the Dina truck producer. Eventually, when foreign investors withdrew, the government had to acquire full ownership of Renault and VAM, and Mexican investors sold their equity to Chrysler.

Second Regime: Transition to Exports

By 1977 the auto industry had undergone important changes in the world market. First, it had become evident that auto producers tended to specialize in producing either cars that fit the tastes of local markets or certain components that they could export efficiently. Second, because this strategy demanded maximum flexibility in defining the local product mix of each plant and affected the plant's profitability, it required total ownership by the auto producer.

By this time it was also evident that the international consensus of policymakers and especially of multilateral organizations favored freer international trade, which limited local industrialization policies. The regulations for the auto industry began to reflect this change but not in a consistent way, giving rise to a transition period in which the original aims of local content seemed to contradict other policy objectives such as efficient exports.

Mexico's Auto Decree of 1977 freed prices of cars in the hope that this would improve competition among producers. The decree, however, also introduced a stricter form of balance-of-payments objectives that included foreign-exchange budget directives not only to control imports and offset them with exports but also to control the cost of services, dividend remittances, and royalties.

This decree was the first one that distinguished protection for Mexican-owned firms from that for foreign-owned firms. It created the distinction between national suppliers and nonnational suppliers, the latter being foreign-owned auto producers and their subsidiaries. In 1983 a new decree linked the foreign-exchange budget with the maximum volume of production permitted to each company. The 1983 decree confirmed, for protection purposes, the distinction between national and nonnational suppliers.

Third Regime: Gradual Opening of Trade, or Selective Protection

The 1989 auto industry decree confirmed all the protective features that had been established by previous decrees as well as the pressure put on producers to export. The distinction between national and non-national suppliers was maintained, giving protection to the former despite the move by the newly elected Carlos Salinas government to dismantle protection as part of its effort to modernize the trade regime. It was the elimination of the protectionist elements in this decree that NAFTA negotiators on the auto-industry side would try to push against the negotiators on the parts-industry side who wanted to prolong protection.

On paper the trade regime of Mexico appeared liberal, but this was not true for the auto industry. Although the 1989 Auto Decree reduced the overall local content required from 50 percent to 32 percent, it redefined national content in a way that excluded purchases from producers' own facilities because such facilities were not "national producers." The 1989 decree made it more difficult, in fact, for producers to meet the national content required.

Under the new regulations, each manufacturer had to meet the national-content requirement of 32 percent on both domestic *and* export sales; therefore purchases from local suppliers simply had to increase. To import, a firm had to achieve a trade balance greater than zero. Given that exports of autos and parts had to be directed mainly to the same corporation as that of the exporter, the 1989 decree boosted intrafirm trade to very high levels. Thus one result of this decree was to enhance trade between Mexico and the United States. Because auto producers loomed large in Mexican trade with the United States even before the 1989 decree, the industry was key to the NAFTA negotiations. The 1989 decree established the basis for NAFTA negotiations.

Long-Run Performance of the Industry

The performance of the industry has been determined largely by income growth and government policy. In the 1950s and 1960s, the nascent Mexican auto industry directed its production toward the developing domestic market. Production of automobiles grew continuously from 10,384 vehicles in 1950 to 48,841 in 1962, the year when the first local-content regulations were introduced.

By 1970 the auto industry represented 4 percent of manufacturing value-added, increasing to 9.4 percent in 1989. Of the total in 1989, 56 percent was produced by the parts industry and 44 percent by the assembly industry, which had seen its share fall from 75 percent in 1981.

Although these figures convey an image of steady growth, the industry's development has been far from smooth. Between 1970 and 1977, the latter period of the first regime, production of vehicles for the domestic market increased 48.6 percent or 5.8 percent per year, as is shown in table 3.1. Production for the export market became significant only in the mid-1980s. This production usually consisted of a product mix slightly different—sometimes of higher quality, with more accessories and more imported components—from that of cars sold in the domestic market. This would only confirm the presence of government restrictions.

From 1977 to 1981, production for the domestic market jumped 109.2 percent or 20.3 percent per year, an improvement fully explained by the high growth in GDP during this oil-boom period. Table 3.1 shows, however, that production fell in 1982–1983 and did not reattain its 1981 level until 1991. The interruption in growth was caused by the major macroeconomic adjustment undertaken by Mexico at the onset of its foreign-debt crisis. The same stop–go pattern was observed during shorter periods between 1981 and 1991, brought about by macroeconomic shifts that hurt domestic demand for automobiles.

Employment in the industry followed the same pattern. As table 3.1 shows, it contracted in 1976 when Mexico devalued its

Table 3.1
Mexican Auto Industry Domestic Production, Sales, and Employment, 1970–1996

| Years | Domestic Market (units) | | Employment | | |
	Production	Sales	Vehicle Assembly	Auto Parts Manufacture	Total
1970	188,986	187,675	29,283	34,722	64,005
1971	211,393	207,506	31,061	38,964	70,025
1972	229,848	233,417	33,998	41,400	75,398
1973	285,618	262,045	42,105	50,832	92,937
1974	350,947	332,370	45,482	63,133	108,615
1975	356,624	345,897	44,617	60,224	104,841
1976	324,979	303,367	42,639	53,984	96,623
1977	280,813	289,240	39,806	50,900	90,706
1978	384,127	351,028	47,823	61,011	108,834
1979	444,426	425,231	50,534	68,468	119,002
1980	490,006	464,411	48,845	75,896	124,741
1981	587,460	571,013	55,488	83,119	138,607
1982	468,009	466,663	49,675	73,354	123,029
1983	284,550	272,815	36,878	62,759	99,637
1984	340,924	330,287	38,734	70,223	108,957
1985	358,830	391,649	42,647	78,831	121,478
1986	262,483	258,835	40,199	68,678	108,877
1987	227,943	242,008	41,665	73,026	114,691
1988	330,956	335,864	41,008	177,099[*]	218,107
1989	433,763	434,669	48,178	217,321	265,499
1990	525,133	532,872	57,670	237,480	295,150
1991	595,529	614,823	60,512	225,728	286,240
1992	660,129	676,176	59,958	285,415	345,373
1993	562,027	576,025	54,944	258,213	313,157
1994	522,350	598,087	49,737	255,505	305,242
1995	152,500	184,937	48,048	214,460	262,508
1996	240,423	333,920	50,682	226,214	276,896

Sources: Mexican Association of Automotive Industry (AMIA); National Institute of Statistics, Geography, and Information (INEGI).

* The original source, INEGI, does not explain this jump in employment, which is caused by the inclusion of in-bond *maquiladoras*. The source does not disaggregate the total after 1987, which makes it impossible to use a comparable time series for the long 1970–1996 period.

currency and started a stabilization program; it grew during the oil boom of 1978–1981; and it declined during most of the 1980s. In 1987 it began to increase again, recording one of the fastest periods of job creation as the new regime fostered a more competitive and export-oriented industry. It then fell again in 1995 with the new peso crisis. A large part of the increase in employment in the late 1980s was the result of more in-bond *maquiladora* plants. The inclusion of these data in the time series makes it impossible to separate employment in the parts industry in *maquiladoras* from such employment in other plants.

By the mid-1980s, Mexico was beginning a radical transformation of its economic regime. Trade flows started to be liberalized and tariffs were reduced, exporters were allowed to import more, and in 1986 Mexico became a member of the General Agreement on Tariffs and Trade (GATT). Nevertheless, when Mexico joined GATT and adopted a tariff reduction schedule, it did so with the exception of autos, which remained subject to a protectionist regime that was reconfirmed in the 1989 Auto Decree.

Auto companies began exporting in the late 1970s, and exports accelerated in 1983 following the collapse of the domestic market and the start of new, large operations to increase export capacity. In the late 1970s, forced by the 1977 decree that created a foreign-exchange budget that included payments for services, producers started to build new plants for engines, cars, and parts designated for export. A large part of the new export capacity added during this period was in response to the extremely bullish expectations, based on the high oil prices, that producers had for the growth in domestic demand. Global competition was increasing and it was no longer possible for firms to operate under the rigid labor contracts that had previously existed. The new plants were located in northern Mexico, where labor unions were new and labor contracts were more flexible. Simultaneously, protracted labor disputes in plants located in traditional centers, especially Mexico City and Puebla, confirmed to producers that locating plants in the north was a good strategy.

The key factor in reducing the bargaining power of unions, however, was the softening of the labor market brought about by the 1982 crisis. Producers considered closing several plants as the crisis deepened and made workers fear the loss of jobs. The perceived risk of losing jobs became the key to the loss of bargaining power for unions, not only vis-à-vis employers but also vis-à-vis the government, which was trying to induce wage moderation to control inflation and meet macroeconomic targets in International Monetary Fund (IMF) programs.

Now, apart from the reduced presence of the Confederación de Trabajadores de México (CTM) that producers wanted to avoid as a counterpart in labor contracts, northern locations offered lower transport cost to the United States, lower operating costs, and a location closer to customs offices at the border.

The oldest plants in the industry are concentrated in Mexico City, Puebla, Cuernavaca, Ciudad Sahagún, and Monterrey and specialize in cars, heavy vehicles, buses, and engines. During the 1980s, new plants were opened by Ford in Chihuahua and Hermosillo and by General Motors in Ramos Arizpe for the production of car parts and engines and the assembly of cars and trucks. Plants in Ciudad Juárez, Nuevo Laredo, and Matamoros have recently undergone upgrades, having started as *maquiladoras*. The proliferation and efficient operation of northern plants eventually facilitated the overhaul and modernization of some plants in the south. For example, the Ford Cuautitlán plant near Mexico City was closed for a large overhaul. This and another Ford plant in Puebla have now been modernized and produce with high efficiency.

In 1970 employment in autos and parts totaled only 64,005 workers, of whom 46 percent were employed by assembler firms and 54 percent by the parts industry. Between 1970 and 1980, employment grew by 94.9 percent. There are no employment data for the 1960s, but, based on ratios of output to employment, we estimate that employment nearly trebled by the end of the 1980s with respect to its level in the 1960s. Production of parts, where much of this employment was created, included glass, plastic, rubber, and aluminum components.

Table 3.1 shows that the increase in employment in the parts industry was greater than that in the assembly industry. The 1980s saw a decline in employment in the assembly sector from peaks in 1974 and 1981, while decreases were much milder in the parts sector. Thus, although 43 percent of automotive industry employees worked in the assembly sector in the 1970s, assemblers accounted for only 31.1 percent in the 1980s. Employment shifted toward the parts sector as the export of auto parts grew, the quality of parts improved, and foreign direct investment (FDI) increased.

In table 3.1, we see a jump in employment in the parts industry in 1988 owing to the incorporation of in-bond *maquiladora* plants. The National Institute of Statistics, Geography, and

Information (INEGI), which is the source of these data, does not caution readers about the cause of such a jump, nor does it provide any basis for making an adjustment of the time series. This renders the series useless for quantitative analysis because it masks two different bases, one before 1988 excluding *maquiladora* jobs and another, from 1988 onward, including them. Any empirical analysis of employment and other variables related to it must therefore exclude the parts industry.

As the industry became more global, auto assemblers regained total ownership of firms in those few cases that had involved a local partner. Total ownership and total control by the foreign party would allow it the necessary flexibility to make decisions about the site of the production, the scale, the product mix, and export and import prices. The rationale in the auto industry worldwide was to specialize plant production for a limited number of models of cars and parts and to import any other models and parts. The cars produced were usually those that had a large domestic market, and the same models could be exported. This was well illustrated in the case of Volkswagen's Beetle; Mexico was the only producer in the world after this model was phased out in the rest of VW's plants. In other cases, companies began to produce certain models solely for export to the U.S. market (for example, Ford's Hermosillo plant) as part of their strategy of globalization and specialization.

This model of operation would naturally lead to more exports as a result of specialization, more imports as domestic production and sales rose, the production of only a few models, and greater efficiency at the plant as production runs became longer and the flow of products and inputs more certain. This entire process is controlled by corporate programs in which unnecessary stocks and interruptions to the production run are minimized. It must not be forgotten, however, that exports initially surged based on the producers' projections of high domestic sales, projects that would prove to be wrong.

Still, Mexico had not fully liberalized its trade regime by the early 1990s; it maintained provisions for local content and supplies, and the scale of plants was small relative to many of their international counterparts. Mexican producers consequently would continue to record higher production costs than international producers. The same problem applied to the production of car parts—where there was also a problem with quality—and it only began to be corrected in the late 1980s; even in the late 1990s it has not been fully corrected.

Consonant with the location of new plants, 85 percent of exports during the late 1980s went to the United States and only 2.4 percent to Canada. Exports to Latin America represented 12 percent, while only 0.6 percent went to Europe and Asia. These figures illustrate the importance of the link between investment and trade: foreign investors eventually export, but in many industries (especially in automobiles) these exports are part of the multinational network of production of the parent companies. During 1981–1989 this industry was responsible for 29.5 percent of Mexico's manufacturing exports and 17.7 percent of imports; parts represented 23.5 percent of exports and 16.5 percent of imports of manufactures.

A dramatic change occurred also in the structure of demand in this industry. The export share of sales jumped from 4.4 percent in the 1970s to 20.4 percent during 1980–1989.

Imports also rose as the domestic industry became more focused on the production of specific models and components. Domestic demand increased, both for new cars and for parts for new cars as well as existing vehicles. The industry trade deficit rose as domestic demand grew, reaching $408 million per year during the 1980s from $2.003 billion of exports and $2.411 billion of imports on average. In some years, however, such as 1986 and 1988 when domestic demand collapsed, trade surpluses were recorded.

It must be remembered that the auto parts industry responded to the demand for parts not only for the assembly industry but also for existing vehicles. For this reason the parts industry suffered fewer fluctuations in activity. As the number of existing vehicles increased, employment in the parts industry grew more steadily than in the auto assembly sector, partly as a result of this lesser volatility but mainly because of increasing *maquiladora* operations.

Intra-Industry Trade

Intra-industry trade is one way to test the hypothesis of increasing specialization in the industry. The previous discussion leads to the expectation that, at a given level of aggregation, trade flows reveal increasing trade in both directions—imports and exports. This is because, unlike the theory of comparative advantage, intra-industry trade permits the same industry to produce one type of product that is exported and at the same time import another type of the same product.

This hypothesis was first formulated by Grubel and Lloyd (1975) and can be expressed as follows:

$$\sigma_i = (X_i + M_i) - |X_i - M_i|,$$

where X and M are exports and imports, respectively. As a share of total trade, intra-industry trade (σ_i) can be expressed as follows:

$$B_i = \sigma_i / (X_i + M_i).$$

The level of aggregation of trade flows is that defined by INEGI, which distinguishes between automobiles and automobile parts. In these broad categories are many models of vehicles, including light trucks, and many types of parts; therefore trade in both directions denotes exports of some types and imports of others. Netting out the difference between exports and imports means that only that part of trade in which exports and imports match each other in value is measured.

Table 3.2 shows that, for cars, intra-industry trade was variable during 1981–1996 mainly because of the low level of imports and their sensitivity in 1995 to the fall in domestic demand. We do not find a pattern, therefore, for intra-industry trade in autos because it is only recently that Mexico has liberalized its restrictions on auto imports and they are growing from a very low level.

In auto parts, however, we find a pattern of increasing intra-industry trade despite changes observed in certain years. We also see an interesting change in the pattern of intra-industry trade. In years when there was a heavy devaluation of the peso and a contraction in domestic demand (1983 and 1986), intra-industry trade declined following the decrease in imports and the increase in exports. Nevertheless, once NAFTA was in effect, the peso devaluation and the contraction in domestic demand in 1995 were not enough to cause a similarly sharp reduction in imports; hence, intra-industry trade actually increased. Imports could not fall because exports were rising, and such exports required imported components.

The Industry at the Start of NAFTA

Once the Mexican, U.S., and Canadian governments began negotiations for a free-trade agreement, the auto industry realized that the main features of the protectionist regime could be removed. Automobile producers viewed the agreement as an

Table 3.2
Intra-Industry Auto and Auto Parts Trade, 1981–1996
(millions of $ and percentages)

Years	Automobiles					
	X_i	M_i	X_i-M_i	X_i+M_i	σ_i	B_i (%)
1981	70	182	(112)	252	140	55.5
1982	67	94	(27)	161	134	83.4
1983	110	15	95	124	29	23.3
1984	119	18	101	137	36	26.0
1985	116	41	76	157	81	51.7
1986	657	37	620	694	74	10.7
1987	1,243	42	1,201	1,285	83	6.5
1988	1,416	66	1,350	1,482	132	8.9
1989	1,642	86	1,556	1,728	172	9.9
1990	2,492	294	2,198	2,785	587	21.1
1991	3,661	297	3,363	3,958	595	15.0
1992	3,378	384	2,994	3,762	769	20.4
1993	4,251	405	3,847	4,656	809	17.4
1994	5,077	1,250	3,827	6,326	2,499	39.5
1995	7,529	446	7,082	7,975	893	11.2
1996	9,816	930	8,886	10,745	1,860	17.3

Sources: Bank of Mexico 1989–1996; INEGI 1993.

Notes: $\sigma_i = (X_i+M_i)- |X_i-M_i|$
$B_i = \sigma_i/(X_i+M_i)$
X = Exports; M= Imports
Imports (M) includes all vehicles

opportunity to crystallize a regime in which investment could move freely and production facilities in the three countries could be rationalized to maximize specialization and reduce costs. Parts producers, by contrast, representing large Mexican business groups close to President Carlos Salinas, sought to prolong the protection afforded by the status quo, in particular, the

Table 3.2 (*continued*)
Intra-Industry Auto and Auto Parts Trade, 1981–1996
(millions of $ and percentages)

Years	Auto Parts					
	X_i	M_i	X_i-M_i	X_i+M_i	σ_i	B_i (%)
1981	347	814	(468)	1,161	693	59.7
1982	449	446	4	895	891	99.6
1983	959	195	764	1,153	390	33.8
1984	1,412	355	1,057	1,767	710	40.2
1985	1,408	496	912	1,904	991	52.1
1986	1,709	199	1,510	1,908	398	20.8
1987	1,864	347	1,517	2,211	694	31.4
1988	2,003	806	1,197	2,809	1,611	57.4
1989	2,196	999	1,197	3,195	1,998	62.5
1990	2,225	1,132	1,093	3,357	2,264	67.4
1991	2,935	1,813	1,122	4,749	3,627	76.4
1992	3,331	2,546	784	5,877	5,093	86.7
1993	3,978	2,482	1,496	6,460	4,964	76.8
1994	4,892	3,272	1,620	8,164	6,544	80.2
1995	5,854	5,333	521	11,187	10,666	95.3
1996	6,363	9,393	(3,030)	15,756	12,726	80.8

Sources: Bank of Mexico 1989–1996; INEGI 1993.

Notes: $\sigma_i = (X_i+M_i) - |X_i-M_i|$
$B_i = \sigma_i / (X_i+M_i)$
X = Exports; M= Imports
Imports (M) includes all vehicles

protection against FDI in the parts industry. This made the automobile section of NAFTA an ambiguous one in terms of trade liberalization.

In the 1989 regime, automobile producers aimed to remove the following features in particular:

- The national content requirement,
- The requirement to achieve a trade balance, and
- The definition of national suppliers in which there was a bias against vertical integration in Mexico, as ownership of a parts producer by a car assembler would exclude such parts from the accounting of domestic value added.

Before the existence of NAFTA, Mexico had made important structural changes, including trade liberalization although this change did not include the auto industry. Other changes were a reduction in state intervention in the economy and the privatization of many state enterprises. To a significant degree, the reforms responded to disenchantment with import-substitution policies as well as a shift in the thinking of multilateral organizations such as the IMF and the World Bank. These institutions were close observers of Mexican economic policy and, as lenders of financial packages and watchers of adjustment programs, had influence in steering Mexico's strategies in a new direction. The key changes in the transformation of the auto industry from a protected one to one part of a global industry remained to be accomplished through NAFTA negotiation.

During the 1990s, developments in the industry have been dominated by two factors: the negotiation and implementation of NAFTA and the adjustment of the auto industry to the financial crisis of 1995–1996. During the 1990s the industry grew at a high rate, influenced by expectations related to NAFTA and that other macroeconomic reforms would create a strong domestic market. Table 3.1 shows that domestic sales grew 78.1 percent from 1988 to 1994, or 10.1 percent per year. Although this was a less impressive rate than in previous cycles, the rise started from a relatively high level.

Table 3.3 shows that high growth in domestic sales was accompanied by a strong increase in exports; output in the industry was growing more rapidly than domestic demand. Growth was 117.2 percent between 1988 and 1994, or 13.8 percent per year, for domestic and export sales.

In 1993 the economy suffered a slowdown induced by a tight fiscal and monetary policy adopted by the government in its effort to prevent the external deficit from increasing before the signing of NAFTA. Domestic production fell 14.9 percent in 1993 and 7.1 percent in 1994. Nevertheless, as table 3.3 shows, exports continued to grow. It is evident that as NAFTA was being negotiated and approved the auto industry in Mexico was already

Table 3.3
Mexican Auto Industry Production,
Domestic and for Exports, 1985–1996
(units of cars and trucks)

Years	Domestic	For Export	Total
1985	358,830	62,970	421,800
1986	262,483	65,620	328,103
1987	227,943	109,532	337,475
1988	330,956	174,246	505,202
1989	433,763	195,467	629,230
1990	525,133	278,558	803,691
1991	595,529	365,354	960,883
1992	660,129	391,050	1,051,179
1993	562,027	493,194	1,055,221
1994	522,350	575,031	1,097,381
1995	152,500	778,678	931,178
1996	240,423	970,874	1,211,297

Source: AMIA.

operating under the assumption that NAFTA would become a reality, which explains the continued exports. Exports maintained their increase despite the strengthening of the peso because, as they represented intrafirm trade, they were planned flows largely insensitive to exchange rates. But, as described later, the presumed stability of export flows is valid only in the short term. A strong exchange rate would invalidate new export programs over the medium term.

The contraction of the auto industry in 1993, long before the economy contracted sharply in 1995, shows its cyclical nature. The fact that its exports continued to increase that year probably confused the Mexican government, which thought that continued export growth was proof that the strong peso was competitive and represented no macroeconomic risk. Both the Bank of Mexico and the IMF validated this view by reading into the high export growth conditions of a sound exchange rate, which would be further strengthened as the structural reforms undertaken in previous years became effective. However, exports of this industry were responding to long-term corporate programs and, being an integral part of multinational production, such exports would continue despite the strength of the peso.

In 1995 domestic sales fell 71.7 percent. Employment in car assemblers fell only 3.4 percent because of shorter work shifts and temporary suspension of production. High export growth of 35.4 percent was key to maintaining employment levels.

As Mexico began to recover in 1996, the industry also recorded a recovery of 70.4 percent in domestic sales. Part of this recovery, however, was somewhat artificially boosted by the reduction in ISAN, a tax applied to the production of "new automobiles" that has proved to have a major influence on demand. Production for export jumped 24.7 percent. Higher domestic demand, aided by a discretionary reduction in the sales tax, allowed firms to dispose of large inventories. Producers, however, had to restrain themselves from increasing prices in parallel to the peso devaluation. While the peso devalued against the dollar by 89.6 percent in 1995, car prices increased by only 68 percent; and it took two years for producers to fully pass on the higher cost in prices.

In 1997 the industry continued to recover. Through August, production for the domestic market grew 46.8 percent and employment has been reported up by firms.

Note that the high growth in domestic sales during the globalization phase and associated with the NAFTA regime came accompanied by an equally high growth in exports. This has made the present cycle of growth in the industry during 1996–1997 different from previous cycles, when exports were sometimes sacrificed to the increase in domestic sales.

The growth in exports has allowed employment to remain at levels that would otherwise have been impossible to maintain. It has also generated valuable dollar revenues for car producers, which, combined with the peso devaluation, boosted profits. Nevertheless, such financial results are not relevant to producers that remain focused on domestic activity and domestic sales, and exports often represent an internal, corporate transaction.

The expansion of the auto industry in Mexico was for many years justified on the grounds that domestic demand was growing. Nevertheless, this growth has not been maintained over the long run, as is demonstrated by a poor average increase in domestic sales of only 2.2 percent per year between 1970 and 1996. Today it is export sales and the integration of industrial processes in Mexico with those in the United States that make production in Mexico attractive. By the same token, were Mexico to enjoy a continued period of sustained growth in domestic sales at rates of 10 percent to 15 percent per annum, the potential for expansion of the industry would appear to be very promising as, clearly, more production capacity would become necessary and investment would follow.

Content and Implications of NAFTA

NAFTA contains the following provisions that affect the auto industry:

- Elimination of tariffs on all automotive goods by 2003;
- New rules-of-origin and a regional-content requirement of 62.5 percent for cars and specific components and 60 percent for other parts, to be reduced over 10 years to 52.5 percent and 50 percent, respectively;
- Elimination of the U.S.-Canada Auto Pact and Canada's duty remission program based on Auto Pact principles;
- Phasing out of the 1989 Mexican automotive decree and other Mexican restrictions over 10 years up to 2003;
- Treatment of Mexican-produced vehicles as "domestic" under the U.S. corporate average fuel economy (CAFE);
- Elimination of restrictions on the importation of used cars to Mexico after 15 years and full elimination of restrictions only after 25 years;
- The new FDI policy in Mexico, also resulting from NAFTA, that eliminates the limit of 49 percent as the maximum foreign-investment share in parts producers, but only after five years; and
- The national-content requirement that is to continue for 10 years, until 2003, except for investments for exports. *Maquiladora* production can count toward national content for up to 20 percent of costs if it is not produced by a plant owned by the car assembler.

The last two regulations illustrate the strong protection by the Mexican government of its national parts producers. The government of President Salinas was very close to vested interests in the auto-parts industry, in particular.

For these reasons the auto industry has its own chapter in NAFTA; and the negotiations focused on Mexico's desire to liberalize at a very gradual pace and the multinational auto industry's desire to remove restrictions on national content and preserve a high regional-content requirement that would operate as a barrier against non-U.S. auto producers. This rule would address the perceived needs of U.S. industry to protect its considerable investments in the region against unrestricted free trade through Mexico and greater competition in U.S. and Canadian markets from producers operating outside of the region.

The Mexican automotive industry decree, which even in its latest version still compels domestic firms to export, is to be phased out over 10 years, a long and generous transition for a regime that grants unnecessary protection to Mexican parts suppliers. It is evident by now that the Mexican industry has adapted more quickly than negotiators had expected and, consequently, will not in fact need such a long transition period.

NAFTA also reserved a market share for the Mexican auto-parts industry. A minimum of 34 percent of total costs must be sourced from these producers. NAFTA also set a limit of 49 percent for foreign investment in national-supplier firms during the first five years of the agreement; therefore domestic-owned firms enjoy double protection: against imports and against foreign investors.

Despite its protectionist bent, the NAFTA market remains attractive to European and Japanese producers but only insofar as domestic demand in those countries justifies increased local assembly. Their strategy would thus be to establish production or assembly facilities with different degrees of local content in the NAFTA countries whose markets they wish to enter. This, by definition, is the United States; it is the largest market with a low import tariff where such producers can still sell autos with a large percentage of imported components but cannot export them to the other two countries under the benefits of NAFTA. This, for example, is the strategy followed by Mercedes Benz and BMW.

At present the auto industry in Mexico has considerable idle capacity. With a capacity of 1.7 million vehicles, it is now producing 1.2 million; 300,000 are for the domestic market and 900,000 are exported. Mexico also imports roughly 100,000 vehicles, a number that could rise in the future. Mexico will benefit from investment by North American producers, but it will not necessarily become a global producer for European or Japanese producers until the protections afforded to national suppliers and the high rules-of-origin are phased out or reduced significantly. The competitiveness of its industry will thus be determined by the competitiveness of North American producers.

The restriction imposed on the sales of *maquiladora* production in the Mexican domestic market is to be phased out over seven years. One year after NAFTA entered into force, a *maquiladora* could sell up to 60 percent of its previous year's exports in the domestic market. This percentage will increase in 5-percent increments to 85 percent in the sixth year. The restriction will be completely removed in the seventh year. This is not, however, a program that will directly discourage the operations of *maquiladoras* nor will it reduce their incentives to expand. That is, *maquiladora* production is determined by many factors, including labor and taxes, as well as by the efficiency in Mexican plants. NAFTA does not necessarily mean the termination of incentives for *maquiladora* production.

After January 1, 2001, the NAFTA drawback rules will apply to the *maquiladoras*. Duty deferred on materials imported from countries other than the United States or Canada will have to be paid at the time that the goods are exported to the United States or Canada. This has no effect on U.S.-owned *maquiladoras*, but it will have a substantial effect on *maquiladoras* owned by third-country investors such as Japan or Germany if they source materials in their home countries instead of NAFTA.

Mexico eliminated its auto transportation decree, which covered larger trucks and buses, with the implementation of NAFTA. Nevertheless, until 1999, restrictions will remain on the importation of these vehicles. Mexico may restrict the number of vehicles imported by an assembler to 50 percent of the number of vehicles the assembler produces in Mexico, and the importing assembler must satisfy a 40-percent national value-added requirement in its Mexican production.

NAFTA contains a general prohibition on import-permit systems. Nevertheless, Mexico is permitted to maintain such import permits on all types of vehicles. For vehicles covered by the automotive decree, the permit system may remain in place for 10 years; for vehicles covered by the auto transportation decree, the permit system may continue for 5 years.

With improvements in infrastructure and the operation of customs, Mexico could become a more attractive location for production and greater value-added than it is at present. One current example of the potential is a producer of components,

Delphi Automotive Systems, a General Motors (GM) subsidiary that employs 2,000 people in design in Ciudad Juarez. Facilities such as this are encouraged by the regulation that suppliers must produce certain components in Mexico. Today Delphi has 60 plants in Mexico; this makes GM the largest *maquiladora* employer, with 90,000 workers out of a total of 160,000.

Trends and Structural Relationships in the Industry

Direction of Trade, 1990–1996

The auto industry including in-bond *maquiladoras* is Mexico's largest export industry, exceeding oil and tourism. Car exports are the largest component, as is shown in table 3.4.

By contrast, table 3.5 shows that on the import side the largest component is material for assembly of vehicles.

On the export side, note the increasing share of trucks and car parts as distinguished from engines. On the import side, note the increasing share of cars (in 1994 the value of car imports reached a high of $1.2 billion) and engines and parts, for both new vehicles as well as replacement parts. From 1990 onward the data include trade of *maquiladoras*, again with no adjustment backward in the time series.

The large increase in car imports cannot be attributed to NAFTA because NAFTA started only in 1994. Nevertheless the increase is part of the same change of regime that was evolving during the 1990s and that NAFTA liberalized further.

The United States was the destination for 72.9 percent of total exports in 1991, 86.7 percent in 1995, and 85.5 percent in 1996; Canada imported approximately 4.2 percent in 1996. It is possible, however, that some of the cars exported to the United States have Canada as their final destination because the U.S. parent company might reexport them.

Employment and Productivity

If the changes in employment in the auto industry since 1970, as shown in table 3.1, are combined with the volume of output, a crude measurement of productivity (output per worker) is obtained. This is done only for the auto industry, however. (The employment figures in the parts industry are distorted by the inclusion in 1988 of the *maquiladoras* without including employment in such plants for prior years.) When the parts industry is excluded, production of cars per worker appears to increase with the business cycle as would be expected, but it falls to much lower levels when domestic activity falls. It is only in recent years that, because of increasing exports, production per worker has risen steadily.

The distortion in the employment series of the parts industry does not allow appraisal of the dynamics of job creation before 1988 (see table 3.1). Employment increased, however, from 218,107 in 1988 to 305,242 in 1994 but then fell in 1996 to 276,896. The largest part of this change was in the parts industry, where employment increased by 78,406 between 1988 and 1994 but then by 1996 fell by 29,291, 37 percent of its advance during the previous six years.

Table 3.6 presents crude measurements of productivity. In the parts industry, from 1988 to 1996, productivity rose by 64.2 percent or 6.3 percent per year. In the assembly industry, the increase in productivity from 1985 to 1996 was 141.6 percent or 8.4 percent per year. Both were significant increases. It is clear, however, that the trend in productivity is distorted by the large cyclical change in production, a cycle caused largely by macroeconomic crisis, including sharp contraction in employment, especially in the parts industry in the short run.

The increase in employment has been much faster in the parts industry than in the auto industry because many assembly operations have been restructured or eliminated. This reconversion, from an industry focused on increasing local content to one focused on increasing efficiency, may appear as a loss of jobs, but this is not the case when we take into account that many of the jobs created are more competitive jobs and of higher levels of efficiency.

Thus trends in employment reflect two forces: one operating over the medium term and reflecting structural changes in the industry; the other depicting a cyclical change owing to macroeconomic conditions. Under these circumstances, the measurement of productivity based on a ratio of output to employment is not appropriate. In fact, the ratio output/employment would result in a downward bias in the short term because industry records the reduced output much faster than it can adjust the labor force downward. In addition, the mix of the output changes over time and the new mix reflects goods produced under more competitive conditions. Despite such caveats, however, it is undeniable that productivity has risen remarkably since the mid-1980s, especially in the automobile sector. This is

Table 3.4
Mexican Auto Industry Exports, 1981–1996
(millions of $)

Years	Cars	Trucks	Chassis with Engine	Car Engines	Springs & Sheets	Car Parts	Engine Parts	Others	Total
1981	70.10	39.40	1.40	61.50	18.60	165.00	21.80	78.30	456.10
1982	67.00	14.10	0.30	214.00	28.30	131.30	27.30	48.00	530.30
1983	109.70	14.40	0.00	602.70	33.90	179.80	40.60	101.60	1082.70
1984	119.20	26.80	0.00	982.60	47.30	270.30	46.80	65.30	1558.30
1985	116.40	24.30	0.10	1,039.40	6.40	240.60	49.00	72.60	1548.80
1986	657.20	29.40	0.00	1,219.20	10.80	293.30	81.00	104.60	2395.50
1987	1,243.00	23.40	0.50	1,222.40	45.70	406.20	98.40	90.70	3130.30
1988	1,416.00	37.00	8.60	1,351.50	49.20	453.90	97.90	41.70	3455.80
1989	1,641.80	32.70	17.50	1,335.90	53.20	397.00	107.80	284.70	3870.50
1990*	2,491.60	39.00	31.60	1,503.00	46.20	416.70	97.30	130.40	4755.80
1991	3,660.60	169.90	44.90	1,197.00	62.20	1,209.10	276.20	145.80	6765.70
1992	3,378.00	588.40	81.00	1,202.70	63.00	1,524.70	271.50	187.80	7297.20
1993	4,251.50	670.50	134.30	1,302.20	106.00	1,889.00	316.80	229.90	8900.10
1994	5,076.80	829.50	212.80	1,777.80	125.70	2,106.90	404.80	263.70	1,0798.00
1995	7,528.50	1,855.50	217.20	2,123.30	126.70	2,298.00	467.80	620.90	1,5237.90
1996	9,815.50	3,462.00	267.50	2,215.80	144.30	2,735.00	552.70	447.50	1,9640.30

Sources: Bank of Mexico 1989–1996; INEGI 1993.   * In-bond *maquila* data are included from 1990 onward.

Table 3.5
Mexican Auto Industry Imports, 1981–1996
(millions of $)

Years	Cars	Light Trucks	Trucks	Car Chassis	Car Assemblies & Parts	Car Engines & Parts	Replacement Parts	Others	Total
1981	182.20	148.60	194.50	6.80	2,010.80	177.10	552.50	77.90	3,350.40
1982	93.60	58.40	64.00	1.50	1,182.70	109.20	296.00	38.90	1,844.30
1983	14.50	10.70	8.40	0.20	674.40	65.50	99.20	29.90	902.80
1984	17.80	55.20	24.50	0.30	1,178.10	112.00	209.80	32.80	1,630.50
1985	40.60	39.30	55.30	0.30	1,650.00	145.80	288.60	60.90	2,280.80
1986	37.10	25.60	28.60	0.70	1,497.00	112.80	28.10	57.20	1,787.10
1987	41.70	47.10	34.00	1.00	1,898.30	102.70	179.90	63.20	2,367.90
1988	65.80	66.60	93.30	2.10	2,364.30	148.00	556.30	99.30	3,395.70
1989	85.80	45.70	30.50	1.50	2,978.00	171.00	639.70	186.90	4,139.10
1990*	293.60	44.60	46.00	2.10	1,009.50	177.60	632.60	319.90	2,525.90
1991	297.30	84.50	29.90	2.90	5,024.20	280.20	1,090.10	440.30	7,249.40
1992	384.30	122.70	58.60	24.90	6,007.10	376.90	1,337.90	806.70	9,119.00
1993	404.60	86.60	32.60	9.40	6,439.30	394.20	1,377.10	701.10	9,444.90
1994	1,249.60	149.20	34.40	50.00	6,733.20	565.50	1,980.60	676.10	11,438.60
1995	446.40	27.10	15.10	17.80	3,649.40	997.70	3,897.20	420.50	9,471.20
1996	929.80	36.20	40.40	42.40	18.80	2,251.90	6,515.60	583.20	10,418.30

Sources: Bank of Mexico 1989–1996; INEGI 1993.   * In-bond *maquila* data are included from 1990 onward.

Table 3.6
Mexican Auto Industry Wages, Employment, and Productivity, 1983–1996
(Indices 1983=1.00, 1988=1.0 and 1985=1.0)

| | WAGES | | | PARTS INDUSTRY | | | ASSEMBLY INDUSTRY | | |
| | Mexico | | U.S. | | | | | | |
Year	Manufac'g real $ (1983=1.0)	Auto Sector current $ (1983=1.0)	Auto Sector current $ (1983=1.0)	Output Volume (1988=1.0)	Employment (1988=1.0)	Productivity per Worker (1988=1.0)	Output Volume (1985=1.0)	Employment (1985=1.0)	Productivity per Worker (1985=1.0)
1983	1.0000	1.0000	1.0000						
1984	0.8916	1.2594	1.0838						
1985	0.8473	0.9558	1.1667				1.0000	1.0000	1.0000
1986	0.7898	0.6788	1.1963				0.7779	0.9426	0.8252
1987	0.7810	0.5574	1.1857				0.8001	0.9770	0.8189
1988	0.7765	0.5629	1.3436	1.0000	1.0000	1.0000	1.1977	0.9616	1.2456
1989	0.8451	0.6104	1.3666	1.1288	1.2271	0.9199	1.4918	1.1297	1.3205
1990	0.8628	0.6634	1.4363	1.1750	1.3410	0.8762	1.9059	1.3523	1.4094
1991	0.9115	0.8532	1.6352	1.3597	1.2746	1.0667	2.2781	1.4189	1.6055
1992	0.9956	0.9967	1.7274	1.3281	1.6116	0.8241	2.4921	1.4059	1.7726
1993	1.0708	1.2561	1.7230	1.2151	1.4580	0.8334	2.5017	1.2883	1.9418
1994	1.0996	1.3631	1.8059	1.3220	1.4427	0.9163	2.6017	1.1662	2.2308
1995	0.9491	0.9382	1.7843	1.2053	1.2110	0.9954	2.2076	1.1266	1.9595
1996	0.8031	1.1457	1.8425	1.4399	1.2773	1.1272	2.8717	1.1884	2.4165

Sources: Bank of Mexico 1997; INEGI; U.S. Department of Commerce.
Notes: Wages for Mexico's auto industry are reported by one large producer.
Productivity is the index of output divided by the index of employment.

partly because, owing to the large swings in domestic demand, firms have not increased employment and the increase in exports has taken up any slack in domestic demand. The effect on employment has been minimized, with the result that employment growth has remained stagnant this decade.

In the parts industry a different pattern operates. The industry was highly protected initially by the trade regime; therefore its output mix and productivity levels would be different from those in the years of trade liberalization. Again, although it is not possible to appraise the trend of productivity before 1988, it is clear that until 1988 (the year of the data distortion) employment was growing in the non-*maquiladora* sector by 4.4 percent per year. This was probably because of the protectionist trade regime, which worked for the benefit of parts producers.

From 1988 onward, employment also grew by 3.1 percent although this rate of growth is influenced by the heavy contraction in 1995–1996. Without these two years, employment increased by 6.3 percent per year. Recall that productivity also increased by 64.2 percent, or 6.4 percent per year, between 1988 and 1996. Nevertheless, employment numbers from 1988 onward include that of *maquiladoras*.

Wages

Wages in Mexico have fallen significantly since the late 1970s, a result of economic crises that have been resolved by reductions in wages as well as the profound industrial restructuring that has weakened the labor market. Over the medium term, industrial restructuring has meant the closure of many industrial operations. Over the short term, macroeconomic adjustments have forced wages down; it will take years for wages to regain their previous levels.

Table 3.6 shows real wages in manufacturing during the 1983–1996 period. The base year (1983) already presents wages sharply reduced—probably in the range of 30 percent—from their level at the end of the 1970s. Nevertheless, following their sluggishness during the early 1980s, real wages in manufacturing rose very quickly—by 6.0 percent per year from 1988 to 1994—more rapidly than wages should have risen in a stabilization program because the economy was still in a recovery phase and policymakers should have avoided a consumption boom. This large increase in wages reflects the distortions of a stabilization policy based on a pegged exchange rate and an incomes policy that made it difficult for the government to see that wage increases were unrealistic while export profits for the manufacturing sector in general were falling. The too-high increase was masked at the time by the notions that wages were too depressed at the beginning of the 1990s and that their past decline could and ought to have been reversed as Mexico entered a new era of high economic growth. Expectations over NAFTA helped to support this notion.

Table 3.6 shows that hourly wages expressed in current dollars grew rapidly during the same 1988–1994 period, that is, by 142.2 percent, or 15.9 percent per year. This compares with growth in U.S. wages of only 34.4 percent, or 5.1 percent per year. Note that these are wages in the auto industry in dollars and not wages of manufacturing industry. The disproportionate growth in Mexican wages is, again, owed to the exchange-rate appreciation, which eventually led wages to fall abruptly in 1995.

Recall that Mexican productivity was rising during the industry's transformation from a protected to a competitive one. The rise, however, was less than the Mexican government and the international organizations believed, partly because the initial point of the productivity increase was when production was low. Furthermore, continued growth in the industry was interrupted by contraction in demand as early as 1993, when the stabilization program encountered its limits. Thus the measurement of productivity is difficult because changes reflect large swings in employment independent of changes in efficiency. It is not surprising, however, that in 1993 when wages increased, employment began to decline even before domestic sales fell. For the manufacturing industry, employment followed the same trend except that its fall was much more pronounced and began before 1993; manufacturing was less able than auto producers to adjust to the strong exchange rate, the industrial restructuring, and the greater international competition.

The large fluctuation in real wages, with a downward trend over the long run, represents changes not only in the auto industry but also in Mexico's economy. Industry, however, is more affected than the economy by specific developments that have an impact on wages in the short run. One development was that the industry was vulnerable to cost pressures as it became gradually exposed to international competition; this weakness was transmitted to wages through a soft labor market. Also, because of the rapid adaptation that the industry had to make to the trade and regulatory regime, producers became reluctant to increase employment, which helped indirectly to depress wages. The most salient effect on wages, however, has been the abrupt change of conditions in the macroeconomy, vitiated by an unsustainable exchange-rate appreciation. This caused the rise in dollar wages to be too high and, then, the fall to be too sharp.

Empirical Analysis

These data on output and sales, employment, trade, average productivity, and wages over the period 1983–1996 will now be used to appraise some structural relationships in the automobile industry. Results are provided in table 3.7 and are discussed below.

The variables chosen are export sales of cars in units and car parts in an index of volume based on dollar exports deflated by U.S. consumer prices. Domestic sales exclude parts and are only of car units because there are no reliable data on parts sales. Employment is the number of workers in the auto industry only, excluding parts, because of the distortion in data described earlier. Output per worker, or crude productivity, could be measured only from 1985 onward because the series of production for domestic and export markets is not broken down for earlier years. The measure of the real peso exchange rate is U.S. dollar per peso in terms of purchasing-power parity, in other words, adjusted for consumer inflation in the two countries with 1983 as the base year.

For wages, data of nominal hourly labor costs in the auto industry (supplied by one of the Big Three U.S. producers) are used. These data are used to investigate a possible relation between Mexican and U.S. wages and Mexican employment. U.S. GDP is expressed in constant prices, as reported by the U.S. Department of Commerce. Real disposable income in Mexico is nominal income deflated by average inflation, as reported by INEGI.

The automobile relative price index is the price of autos divided by the average national consumer price index, as reported by the Bank of Mexico. Productivity is the measure of output in volume divided by employment, in the auto industry only. All data are shown in the appendix to this chapter, and all regressions are in logarithmic form for the 1983–1996 period. In the case of estimates involving productivity, only the period 1985–1996 is used, as was explained earlier.

Table 3.7
Mexican Auto Industry Sales, Exports, Employment, and Wages: Regression Results

Dependent Variable	Constant	Explanatory Variables									Adjusted R-squared	Durbin-Watson
		X	r	Y	A	Y_{US}	L	S	P	W_{US}		
1. Car domestic sales	-29.396 (-1.727)			3.609 (1.736)	0.192 (0.202)						0.430	0.840
1a. Car domestic sales	-(4.183) 26159		1.107a (2.440)	3.21a (4.220)							0.629	0.977
1b. Car domestic sales	-22.021 (-1.501)		1.143a (2.800)	2.704 (1.508)	-0.260 (-0.315)						0.596	1.021
2. Car exports	0.018 (0.140)		0.199 (0.522)			10.688b (19.308)					0.967	1.550
2a. Parts exports	-0.19 (-0.264)		-0.164 (-0.773)			3.743b (12.153)					0.924	1.099
3. Car employment	0.003 (0.080)	0.088b (4.847)						0.212b (4.233)			0.808	1.694
3a. Car employment	-0.010 (-0.216)	0.077b (3.544)					0.070 (0.891)	0.221a (4.287)			0.804	1.710

Table 3.7 (continued)
Mexican Auto Industry Sales, Exports, Employment, and Wages: Regression Results

Dependent Variable	Constant	Explanatory Variables									Adjusted R-squared	Durbin-Watson
		X	r	Y	A	Y_{US}	L	S	P	W_{US}		
4. Wages in car industry	0.078 (0.219)	-0.376 (-1.873)						-0.027 (-0.160)	1.134 c (2.214)		0.287	0.991
4a. Wages in car industry	-0.047 (-0.105)	-0.366 (-1.729)						-0.366 (-1.729)	0.962 (1.522)	1.340 (0.517)	0.216	1.260

Source: Ecanal S.A.
Notes: t values in parentheses

a 95% of 2-tail significance
b 99% of 2-tail significance
c 90% of 2-tail significance

X = Car exports
r = Real exchange rate
Y = Real personal disposable income
A = Automobile relative price index
Y_{US} = Real U.S. GDP
L = Ratio of real wage index in auto industry U.S./Mexico in dollars (deflated by U.S. consumer price index [CPI])
S = Car domestic sales
P = Productivity (index of output divided by the index of employment)
W_{US} = Real hourly U.S. wage in auto industry

Table 3.7 shows that domestic sales of the industry (line 1) may depend on disposable income (but the coefficient is insignificant) while the real automobile price is insignificant and the fit is poor. When the real peso exchange rate was used as a proxy indicator of real prices (line 1a, table 3.7), however, an improved explanation and a much better fit was found; income became a significant explanation. The reason is not only that car costs are determined largely by the exchange rate but also that real income of consumers is boosted when the peso is strong. That is when domestic sales rise because auto prices reflect lower import costs.

The second relation that was tested was that of exports with respect to an indicator of external demand and the peso exchange rate. For external demand, GDP in the United States was used. Line 2 of table 3.7 shows that the coefficient of foreign income (Y_{US}) is very high and highly significant while that of the real exchange rate is positive but insignificant. This suggests that exports, being largely intrafirm trade, are unlikely to change when the strong exchange rate makes them less competitive because the production network cannot change sources of supply over the medium term. Such a change involves strategic corporate decisions that take a longer time to materialize.

Furthermore, since the late 1980s, exports have risen as a result of producers' plans that had been laid out in previous years; these plans coincided with the expectation of the adoption of NAFTA (from 1991 onward) and with the appreciation of the peso that resulted from the stabilization plan on which Mexico embarked in December 1987. Exports and the strong peso were a coincidence; for that reason, this should not necessarily lead to the conclusion that exports are insensitive to movements in the real exchange rate. In a separate regression for auto parts (line 2a), where intrafirm trade is less than in automobiles, the exchange rate has the correct sign but it still lacks significance. The presence of car engines (between producers of the same corporation) and of parts that are integrated to programmed production suggests that not only has intrafirm trade become much more significant over time but also that the scope for changes in prices or volumes in response to exchange-rate movements is very limited.

Thus the exchange rate does not seem to affect the trade flows, but it must be said that a consistently strong exchange rate might compel firms to revise their long-term export plans if such exports were regarded as too costly. It might, therefore, affect the allocation of investment over the long term, as was confirmed by industry participants during interviews.

The third relation investigated is that among employment, output, and sales in the auto industry only. Lines 3 and 3a of table 3.7 show that higher employment is associated with increased exports and even more with increased domestic sales. This would seem consistent with the large fluctuation in employment in the years of heavy contraction in the domestic market.

An alternate estimate of employment (line 3a) confirmed the significance of exports and domestic sales but failed to show a relation with U.S. wages relative to Mexican wages. This is a finding that serves to reject the notion that growth in employment in Mexico is motivated by the need for producers to reduce wages in the United States or that low Mexican wages contribute to job creation in Mexico as producers move facilities away from the United States.

Recall that real wages in manufacturing during the 1980s and 1990s have fluctuated greatly, such that any estimation in relation to other variables has proven meaningless. Real (dollar) wages in line 4, table 3.7, are negatively correlated with exports, which is consistent with the effects of peso devaluations although the coefficients lack significance. They are also negatively correlated with domestic sales for the same reason and seem only weakly related to productivity, but with very poor fits. The main reason is that wages in the industry depend on wages in Mexico, and since the mid-1970s the latter have experienced a long decline with variations during short periods in which cyclical factors and the real exchange rate contributed to sharp gyrations. Even though wages have failed to rise on a sustained basis—this in spite of the export drive of the 1980s—it is clear that this issue is beyond the reach of NAFTA. The trade agreement might contribute to wage increases in Mexico, but, if this is so, it will be over the long term and possibly not independent of the improvement in other indicators of performance more directly connected with the structure of the economy.

These relations need further exploration in light of the strategies adopted by auto producers in Mexico. There seems to be a very clear association between employment and exports, and between export growth and trade liberalization. Productivity is clearly associated with exports as stated by auto producers, but such a relation must be explored with more data than used in this study so that the effect on employment of macroeconomic fluctuations and company restructuring can be controlled properly.

Conclusions

NAFTA went one step farther in the removal in Mexico of protectionist policies in the auto industry because such protection was inconsistent with being a producer for the global market. Nevertheless, NAFTA's effects are slow to be seen because of the long period for the phaseout of preexisting restrictions on both trade and investment. NAFTA followed a long import-substitution period and a transition during the 1980s to a regime in which exports of the industry gradually became more important.

The gradualism of NAFTA allowed the Mexican auto industry to adapt because some restrictions against imports were maintained while Mexican producers were reassured by the certainty of their access to an enlarged regional market. This has enabled the auto industry to achieve levels of efficiency and exports that had not been attained during the earlier period of import substitution nor during the transition period in the early 1980s.

The performance of the industry in the long run has been affected by the poor macroeconomic performance of Mexico, and the change in regime became apparent in numerous industry decrees that added or changed restrictions on operations of producers. The regimes maintained a protectionist stance although they have been gradually adapting to the global reality of the industry. This is partly because by the mid-1980s Mexican domestic demand had failed to materialize as producers and the government had expected. Exports were the only way to maintain employment levels; and this forced the government to open up the trade regime. Mexico became a member of GATT in 1986, and trade liberalization proceeded on a firmer ground. The auto industry started to rationalize its operations based on international specialization, eliminating lines of vehicles and cars from domestic production and increasing output of selected products. The shift to being a global, efficient producer, however, will not be complete until a phaseout of the protectionist measures, in particular the national-producer content, the restrictions on car imports, and the restrictions on equity foreign investment in the parts industry that are still in existence under NAFTA.

The poor macroeconomic performance led to high growth in

domestic sales during the upward part of the economic cycle; this was followed by sharp falls, with the result that growth was poor over the long run, that is, only 2.2 percent per year during 1970–1996. Employment expanded at a faster pace because of growth in the parts industry and the expansion of *maquiladoras.* This explains that, for employment, the parts sector is now more important than the car sector.

The automobile industry has become the largest exporter in Mexico, surpassing oil and tourism as a source of foreign exchange revenues. It has also imported more, but exports now seem to outpace imports as the industry has become an established supplier to the other NAFTA partners. The level of intra-industry trade has always been high in the parts industry, but it has reached much greater levels in recent years as the evolving trade regime has forced auto producers to export while their specialization has pushed imports up.

Employment in the industry is positively related to domestic sales, as would be expected, but its relation with exports is also very important. This conclusion holds despite the estimates being influenced by large fluctuations in domestic sales during the past 13 years (1983–1996), which have dictated employment trends. Exports, however, have maintained steady growth. In 1995, employment fell only 3.4 percent in the auto industry as domestic sales of vehicles fell 69.1 percent and exports increased 41.5 percent. By contrast, in the parts industry, employment fell 16.1 percent, which illustrates the greater exposure of this sector of the industry to the domestic market.

In a dependence greater than that of domestic sales on Mexico's economic activity, exports of the industry depend on the increase in economic activity in the United States. The high significance of U.S. economic activity is encountered in all estimates of Mexican exports, but in the auto industry the relation appears to be even stronger: auto exports increase by 10.7 times the increase in U.S. GDP, with a high statistical significance. Such a high growth in exports, especially during the 1990s, is closely associated with implementation of NAFTA because producers cemented their export plans as soon as negotiations started in 1991.

Wages in Mexican manufacturing have been stagnant during the 1983–1996 period. They fell 22.4 percent between 1983 and 1988, recovered through 1994, only to fall again in 1995. Nevertheless, dollar wages grew quickly during 1988–1994 because of the appreciation of the peso, only to fall again in 1995.

The relation of wages with productivity is not clear and must be examined further to establish whether or not the industry's productivity influences employment and wages positively. It must be admitted that this is not possible yet because employment in auto production has increased very mildly since the end of the 1980s and the industry has been adapting for years not only to regime changes but also to macroeconomic fluctuations. Because productivity is positively associated with exports, according to company interviews, the possibility exists that further development of the auto industry will lead not only to higher employment but also to higher wages once excess capacity in the industry begins to be eliminated. In this light, to facilitate a less volatile expansion in domestic sales, the Mexican government should try to maintain a stable tax regime for the auto industry.

Despite the fact that in this industry the effects of NAFTA on international trade are clear, much still needs to be learned from employment. There is no doubt that productivity has increased at high rates for the past 5 years, especially in the auto sector. Nevertheless, until now it has apparently not affected wages because of the substantial restructuring that has taken place and that will probably prevail during the next few years. There is a need, however, for industry-specific data supplemented by interviews with producers in order to examine the relation between pay and productivity in more depth.

Equally important is the relation between the exchange rate and exports, which appears to be insignificant but could be more significant for investment plans as companies determine their strategies and focus on the need to minimize costs and meet their global competition. Most industry exports are now part of a process of industrial integration between the U.S. parent companies and their Mexican subsidiaries. The subsidiaries developed their export plans in a long-term setting that would not change in the short period of the strong peso of the 1990s. Nonetheless, the stronger peso brought about by the stabilization economic pact in force during 1987–1994 and the rising exports were more a coincidence than they were a stable, structural relationship. As such, exports resulted largely from the maturing of investment projects focused on the U.S. market that were laid out years back, in the late 1970s and early 1980s.

Producers confirm this interpretation, arguing that, despite high local costs in the early 1990s, they kept exporting because exports were part of corporate plans and most were intrafirm. This is a very important result, as it would imply that the

Mexican government, the Bank of Mexico, and the IMF were wrong in believing that because of the continuing growth in exports the peso exchange rate represented no problem for the macroeconomy. This interpretation of these results is worthy of consideration because the auto industry looms large in total exports of manufactures and a similar phenomenon is likely to be encountered in other engineering industries.

Producers, however, hasten to say that, although the real exchange rate may not affect existing export plans, it does affect *future* export plans. That is, the implementation of new investment or the expansion of export operations will be influenced by the view of producers regarding the competitiveness of the real exchange rate. Because this rate cannot be accurately forecast, periods of real exchange-rate appreciation might induce producers to expect a strong rate in the future and deter new investment for export. This would happen even if, in the end, the real exchange rate adjusts down.

The effect on Mexico's industry of U.S. labor costs, which could induce U.S. industry to shift production to Mexico, is a relevant issue. Results indicate that employment in the auto industry in Mexico is not associated at present with relative U.S.–Mexico wages; therefore the claim that jobs are exported from the United States to Mexico to reduce wage costs remains unsupported by evidence. Testing this for the parts industry is not possible because of inconsistent data but, given its small size relative to that of the U.S. industry, the claim seems unlikely.

Mexico has ample room for policy improvements that would increase the benefits from the auto industry spin-offs. One area in particular is value-added and jobs of higher skills.

Design activities by GM's Delphi Automotive Systems in Ciudad Juarez show that certain engineering tasks can be carried out efficiently in Mexican plants. There is a need, however, for a well-coordinated effort by federal and state authorities to improve infrastructure and encourage technical education and training while they maintain a consistent and stable tax regime. Greater flexibility in labor hiring and training is needed.

Productivity increases are possible through the automation and electronic operation of customs. For auto producers, in particular, transit of products can be made much more efficient and less costly than at present if Mexico and the United States copy the electronic account system that is operational between the U.S. and Canadian customs services for imports and exports of cars and parts.

Appendix
Data Used in Chapter 3

Years	A	CS	TS	S	E	Y_{US}	H_M	b	H_{US}	d	L	Y	P
1983	1.0000	192,052	80,763	272,815	1.0000	3,907	4.53	1.0000	22.67	1.0000	1.0000	3273.7	1.0000
1984	1.0205	217,650	112,637	330,287	1.0503	4,149	5.71	1.2594	24.57	1.0838	0.8606	3414.5	1.2085
1985	1.0851	242,187	149,462	391,649	1.1564	4,280	4.33	0.9558	26.45	1.1667	1.2206	3521.5	1.4104
1986	1.1360	160,670	98,165	258,835	1.0901	4,405	3.08	0.6788	27.12	1.1963	1.7623	3276.0	1.0900
1987	1.2893	154,152	87,856	242,008	1.1298	4,540	2.53	0.5574	26.88	1.1857	2.1272	3371.7	1.1627
1988	1.1912	211,122	124,742	335,864	1.1120	4,719	2.55	0.5629	30.46	1.3436	2.3869	3481.4	1.4734
1989	1.0103	274,505	160,164	434,669	1.3064	4,838	2.77	0.6104	30.98	1.3666	2.2389	3658.2	1.7089
1990	0.8789	352,608	180,264	532,872	1.5638	4,897	3.01	0.6634	32.56	1.4363	2.1651	3920.9	1.7674
1991	0.8054	392,110	222,713	614,823	1.6409	4,888	3.87	0.8532	37.07	1.6352	1.9165	4044.7	2.0712
1992	0.6590	445,303	230,873	676,176	1.6258	4,979	4.52	0.9967	39.16	1.7274	1.7331	4128.2	2.3195
1993	0.7394	399,143	176,882	576,025	1.4899	5,135	5.69	1.2561	39.06	1.7230	1.3717	4104.1	2.4767

Appendix (*continued*)
Data Used in Chapter 3

Years	A	CS	TS	S	E	Y_{US}	H_M	b	H_{US}	d	L	Y	P
1994	0.7327	414,654	183,433	598,087	1.3487	5,344	6.18	1.3631	40.94	1.8059	1.3248	4301.1	2.7606
1995	0.8622	117,393	67,544	184,937	1.3029	5,519	4.25	0.9382	40.45	1.7843	1.9019	3780.7	2.3451
1996	0.8059	200,102	133,818	333,920	1.3743	5,651	5.19	1.1457	41.77	1.8425	1.6082	3992.4	3.1334

Notes: A   Relative car prices in Mexico
CS Domestic car sales in Mexico (units)
TS Domestic truck sales in Mexico (units)
S   Domestic car and truck sales in Mexico (units)
E   Employment in car industry in Mexico (index)
Y_{US} GDP in U.S. constant 1990 dollars
H_M Hourly Mexican labor cost in assembly plants, in U.S. dollars
b   Index of H_M
H_{US} Hourly U.S. labor cost in assembly plants, in U.S. dollars
d   Index of H_{US}
L   Ratio of H_{US}/H_M
Y   Personal disposable income in Mexico in constant pesos
P   Output (including domestic sales and exports) of cars per worker (index)

(*continued*)

Appendix (continued)
Data Used in Chapter 3

Years	NE	MI	R	X	XA	XP	USI	CP	CW	PP	PW	V	NW
1983	150.3	1.64	100.0	1,083	22,456	1.0000	1.0000	1.0000	0.40	1.0000	0.60	1.0000	45.2
1984	185.2	2.71	128.7	1,558	33,635	1.4121	1.0433	1.2701	0.40	1.2593	0.60	1.2636	66.6
1985	310.3	4.28	117.0	1,549	58,423	1.3584	1.0814	1.6333	0.40	1.4730	0.60	1.5371	100.0
1986	637.9	7.97	104.0	2,396	72,429	1.6191	1.1010	1.1914	0.40	1.2772	0.60	1.2429	173.4
1987	1405.8	18.47	105.5	3,130	163,073	1.7213	1.1417	1.3166	0.40	1.2656	0.60	1.2860	397.6
1988	2289.6	39.55	133.4	3,456	173,147	1.7592	1.1877	1.6422	0.41	1.4762	0.59	1.5436	846.1
1989	2483.3	47.47	140.8	3,871	196,999	1.8394	1.2454	2.2343	0.41	1.6646	0.59	1.8976	1107.0
1990	2846.6	60.12	147.6	4,756	276,859	1.7688	1.3123	2.7674	0.45	1.7693	0.55	2.2195	1432.0
1991	3016.2	73.74	165.8	6,766	350,661	2.2392	1.3675	3.4025	0.50	2.0053	0.50	2.7039	1852.8
1992	3094.9	85.18	181.4	7,297	388,739	2.4653	1.4094	3.7764	0.49	1.9598	0.51	2.8572	2337.5

Appendix (*continued*)
Data Used in Chapter 3

Years	NE	MI	R	X	XA	XP	USI	CP	CW	PP	PW	V	NW
1993	3118.4	93.49	191.8	8,900	471,483	2.8592	1.4514	3.6959	0.51	1.7926	0.49	2.7595	2761.7
1994	3390.7	100.00	183.9	10,796	567,107	3.422	1.4882	3.7291	0.49	1.9503	0.51	2.8255	3030.5
1995	6509.2	135.00	125.8	15,276	781,082	3.9902	1.5302	3.0602	0.50	1.7783	0.50	2.4192	3529.9
1996	7600.6	181.41	140.8	17,853	975,408	4.2152	1.5748	4.3131	0.50	2.1242	0.50	3.2187	4017.5

Notes: NE Nominal exchange rate; Ps/$ (old pesos)
MI Consumer price index in Mexico, 1994=100
R Real exchange rate, $/Ps, 1983=1.0
X Exports of cars, trucks and parts from Mexico (current dollars)
XA Car exports (volume units)
XP Car parts in volume index ($ exports deflated with U.S. CPI)
USI U.S. CPI, 1983=100
CP Car and truck production index, 1983=1
CW Weight of vehicles in combined vehicle and parts output
PP Parts production index, 1983=1
PW Weight of parts in combined vehicle and parts output
V Estimated output in combined vehicles and parts industry
NW Nominal wage index in machinery and equipment industry in Mexico

(*continued*)

Appendix (*continued*)
Data Used in Chapter 3

Years	A	S	E	H_M	H_{MR}	H_{US}	H_{USR}	LR
1983	1.0000	272,815	1.0000	1.0000	1.0000	1.0000	1.0000	1.0000
1984	1.0205	330,287	1.0503	1.2594	1.2071	1.0838	1.0388	0.8606
1985	1.0851	391,649	1.1564	0.9558	0.8839	1.1667	1.0790	1.2206
1986	1.1360	258,835	1.0901	0.6788	0.6165	1.1963	1.0865	1.7623
1987	1.2893	242,008	1.1298	0.5574	0.4882	1.1857	1.0385	2.1272
1988	1.1912	335,864	1.1120	0.5629	0.4740	1.3436	1.1313	2.3869
1989	1.0103	434,669	1.3064	0.6104	0.4901	1.3666	1.0973	2.2389
1990	0.8789	532,872	1.5638	0.6634	0.5055	1.4363	1.0944	2.1651
1991	0.8054	614,823	1.6409	0.8532	0.6239	1.6352	1.1958	1.9165
1992	0.6590	676,176	1.6258	0.9967	0.7071	1.7274	1.2256	1.7331

Appendix (*continued*)
Data Used in Chapter 3

Years	A	S	E	H_M	H_{MR}	H_{US}	H_{USR}	LR
1993	0.7394	576,025	1.4899	1.2561	0.8654	1.7230	1.1871	1.3717
1994	0.7327	598,087	1.3487	1.3631	0.9160	1.8059	1.2135	1.3248
1995	0.8622	184,937	1.3029	0.9382	0.6131	1.7843	1.1661	1.9019
1996	0.8059	333,920	1.3743	1.1457	0.7275	1.8425	1.1700	1.6082

Notes: A   Relative car prices in Mexico
      S   Domestic car and truck sales in Mexico (units)
      E   Employment in car industry in Mexico (index)
     H_M Index of hourly Mexican labor cost in car plants (in dollars)
    H_{MR} Real hourly Mexican labor cost deflated by U.S. CPI (in dollars)
    H_{US} Hourly U.S. labor cost in car plants (in dollars)
   H_{USR} Real hourly U.S. labor cost (in dollars)
     LR   Ratio of indices of real wages in car industry, U.S./Mexico

(*continued*)

Appendix (*continued*)
Data Used in Chapter 3

Years	R	XA	XP	Y	P	Y_{US}
1983	100.0	22,456	1.0000	3273.7		3,907
1984	128.7	33,635	1.4121	3414.5		4,149
1985	90.8	58,423	1.3584	3521.5	1.0000	4,280
1986	89.0	72,429	1.6191	3276.0	0.8252	4,405
1987	101.4	163,073	1.7213	3371.7	0.8189	4,540
1988	126.4	173,147	1.7592	3481.4	1.2456	4,719
1989	105.5	196,999	1.8394	3658.2	1.3205	4,838
1990	104.9	276,859	1.7688	3920.9	1.4094	4,897
1991	111.1	350,661	2.2392	4044.7	1.6055	4,888
1992	109.2	388,739	2.4653	4128.2	1.7726	4,979
1993	105.8	471,483	2.8592	4104.1	1.9418	5,135
1994	95.9	567,107	3.422	4301.1	2.2308	5,344
1995	68.4	781,082	3.9902	3780.7	1.9595	5,519
1996	111.8	975,408	4.2152	3992.4	2.4165	5,651

Notes: R   Real exchange rate, $/Ps (1983=1.0)
       XA   Car exports (in volume units)
       XP   Car parts, $ exports deflated with U.S. CPI (in volume index)
       Y   Personal disposable income in Mexico (in constant pesos)
       P   Output of cars per worker (domestic sales and exports) (index)
       Y_{US} GDP (in U.S. constant 1990 dollars)

Bibliography

Bank of Mexico. 1997. *Indicadores Económicos*. Mexico: Bank of Mexico. January.

―――. 1989–1995. *Indicadores del Sector Externo*. Mexico: Bank of Mexico.

Globerman, Stephen, ed. 1993. *Assessing NAFTA: A Tri-national Analysis*. Studies on the Economic Future of North America. Vancouver, Canada: The Fraser Institute.

Grubel, H. G., and P. J. Lloyd. 1975. *Intra-Industry Trade: Theory and Measurement of International Trade of Differentiated Products*. London: MacMillan.

International Monetary Fund. 1997. *International Financial Statistics Yearbook 1996*. Washington, D.C.: International Monetary Fund. February.

Mexican Association of Automotive Industry (AMIA). *Bulletin*. Various numbers.

National Institute of Statistics, Geography, and Information (INEGI). 1993. *Anuario Estadístico de los Estados Unidos Méxicanos*. Mexico: INEGI.

―――. 1996. *Balanza Comercial de México*. Mexico: INEGI. December.

―――. 1996. *Encuesta Industrial Mensual*. Mexico: INEGI. January–June.

―――. 1996. *Sistema de Cuentas Nacionales de México*. Mexico: INEGI. August.

U.S. Department of Commerce. *Survey of Current Business*. Various issues.

4

The Impact of NAFTA on the Auto Industry in Canada

Pradeep Kumar and John Holmes

During the past decade, the automotive industries in Canada and the United States have faced a number of common challenges. The long-standing expectation that growth in the North American auto industry would continue indefinitely was shattered during the early 1980s as the Big Three North American automakers—General Motors (GM), Ford, and Chrysler—entered a period of serious competitive decline. The 1980s were marked by intensified competition for market share; the challenge came first from vehicles imported from Japan and then from the transplant assembly facilities built in North America by the Japanese automakers. Imports rose to nearly 27 percent of total North American vehicle sales in 1987 while transplant production increased from approximately 96,000 vehicles in 1982 to almost 2 million by 1991. In 1978 North America–based automakers accounted for more than 85 percent of vehicle sales in the North American market, but by 1990 this figure had declined to 67 percent (representing a loss of well over 2 million vehicles a year). This loss of market share to foreign producers was compounded at the beginning of the 1990s by the severe recession that gripped the economies of the United States and Canada and seriously depressed the demand for new automobiles.

The intensified international competition of the 1980s set off a chain of restructuring in the North American auto industry, particularly in the Big Three. The restructuring process was designed to achieve cost efficiencies and operational flexibility and entailed large capital investments in plant modernization and new technology; the introduction of lean production, closer collaboration with suppliers in the design and delivery of high quality, and more cost competitive component parts; work force rationalization and downsizing in both the assembly and parts sectors; and a wide variety of changes in work systems and industrial relations practices.

The final challenge, and the one that lies at the center of the analysis in this chapter, is the impending full integration of Mexico into the North American auto industry. In North America, the sea change in the global political economy toward a greatly liberalized investment and trade regime led to the 1989 Canada-U.S. Free Trade Agreement (CUFTA), closely followed by the North American Free Trade Agreement (NAFTA) in 1994. By the time NAFTA is fully implemented in 2004, the North American auto industry will consist of the United States, Canada, and Mexico and production will be fully integrated across the continent. It is important to recognize, however, that the momentum toward Mexico's integration into the continental auto industry began in the early 1980s and was already well under way before the formal signing of NAFTA. Under the trade regime ushered in by the 1965 Canada-United States Automotive Products Trade Agreement (commonly known as the Auto Pact), the vitality and fortunes of the Canadian automotive industry have for the past 30 years been inextricably linked to the relatively large share of the combined Canada-U.S. market that it has been able to command.

In this chapter we examine how the Canadian automotive industry has responded and adapted to changes in the competitive environment since 1985.[1] The choice of this time period provides sufficient perspective to be able to assess what impact the implementation of NAFTA has had on the industry. The start date precedes both CUFTA and the last major cyclical downturn in the industry and, thus, provides a good baseline for our analysis. The emphasis will be on the role played by Canada in the integrated North American auto industry and how this role might change as a result of the full economic integration of Mexico into the industry.

The Canadian auto industry was stronger in 1995 and 1996 than it had been for some years, primarily because of a sharp rise in vehicle production and exports fueled by the market recovery in the United States. The production-to-sales ratio was at a record level of 2:1, the highest of any of the major vehicle-producing nations in the world. Between 1991 and 1995 the number of vehicles produced increased by 27.6 percent and the constant dollar value of Canadian shipments of motor vehicles (Standard Industrial Classification [SIC] 3231) rose by 50.7 percent. Following a significant shakeout that took place between 1989 and 1991, the Canadian automotive parts sector also rebounded and has registered significant increases in both shipments and new investment. Its performance since 1991 parallels and is linked to the strong growth in the Canadian assembly sector but is also a function of the improved competitiveness of those parts companies that survived the shakeout at the beginning of the 1990s. A number of factors have contributed to this success: besides being the sole source for a number of the most important and popular models sold in the United States, Canadian assembly plants enjoy good manufacturing capability, positive labor–management relations, and a significant unit-cost advantage.

Although the Canadian and Mexican auto industries remain dwarfed by the United States in terms of both market and production shares (figure 4.1), there is evidence that high levels of intra-industry and intra-firm trade in the industry are leading to some degree of regional production specialization, especially with respect to vehicle assembly. For example, Mexican assembly plants produce mainly subcompact and compact cars while Canadian plants produce a disproportionate share of minivans and trucks. There is no question that NAFTA will reinforce and probably accelerate the trend toward the continental economic integration of the auto industry, which was already well under way by 1994. Based on the data collected to date in our research, however, it is difficult to discern any significant changes in the Canadian auto industry's key performance indicators that can be ascribed directly to NAFTA. The only possible exception, and this is more in terms of what it might portend for the future rather than its present significance, is the recent growth in the number of vehicle imports into Canada from Mexico.

We conclude that the Canadian auto industry in the mid-1990s is robust and performing as well as ever. The challenge will be for the industry to preserve its present share of North American production, value added, and employment as Mexican production is rationalized and integrated into the rest of the continental auto industry. This hinges on whether the industry is able to retain its present share of the key U.S. market. Canada's ability to compete in a fully integrated North American auto industry will be dependent on the decisions about vehicle assembly and, especially, the allocation of new models among assembly plants, as well as the continuing cost competitiveness of Canadian assembly and parts plants. The challenges of integration are particularly serious for component-parts producers that are facing both intense competition from Mexican and offshore producers in the market for technologically less

Figure 4.1
Canadian, U.S., and Mexican Shares of North American
Production and Vehicle Sales, 1986–1995
(percentages)

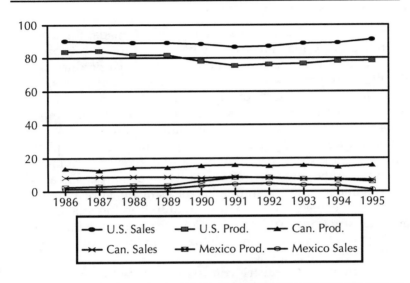

Sources: Industry Canada 1996 2, b; Ward's Communications 1996.

sophisticated parts and components and growing pressures from assemblers to reduce the cost and improve the quality of parts as one element of the new supply-chain management system.

The first of this chapter's four major sections provides a descriptive profile of the Canadian auto industry as it stood in 1996; the second section presents a statistical overview of the changes in production, investment, employment, productivity, and real wages that have taken place in the 1985–1996 period. The third section focuses on patterns of Canadian automotive trade, the extent of regional specialization, and the role that Canada plays within the continental industry. Labor issues and especially the effects on labor of continental integration and NAFTA are the subjects of the fourth section. In particular, we focus on cross-national variations in labor relations/human resource management policies and practices and the challenges facing workers and the unions owing to the growing diffusion of lean production and the increasing emphasis on outsourcing in the industry. The chapter concludes with a summary of research findings and identifies issues that merit further investigation.

Overview of the Auto Industry in Canada: Size, Structure, and Significance

The automobile industry is a key industry in Canada. It plays a vital role in the Canadian economy because of its size, its backward and forward linkages with other sectors that produce significant multiplier effects, and its substantial contribution to international trade. The industry accounts for 11.5 percent of Canada's manufacturing gross domestic product (GDP), more than 4 percent of the total GDP, one-third of all retail sales and manufacturing exports, and nearly 5 percent of total employment. The industry's contribution to the economy is much greater when the multiplier effects of its input–output linkages are taken into account. According to one estimate, $1 of automotive output generates more than $3 of output in the total economy (Industry Canada 1996a). A unique feature of the industry is its high level of integration with the U.S. industry with regard to both production and sales.

The automotive industry consists of automobile manufacturers (SIC 3231 and 325); automotive dealers (SIC 631); and aftermarket sales, service stations, and repair shops (SIC 552, 633, 634, and 635). Automobile manufacturing, the focus of this chapter, is composed of two major industries: motor vehicle assembly (SIC 3231) and automotive parts and accessories (SIC 325). The two industries produce a wide array of products: a variety of passenger cars and light-duty trucks (vans, minivans, sport-utility vehicles, and pickup trucks) as well as a wide range of component parts (engines, transmissions and related drivetrain components, steering and suspension parts, wheels and brakes, stampings, plastic parts, interior and exterior trims, and electrical parts and wiring assemblies). The parts production is primarily geared to the assembly sector. In 1994, the latest year for which information is available, the motor vehicle assemblers purchased 80 percent of parts shipments.

The Motor Vehicle Assembly Industry

The motor vehicle assembly segment of the industry, which accounts for nearly 70 percent of total industry shipments, includes 14 major car and light-duty truck assembly plants; 10 of these are owned by the Big Three. General Motors owns four plants, Ford and Chrysler each has three, and the remaining four are transplants of Toyota, Honda, Volvo, and CAMI, a joint venture of General Motors and Suzuki of Japan (see table 4.1 for a detailed profile of the plants). All vehicle assemblers (except Volvo) also have in-house component-parts production facilities that account for over one-third of the total parts production in Canada. The Big Three have 12 parts plants (Ford, 5; General Motors, 4; and Chrysler, 3). All three Japanese assembly plants have on-site stamping facilities. Toyota also has an engine plant on-site. Twelve of the 14 plants are located in southwestern Ontario, adjacent to the state of Michigan, the heartland of the U.S. auto industry. One plant (GM's Ste. Thérèse plant) is located in Quebec, and the small Volvo plant is in Halifax, Nova Scotia.

The total combined production capacity of the 14 assembly plants is currently 2.7 million vehicles a year and is expected to reach 3.0 million by the year 2000, when plant expansion at Toyota, Honda, and Ford is completed. In 1996, they produced a total of 2.37 million vehicles (1.28 million passenger cars and 1.09 million light-duty trucks), accounting for 16 percent of North American vehicle production and nearly 5 percent of total world output. Of the 2.37 million vehicles produced, nearly 2.0 million, or 84 percent, were assembled at the Big Three plants. Transplants accounted for 16 percent of the total vehicle production (25 percent of passenger cars and 5 percent of light-duty trucks). General Motors was the largest producer, with a total production of 752,371 units in 1996 (483,489 cars and 258,882 trucks) or 32 percent of total vehicles and 38 percent of passenger car output. However, Chrysler, the second largest producer, was the leading assembler of light-duty trucks, especially minivans, accounting for 43 percent of total Canadian truck output.

The Big Three and transplants differ in the type of vehicles produced. While the Big Three primarily assemble large or mid-size passenger cars, minivans, and full-size pickup trucks, the transplants (except Volvo, which assembles large 850-series cars) currently produce subcompact and compact cars (see table 4.1). Most products produced in Canadian plants are sole-sourced for export to the U.S. market. The exceptions are Honda Civic, Dodge Intrepid, Chrysler minivans, and Ford and GM pickup trucks that are made in both U.S. and Canadian plants.

Table 4.1
Vehicle Assembly Plants in Canada

CAR PLANTS

Location	Bramalea ON[a]	St. Thomas ON	Oshawa #1 ON	Oshawa #2 ON	Ste. Thérèse QC	Alliston ON	Cambridge ON	Ingersoll ON	Halifax NS
Ownership	Chrysler	Ford	GM	GM	GM	Honda	Toyota	GM (50%) Suzuki (50%)	Volvo
Year of start	1987	1967	1955	1957	1965	1986	1988	1989	1963
Current product line	Concord, Intrepid, LHS New Yorker, Vision	Crown Victoria, Grand Marquis	Lumina, Monte Carlo	Lumina Regal	Camaro Firebird	Honda Civic, Acura EL	Corolla	Metro, Swift Firefly	Volvo 850 Series
Current capacity	252,000	226,000	248,000	248,000	210,000	150,400	97,760	141,752	8,500
Line speed (units per hour)	67	60	66	66	56	40	26	38	NA
No. of shifts	2	2	2	2	1	2	2	2	2
Total production in '000 (1998)	239.0	226.2	217.6	187.9	88.6	144.0	97.3	80.4	7.6

Table 4.1 (*continued*)
Vehicle Assembly Plants in Canada

CAR PLANTS

Location	Bramalea ON[a]	St. Thomas ON	Oshawa #1 ON	Oshawa #2 ON	Ste. Thérèse QC	Alliston ON	Cambridge ON	Ingersoll ON	Halifax NS
Total employment in 1996	2,726	2,888	2,830	3,111	1,588	1,100	927	1,144	200
(*hourly*)	2,506	2,650	2,629	2,905	1,398	950	777	964	
Labor productivity (worker per vehicle) 1996	2.54	3.01	2.68	2.95	3.54	2.44	2.35	3.51	NA
Quality (1996)									
Problems per 100 vehicles	97	85	99	91	141	69	63	97	NA
Ranking[b]	20	10	21	14	39	2	1	19	NA

[a] A new plant built in 1987 under American Motors ownership and acquired by Chrysler after the merger of the two companies.
[b] Based on ratings of 42 car plants in the United States, Canada, and Mexico.

(*continued*)

Table 4.1 *(continued)*
Vehicle Assembly Plants in Canada

LIGHT-DUTY TRUCK PLANTS

Location	Windsor ON^c	Windsor ON (Pillette Road)	Oakville #1 ON^d	Oakville #2 ON (Ontario Truck)	Oshawa ON	Ingersoll ON
Ownership	Chrysler	Chrysler	Ford	Ford	GM	CAMI
Year of start	1925	1975	1953	1965	1965	1989
Current product line	Caravan Voyager (minivan)	Ram Van Ram Wagon	Windstar (minivan)	F-Pickup Trucks	Chevrolet K Sierra	Geo Tracker Sidekick Sunrunner
Current capacity	325,000	120,000	282,000	169,000	229,360	83,472
Line speed (units per hour)	72	30	75	45	61	22
No. of shifts	3	2	2	1	2.5	2
Total production in '000 (1998)	373.2	93.3	236.5	74.4	258.9	47.9
Total employment in 1996	4,966	1,625	3,421	1,353	3,608	1,089
(hourly)	4,698	1,536	3,110	1,216	3,362	962

Table 4.1 (*continued*)
Vehicle Assembly Plants in Canada

LIGHT-DUTY TRUCK PLANTS

Location	Windsor ON[c]	Windsor ON (Pillette Road)	Oakville #1 ON[d]	Oakville #2 ON (Ontario Truck)	Oshawa ON	Ingersoll ON
Labor productivity (worker per vehicle) 1996	3.42	3.69	2.85	3.68	3.06	4.61
Quality (1996)						
Problems per 100 vehicles	154	176	111	170	110	107
Ranking[e]	27	32	12	31	11	9

[c] The plant started producing minivans in 1983. Before that it produced passenger cars.
[d] The plant was converted from a car assembly operation to an all-new mid-size Windstar minivan plant in February 1994.
[e] Based on ratings of 33 light truck plants in the United States, Canada, and Mexico.

Sources: Ward's Communications 1996; Harbour and Associates 1997.

The vehicle assembly industry is totally foreign owned, highly oligopolistic, and dominated by the Big Three that account for more than four-fifths of total production, three-quarters of Canadian vehicle sales, and nearly 60 percent of total employment. The industry has the highest foreign direct investment concentration in the economy. The total productive stock of foreign investment was Can$17 billion in 1994, of which 86 percent was from the United States (Industry Canada 1996a).

Both the production and sale of vehicles in Canada are highly integrated with the United States. Of the 2.4 million vehicles produced in 1996, almost 96 percent were exported to the United States. Similarly, of the 1.2 million vehicles sold in Canada in 1996, nearly two-thirds were imported from the United States. However, although the Big Three operations in Mexico are covered under the Auto Pact and NAFTA, there is minimal integration with Mexico. Mexican vehicle exports to Canada constitute only 9 percent of total Canadian vehicle sales (15 percent of passenger car sales and 2 percent of truck sales). Canadian exports to Mexico were marginal, a little more than one-fourth of 1 percent of total vehicle imports into Mexico.

Canada is a net exporter of motor vehicles. In 1996, Canada had a net trade surplus of Can$27.5 billion (Can$30.7 billion with the United States). The total value of exports was Can$47.2 billion (Can$46.5 billion to the United States). Imports were valued at Can$19.7 billion (Can$15.8 billion from the United States). The United States is Canada's principal trade partner, accounting for 97 percent of the exports and 80 percent of the imports of vehicles. Exports to Canada similarly constitute nearly three-fifths of total U.S. vehicle exports, and close to one-half of vehicles imported into the United States are from Canada. A large part of this trade is intra-firm. Mexico, since 1995, is Canada's second largest automotive trading partner (replacing Japan) although the volume of trade is small, with Can$64 million of exports (one-eighth of 1 percent of total exports) and Can$1.67 billion of imports (8.4 percent of total imports). Nearly 80 percent of the imports from Mexico were under the Auto Pact, as a part of Big Three operations. Unlike the United States, with which Canada enjoys a trade surplus, Canada has a trade deficit with Mexico that amounted to Can$1.6 billion in 1996.

Although still relatively labor intensive, the vehicle assembly industry is a high value-added and modernized industry, a result of nearly Can$25 billion in investments in plant modernization, automation, and rationalization over the past 15 years.

In 1995, the latest year for which data are available, value added by manufacturing per worker in the vehicle assembly industry was Can$200,289, more than 60 percent higher than the manufacturing average. It was the highest value-added manufacturing industry with the highest value of shipments of any manufacturing industry in Canada. Labor costs were 36 percent of the total value added by manufacturing, compared with 29 percent for all manufacturing.

The Canadian vehicle assembly industry is also highly unionized, noted for its above-average wages, benefits, working conditions, and pattern setting in collective bargaining. Overall, union density is approximately 72 percent, nearly twice the average density for Canada. All assembly plants with the exception of Honda and Toyota are unionized. The Canadian Auto Workers (CAW) union, the largest private-sector union in Canada, is the principal union in the industry. The CAW was formed in 1985 following a split in the United Auto Workers (UAW), an international union based in the United States that had represented the Canadian auto workers since 1937. The CAW is a strong and progressive union, noted for its hard and innovative bargaining and its "social unionism" philosophy with a clearly articulated agenda for workplace change and macroeconomic and social reforms.

Hourly earnings in the industry average more than Can$25.00 an hour, nearly 54 percent above the industry average for manufacturing. The industry provides generous benefits in the form of paid time off, cost-of-living adjustments, supplementary unemployment benefits and other related income security benefits, an indexed pension, and extended medical benefits—all totally financed by employers. The industry is also characterized by flexible work scheduling through extended shifts, weekend work, and other forms of alternative work arrangements. Workers also enjoy opportunities for both technical and social training (health and safety, human rights, and literacy training). Non-union Japanese-owned assembly plants conform to the same wage-and-benefits pattern established by collective bargaining between the Big Three and the CAW. In national currencies, Canada and U.S. average hourly labor costs are similar, but when these costs are expressed in U.S. dollars, the Canadian costs are nearly 26 percent lower. The differential, which is estimated to be about Can$11.00 an hour in favor of Canada, is attributable to lower health care insurance costs and the exchange rate (Industry Canada 1996a).

The Canadian vehicle industry is also noted for its high productivity and product quality levels despite the absence of such "high performance work organization" practices as team concepts, job rotation, contingent compensation, employee involvement, and "partnership" with management in shop-floor decisionmaking (Pil and MacDuffie 1996; see table 4.2 for a comparison of Big Three plant practices in the United States and Canada). Overall, Canadian plants are ranked higher with regard to productivity, as measured by either hours per vehicle (table 4.2) or workers per vehicle (Harbour and Associates 1997).[2]

The Motor Vehicle Parts Industry

The auto parts industry, unlike the vehicle assembly industry, is highly diverse in its product array, ownership structure, and institutional characteristics. The product line includes engines, transmissions, stampings, steering and suspension, wheels and brakes, seats, electrical equipment, and plastic parts. A total of 567 establishments in 1994 manufactured auto parts and accessories. Nearly two-fifths were small establishments, employing less than 50 workers and accounting for 4 percent of total employment and total shipments. On the other hand, there were 36 large establishments with 500 or more employees that accounted for nearly one-third of total employment and one-half of total shipments. Ownership was divided equally between Canadian and foreign-owned firms including the Big Three. Nearly 20 firms, both U.S. multinationals and Canada-based companies, dominate the industry as Tier One and Tier Two suppliers. (Tier One companies are those that sell directly to assemblers; Tier Two companies sell to Tier One suppliers.) Magna International, a Canadian multinational that, in terms of sales, is ranked 26th in the top 50 global parts producers, is the largest and most diversified systems developer and integrated producer. Nearly three-quarters of parts manufacturers are located in Ontario, near assembly manufacturers and the midwestern auto industry in the United States. The industry employed 100,673 workers in 1995, 65 percent of total automobile manufacturing employment. Total shipments were valued at Can$22.77 billion, 30 percent of total industry shipments.

The auto parts industry, like the vehicle assembly industry, is also highly integrated and rationalized with its counterpart in the United States. (The imports and exports of parts and accessories, except tires and tubes, for use as original equipment in the

Table 4.2
Characteristics and Practices in Big Three Assembly Plants in Canada and the United States, 1995

	Big Three in U.S.	Big Three in Canada
Number of plants surveyed	19	8
Plant Characteristics		
Capacity per shift	488	467
Product variety	Low	Low
No. of platforms	1.4	1.0
No. of models	2.1	1.8
Parts variety	High	Low
No. of export markets	6.2	2.3
No. of wireharness part numbers	12.9	7.7
No. of engine transmission combinations	34.2	5.8
Production and Management Systems		
Lean production:	Lean	Lean
Inventory level (days)	1.4	1.3
Paint/assembly buffer (percentage of one shift production held)	38.5	25.4
Corrected repair area (percentage of assembly)	11.7	14.2
Automation	High	High
Percentage of direct production steps automated	33.8	32.2
By area		
Welding	78.9	74.6
Paint	48.0	41.7
Assembly	1.1	2.3

(continued)

Table 4.2 (*continued*)
**Characteristics and Practices in Big Three Assembly Plants
in Canada and the United States, 1995**

	Big Three in U.S.	Big Three in Canada
Robots/vehicle/hour	3.3	3.1
Performance		
Productivity (hours/vehicle)	23.2	19.8
Quality (defects/100 vehicles)		
1995	62.2	56.1
1989	86.8	80.7
Change (percent)	-28	-31
HRM/Work Systems		
HRM philosophy (100=high commitment; 0=low commitment)	30.0	19.9
Number of plants with teams	8	1
Percent of workforce in teams where teams present	52.4	25.2
Percent of workforce in EI/QC	38.0	6.1
Contingent compensation (0=none; 6=extensive)	1.5	0.7
Percent of multiskilling	27.8	26.9
Extent of job rotation (1=none; 5=frequent)	2.1	1.8
Responsibility for quality inspection (0=specialists; 4=workers)	2.1	3.1
Responsibility for programming technology (0=specialists; 4=workers)	1.4	1.4
Training hours for workers		
Newly hired	72	55
Experienced	67	17

Table 4.2 (*continued*)
**Characteristics and Practices in Big Three Assembly Plants
in Canada and the United States, 1995**

	Big Three in U.S.	Big Three in Canada
Training hours for supervisors		
Newly hired	236	194
Experienced	69	63
Hourly wages (1994) (U.S.$)	17.47	15.63
Percent of employees older than 45	55	36
Downsizing Efforts		
Plant closings (percent)	50	40
Hiring freeze (percent)	62	80
Layoffs (percent)	62	80
Early retirement incentives (percent)	100	100
Perceived worker influence (1=none; 5=extensive)		
New investment plans	1.7	1.8
Design of new technology	2.5	2.3
Restructuring of jobs	3.3	2.5
Planning and coordination	3.6	3.5
Work allocation changes	2.8	2.8
Overtime work	2.6	2.5
Subcontracting	3.7	4.0

Source: Pil and MacDuffie 1996.

manufacturing of vehicles by the Big Three are duty-free under the Auto Pact and NAFTA.) Nearly 70 percent of the parts produced in Canada are exported, 63 percent to the United States. Similarly, over 80 percent of parts and accessories used in Canada are imported, nearly 74 percent from the United States. More than four-fifths of the imports come duty-free under the Auto Pact. Unlike vehicle assembly, Canada is a net importer of component parts products and in 1996 ran a trade deficit of Can$20.1 billion in parts and accessories, Can$17.2 billion or 86 percent with the United States and another Can$1.42 billion or 7 percent with Mexico.

Relative to vehicle assembly manufacturing, the auto parts industry in Canada is much more labor intensive, adds less value, and is only partially unionized. Labor costs in 1995 constituted 43 percent of total value added by manufacturing, nearly 12 percent higher than vehicle assembly. Total value added by manufacturing per production worker was Can$107,502, only 57 percent of value added per worker in vehicle assembly. Hourly earnings averaged nearly Can$18.00 an hour, 9 percent over the manufacturing average but 30 percent below the average in vehicle assembly.

Nearly one-half of the auto parts workers are unionized. The unionization rate is greater than 80 percent in parts facilities operated by the Big Three and CAMI but only 45 percent in independent parts establishments. Almost all of the large parts producers are unionized in different degrees. Unionization rates vary between less than 1 percent at Magna to 70–85 percent at large auto parts companies such as A. G. Simpson, Johnson Controls, and Budd Canada. The CAW is the principal union in the industry.

Wages, benefits, and working conditions in the industry vary according to the degree of unionization, size of the plants, and the nature of employers. The terms and conditions of employment at the captive parts facilities of the Big Three are identical to their vehicle operations. Workers in these facilities therefore enjoy above average wages, benefits, and working conditions. Labor conditions, including wages and benefits at other unionized plants, vary considerably. Non-union plants generally pay lower wages and provide few benefits to their workers.

According to a recent report by the Automobile Parts Manufacturers Association of Canada (APMA 1997, 45), the major strengths of the Canadian parts industry include the following:

- a strong materials supply base for high-quality steel, powdered metals, nonferrous metals, and plastic feedstock;
- availability of casting, stamping, and plating operations and heat treatment facilities;
- a world-class tool and die industry;
- strong Tier Two manufacturers that produce components for Tier One suppliers;
- a highly skilled workforce;
- an abundant supply of low-cost energy;
- a reputation for quality production;
- a well-developed transportation infrastructure;
- a supportive public policy environment;
- an expanding vehicle assembly industry;
- location of plants close to major customers and in proximity to the large and expanding U.S. market;
- availability of capital; and
- the presence of companies with the expertise and technology to develop systems capabilities.

Many of these competitive advantages have been highlighted in a number of comparative studies conducted by consultants (see, for example, KPMG 1996; Industry Canada 1992; and Booz, Allen, Hamilton 1990).

The APMA publication also highlights the weaknesses of the Canadian parts industry, which include

- a preponderance of small manufacturers with limited research and product development capabilities;
- a very limited number of true Tier One systems suppliers;
- a growing shortage of skilled workers;
- an overreliance for sales on the Big Three and Canada;
- growing competition from parts makers in both low-wage and high-wage countries; and
- a lack of presence in global markets and a limited ability to expand globally.

Changes in the Canadian Automotive Industry, 1985–1995

Two dynamics at work within the broader North American auto industry have been important in shaping the Canadian auto industry during the past decade: the restructuring in response to competitive decline and the growing momentum toward continental economic integration under CUFTA and NAFTA. Within this broader context this section examines trends in the Canadian auto industry with regard to production, sales, investment, employment, productivity, and wages.

The analysis of industry structure and characteristics in this section is based on data drawn from Statistics Canada's *Census of Manufacturing*, which are presented by SIC codes. The two principal divisions of the industry correspond to SIC 3231 (motor vehicle industry) and SIC 325 (motor vehicle parts and accessories industries). SIC 325 is further divided at the four-digit SIC level into eight subindustries (see table 4.3 for a complete list). The most recent year for which data presently are available is 1995.

When the data for the automotive parts sector as a whole (SIC 325) is disaggregated to the four-digit SIC level, there are some quite marked differences in the performances of the various subindustries. Although some of the more striking of these differences are highlighted in this chapter, limits of time and space preclude a detailed analysis at this level of disaggregation. It would be both useful and instructive to conduct further analysis of data at both the four-digit SIC level and the harmonized commodity code level, especially with regard to questions related to intra-industry trade and regional specialization within the auto industry.

Production and Sales

Motor vehicle production and sales data for Canada exhibit quite different trends during the period 1985–1996 (table 4.4 and Appendix). With regard to changes in the Canadian market for motor vehicles there are three key aspects. First, the market has been depressed since the late 1980s, and it was not until 1996 that it began to show any sign of recovery. From a record high of 1.57 million units sold in 1988, the domestic sales market declined in six of the past seven years. By 1995 it stood at 1.17 million vehicles—a decline of more than 30 percent and the weakest market since 1983. Second, although markets have been depressed, the composition of these sales has changed significantly over the past 10 years. The Big Three's share of the market recovered from a low of 64.1 percent in 1991 to 75.6 percent in 1995, while the share taken by imports reached a peak of 30.2 percent in 1991 and then rapidly slipped to 12.1 percent by 1995.

Table 4.3
Canadian Auto Industry: Standard
Industrial Classification (SIC) Codes

SIC 3231	Motor Vehicle Industry
SIC 325	Motor Vehicle Parts and Accessories Industries
SIC 3251	Motor Vehicle Engine and Engine Parts Industry
SIC 3252	Motor Vehicle Wiring Assemblies Industry
SIC 3253	Motor Vehicle Stampings Industry
SIC 3254	Motor Vehicle Steering and Suspension Industry
SIC 3255	Motor Vehicle Wheel and Brake Industry
SIC 3256	Motor Vehicle Plastic Parts Industry
SIC 3257	Motor Vehicle Fabric Accessories Industry
SIC 3259	Other Motor Vehicle Accessories and Parts

Part of this decline in imports was due to the substitution of vehicles produced by the North America-based Japanese transplants, whose share rose steadily throughout the period to a high of 12.1 percent in 1995. Third, since 1985, compact and subcompact cars have accounted for 45–60 percent of the Canadian car market, and the share taken by intermediate-size cars slipped below 20 percent in the early 1990s. This is in sharp contrast to the United States, where intermediate-size cars alone account for 50 percent of sales and compact and subcompacts for less than 30 percent. The Mexican market is overwhelmingly dominated by sales of subcompacts and compacts.

Notwithstanding the weak domestic market for new vehicles through the first half of the 1990s, Canadian vehicle production in 1995 reached an all-time high of 2,407,155 vehicles, and the value of shipments measured in constant dollars was more than 60 percent higher than it had been in 1985. Even during the 1988–1991 downturn in North American auto production, production levels in Canada remained buoyant. While North American production of motor vehicles fell from 14 million units in 1985 to a low of 11.7 million units in 1991, Canadian vehicle production (except for 1987) remained fairly steady, in the 1.85–1.95 million range between 1985 and 1992 before rising over the 2 million mark for the first time in 1993. With more than 85

Table 4.4
Canadian Motor Vehicle Sales and Production,
1985–1996
(thousands)

SALES

Year	North American-Built		Imports			Total as % of North American
	Cars	Trucks	Cars	Trucks	Total	Market
1985	795	345	342	48	1,530	8.6
1986	762	368	329	51	1,510	8.3
1987	701	412	364	51	1,528	9.0
1988	725	460	332	49	1,566	8.8
1989	674	422	319	68	1,483	8.8
1990	580	361	305	72	1,318	8.4
1991	573	348	300	67	1,288	9.0
1992	507	370	291	59	1,227	8.3
1993	494	402	245	52	1,193	7.6
1994	573	475	175	36	1,259	7.4
1995	553	469	116	27	1,165	7.1
1996	573	518	88	26	1,205	7.2

percent of the vehicles built in Canadian plants shipped to the United States and with Canadian plants building 6 of the 20 best-selling vehicles in the U.S. market—several of which are single sourced—production for export to the United States remained the saving grace of the Canadian auto industry. During the past decade there has been a progressive shift in the composition of vehicle output—from cars toward light trucks (a category that includes the popular minivans)—so that by 1995 trucks constituted approximately 45 percent of all vehicles produced in Canada. Also, within remaining car production, there has been a progressive shift toward intermediate-size cars.

These trends in sales and production are reflected in the changing country shares of total North American sales and

Table 4.4 (*continued*)
**Canadian Motor Vehicle Sales
and Production, 1985–1996**
(thousands)

PRODUCTION

Year	Passenger Cars	Trucks	Total Vehicles	Total as % of North American Production
1985	1,071	856	1,930	13.8
1986	1,062	793	1,859	13.8
1987	811	838	1,648	12.7
1988	1,028	950	1,977	14.4
1989	1,002	938	1,940	14.5
1990	1,098	850	1,948	15.5
1991	1,060	827	1,887	16.1
1992	1,020	938	1,958	15.4
1993	1,353	893	2,246	15.8
1994	1,216	1,106	2,322	14.8
1995	1,337	1,077	2,414	15.8
1996	1,280	1,117	2,397	15.4

Source: Ward's Communications 1996.

production (figure 4.1). The picture is quite striking. The United States (at around 90 percent) is the overwhelmingly dominant core market while Canada (now around 7 percent) and Mexico (which even before the market collapse following the devaluation of the peso in 1995 never got higher than 4.2 percent) are very much secondary markets. During the 1985–1995 period, the U.S. share of sales remained flat while its share of production declined until 1992. During the same period, Canada's share of production rose steadily while its share of the market declined steadily. Until the peso crisis of 1995, Mexico saw its shares of both production and sales grow quite significantly. At first glance it might be concluded that a portion of U.S. demand for vehicles is supplied by excess production in Mexico and Canada

Figure 4.2
Canadian Auto Industry Capital and Repair Expenditures,
1980–1995
(Can$ millions)

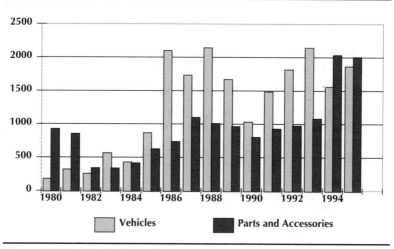

Source: Statistics Canada: Cat. 61–214.

or, put another way, that Canada and Mexico both produce more vehicles than they sell locally and export their surplus to the United States. As we shall see shortly, however, this would be a simplistic interpretation, and the actual pattern of intra-industry trade and specialization is considerably more complex.

The Canadian automotive components and accessories sector also grew substantially during the 1980s, with the value of shipments increasing more than threefold and employment rising from 52,000 in 1980 to more than 96,000 in 1989. This was somewhat surprising given that U.S. production costs were being driven down through intense wage competition and the non-union segment of the parts industry was growing. The recession of the early 1990s had a significant impact on the parts sector and produced a sharp downturn in both production and employment (a loss of 18,000 jobs) between 1989 and 1991. During 1991–1995, however, the value of parts production rose to new highs, employment in the industry reached a record high, and there was significant capital investment in new production equipment (tables 4.5 and 4.6; figure 4.2).

Table 4.5
Canadian Auto Industry Value of Shipments (Production) by SIC Industry, 1985–1995
(in constant 1986 Can$, millions)

	SIC 3231 Vehicle Assembly	SIC 325 Parts and Accessories	SIC 3251 Engine and Engine Parts	SIC 3252 Wiring Assemblies	SIC 3253 Stampings
1985	25,103.3	13,214.2	3,894.6	294.7	1,992.4
1986	24,286.6	12,921.7	3,363.6	398.1	2,103.2
1987*					
1988	29,531.3	14,790.8	3,817.5	374.4	2,351.5
1989	29,090.1	15,876.0	4,170.9	499.8	2,328.1
1990	28,612.2	14,376.4	3,019.6	458.1	2,212.5
1991	26,793.8	13,005.7	1,561.5	387.5	2,207.2
1992	28,264.0	14,127.3	1,696.2	432.6	2,207.2
1993	33,483.2	16,518.9	2,387.3	815.6	2,754.6
1994	37,008.2	18,881.7	2,718.2	1,046.6	3,111.3
1995	39,706.1	20,451.6	2,867.9	1,101.6	3,421.7

	SIC 3254 Steering and Suspension	SIC 3255 Wheel and Brakes	SIC 3256 Plastic Parts	SIC 3257 Fabric Accessories	SIC 3259 Other Parts Accessories
1985	681.8	1,014.4	1,025.2	887.3	3,423.8
1986	662.9	924.7	1,263.9	958.8	3,246.5
1987*					
1988	872.3	1,075.9	1,372.3	1,037.2	3,889.6
1989	903.6	1,127.6	1,478.0	1,143.3	4,224.8
1990	851.8	1,017.1	1,178.7	1,261.1	4,377.5
1991	712.3	878.3	1,056.4	1,243.5	4,959.0
1992	851.0	972.2	1,109.6	1,464.4	5,235.0
1993	1,086.0	1,079.7	1,385.4	1,596.2	5,414.0
1994	1,361.4	1,259.6	1,630.4	1,906.8	5,847.4
1995	1,472.0	1,336.3	1,716.1	1,937.0	6,599.1

Source: Statistics Canada 1997.
* No data were published for 1987.

Table 4.6
Canadian Auto Industry Employment by SIC Industry, 1985–1995
(total, hourly, salaried, and ratio of hourly workers
to total employment)

A. Total employment:

Year	SIC 3231 Vehicle Assembly	SIC 325 Parts and Accessories	SIC 3251 Engine and Engine Parts	SIC 3252 Wiring Assemblies	SIC 3253 Stampings
1985	56,871	84,374	15,450	4,105	11,633
1986	53,534	85,241	15,566	5,645	12,098
1987	52,034	88,550	15,992	5,120	12,652
1988	52,681	94,335	15,121	4,906	12,008
1989	55,392	96,254	15,622	5,441	11,804
1990	56,089	86,396	10,990	5,064	11,630
1991	55,678	78,264	6,032	3,891	10,874
1992	54,738	83,376	6,043	3,693	11,522
1993	54,192	87,974	6,625	4,898	13,372
1994	54,349	92,610	7,140	5,254	14,402
1995	54,088	100,673	8,367	5,596	15,947

	SIC 3254 Steering and Suspension	SIC 3255 Wheel and Brakes	SIC 3256 Plastic Parts	SIC 3257 Fabric Accessories	SIC 3259 Other Parts and Accessories
1985	5,606	7,029	9,530	6,423	24,598
1986	5,069	6,647	11,202	6,483	22,531
1987	5,376	7,339	12,309	6,389	23,373
1988	6,574	8,116	12,971	6,903	27,736
1989	6,963	7,786	12,915	7,487	28,236
1990	6,493	6,861	10,317	6,692	28,349
1991	5,517	6,315	9,560	6,808	29,267
1992	6,403	6,775	10,220	7,175	31,545
1993	6,857	6,971	11,595	6,892	30,764
1994	7,617	6,869	11,771	7,541	32,016
1995	8,309	6,694	12,519	7,780	35,461

Table 4.6 (*continued*)
Canadian Auto Industry Employment by SIC Industry, 1985–1995
(total, hourly, salaried, and ratio of hourly workers
to total employment)

B. Number of hourly employees:

	SIC 3231 Vehicle Assembly	SIC 325 Parts and Accessories	SIC 3251 Engine and Engine Parts	SIC 3252 Wiring Assemblies	SIC 3253 Stampings
1985	44,358	71,128	13,255	3,363	9,950
1986	41,597	72,359	13,337	4,711	10,557
1987*					
1988	41,351	80,307	13,090	3,829	10,021
1989	43,890	82,162	13,605	4,667	9,946
1990	44,344	73,098	9,263	4,333	9,762
1991	44,587	66,176	4,950	3,245	9,145
1992	43,573	72,870	5,117	3,248	9,851
1993	43,302	76,810	5,666	4,316	11,636
1994	43,445	80,413	6,028	4,699	12,267
1995	43,532	86,781	6,820	5,009	13,620

	SIC 3254 Steering and Suspension	SIC 3255 Wheel and Brakes	SIC 3256 Plastic Parts	SIC 3257 Fabric Accessories	SIC 3259 Other Parts and Accessories
1985	4,468	5,644	8,219	5,656	20,573
1986	4,156	5,292	9,699	5,720	18,887
1987*					
1988	5,407	6,732	11,052	6,322	23,854
1989	5,628	6,424	11,045	6,866	23,981
1990	5,466	5,725	8,678	6,059	23,812
1991	4,653	5,203	8,203	6,142	24,635
1992	5,598	5,732	9,037	6,370	27,917
1993	5,913	6,102	10,476	5,983	26,718
1994	6,639	6,077	10,525	6,604	27,574
1995	7,210	5,743	11,142	6,779	30,458

(*continued*)

Table 4.6 (*continued*)
Canadian Auto Industry Employment by SIC Industry, 1985–1995
(total, hourly, salaried, and ratio of hourly workers
to total employment)

C. Number of salaried employees:

	SIC 3231 Vehicle Assembly	SIC 325 Parts and Accessories	SIC 3251 Engine and Engine Parts	SIC 3252 Wiring Assemblies	SIC 3253 Stampings
1985	12,513	13,246	2,195	742	1,683
1986	11,937	12,882	2,229	934	1,541
1987*					
1988	11,330	14,028	2,031	1,077	1,987
1989	11,502	14,092	2,017	774	1,858
1990	11,745	13,298	1,727	731	1,868
1991	11,091	12,088	1,082	646	1,729
1992	11,165	10,506	926	445	1,671
1993	10,890	11,164	959	582	1,736
1994	10,904	12,197	1,112	555	2,135
1995	10,556	13,892	1,547	587	2,327

	SIC 3254 Steering and Suspension	SIC 3255 Wheel and Brakes	SIC 3256 Plastic Parts	SIC 3257 Fabric Accessories	SIC 3259 Other Parts and Accessories
1985	1,138	1,385	1,311	767	4,025
1986	913	1,355	1,503	763	3,644
1987*					
1988	1,167	1,384	1,919	581	3,882
1989	1,335	1,362	1,870	621	4,255
1990	1,027	1,136	1,639	633	4,537
1991	864	1,112	1,357	666	4,632
1992	805	1,043	1,183	805	3,628
1993	944	869	1,119	909	4,046
1994	978	792	1,246	937	4,442
1995	1,099	951	1,377	1,001	5,003

Table 4.6 (*continued*)
Canadian Auto Industry Employment by SIC Industry, 1985–1995
(total, hourly, salaried, and ratio of hourly workers
to total employment)

D. Ratio of production workers to total employment:

	SIC 3231 Vehicle Assembly	SIC 325 Parts and Accessories	SIC 3251 Engine and Engine Parts	SIC 3252 Wiring Assemblies	SIC 3253 Stampings
1985	0.78	0.84	0.86	0.82	0.86
1986	0.78	0.85	0.86	0.83	0.87
1987*					
1988	0.78	0.85	0.87	0.78	0.83
1989	0.79	0.85	0.87	0.86	0.84
1990	0.79	0.85	0.84	0.86	0.84
1991	0.80	0.85	0.82	0.83	0.84
1992	0.80	0.87	0.85	0.88	0.85
1993	0.80	0.87	0.86	0.88	0.87
1994	0.80	0.87	0.84	0.89	0.85
1995	0.80	0.86	0.82	0.90	0.85

	SIC 3254 Steering and Suspension	SIC 3255 Wheel and Brakes	SIC 3256 Plastic Parts	SIC 3257 Fabric Accessories	SIC 3259 Other Parts and Accessories
1985	0.80	0.80	0.86	0.88	0.84
1986	0.82	0.80	0.87	0.88	0.84
1987*					
1988	0.82	0.83	0.85	0.92	0.86
1989	0.81	0.83	0.86	0.92	0.85
1990	0.84	0.83	0.84	0.91	0.84
1991	0.84	0.82	0.86	0.90	0.84
1992	0.87	0.85	0.88	0.89	0.88
1993	0.86	0.88	0.90	0.87	0.87
1994	0.87	0.88	0.89	0.88	0.86
1995	0.87	0.86	0.89	0.87	0.86

Source: Statistics Canada 1997.
* No data were published for 1987.

The data reveal that there was a significant shakeout of the auto parts sector between 1989 and 1992. Virtually all of the four-digit industries experienced a reduction in the number of establishments between 1989 and 1991, this phenomenon being especially pronounced in the wiring assemblies and plastic parts industries and among small plants (table 4.7). The strong recovery in the value of shipments and employment that occurred in these industries between 1991 and 1996 was not accompanied by a corresponding increase in the number of establishments. Thus by 1996 virtually all the industries that make up the Canadian auto parts sector had fewer but, in terms of employment, larger establishments compared with 1989.

The strong performance of the auto parts sector during the past five years clearly is linked to the growth in overall vehicle production in North America and, in particular, to the healthy state of the vehicle assembly industry in Canada. The rules on Canadian value added (CVA) attached to the Auto Pact mean that an expansion of vehicle production in Canada is accompanied almost automatically by an expansion of the Canadian parts sector. Part of the growth may be attributable to the increased outsourcing of subassembly work such as seat and fascia assembly from assembly plants, especially by GM. In addition, plant modernization and the shakeout of less competitive plants in the early 1990s produced a much more competitive industry; this is especially true of the suppliers to the larger original equipment manufacturers (OEM). While Canada's share of the total output of combined Canadian and U.S. automotive parts has remained steady at around 10 percent over the past decade, a recent study (APMA 1997, 14–15) estimated that Canada's share of OEM parts sales grew from 12.7 percent in 1986 to 17.6 percent in 1995.

Employment, Productivity, and Wages

For a variety of reasons, the vehicle assembly industry in Canada was spared much of the dislocation that accompanied assembly plant closings in the United States during the 1980s. Canadian Big Three capacity increased during this period and Canada's share of total North American vehicle production rose. There was much new capital investment in the assembly sector during the mid-1980s (figure 4.2 and Appendix). During the recovery from the deep recession of the early 1980s, employment in the vehicle assembly sector increased from 42,168 in 1982 to 56,871 in

1985. Employment then remained relatively stable over the next 10 years, registering a small decline to 54,088 in 1995. Most of this decline was attributable to a loss of salaried employees, not production employees. Note that the 1989–1991 recession had no significant effect on employment in the Canadian assembly sector because output remained high. Given the steady levels of production employment in the industry combined with strong growth in the value of shipments, it is not surprising that the past five years have produced a significant increase in labor productivity. Manufacturing value added per production worker in constant dollars increased by more than 50 percent between 1991 and 1995 and value added per production hour paid rose from Can$44.71 to Can$69.10 (table 4.8).

The growth of the vehicle assembly industry during the 1980s and 1990s was helped by a favorable model mix of large cars and minivans that sold well in the U.S. market, continuous improvements in productivity and product quality, high capacity utilization, and the more recent vintage of much of the capital stock in Canada. The strong performance of the industry is also attributable in large measure to a significant advantage in hourly labor costs enjoyed by Canada over the United States. Industry Canada (1996a) estimates that, when expressed in U.S. dollars, Canada's auto industry labor costs in 1994 were 32 percent less than those in the United States. Base pay accounted for 2.4 percent of this advantage while benefits, and especially health care costs, accounted for 29.6 percent. According to a CAW study (CAW 1996a), each vehicle assembled in Canadian Big Three plants in 1995 cost Can$480 or U.S.$356 less than the average cost in U.S. plants. No less than 56 percent of the savings was due to lower benefits costs, approximately 2 percent was due to wage differentials, and 29 percent was attributed to higher productivity. Transplant assembly plants in Canada have a smaller labor cost advantage over their counterparts in the United States owing to the latter's lower benefit costs tied to a much younger labor force.

Once again, the trends for the automotive parts sector differ from those in the assembly sector. The most obvious difference is with regard to the impact of the 1989–1991 recession, which triggered a major shakeout in several segments of the parts industry. This shakeout produced a sharp reduction in the number of establishments in virtually every sector of parts production (table 4.7), reflecting a trend toward mergers and acquisitions that led to rationalization and the closure of less profitable

Table 4.7
Canadian Auto Parts Industry, Number of Establishments by Size by SIC Industry, 1985, 1989, and 1994

Number of Establish-ments	SIC 3251 Engine and Engine Parts			SIC 3252 Wiring Assemblies			SIC 3253 Stampings		
	1985	1989	1994	1985	1989	1994	1985	1989	1994
1–49	18	34	13	14	17	10	30	31	18
50–199	13	22	15	7	11	9	38	40	46
200+	7	5	6	7	8	8	12	15	18
Total	38	61	34	28	36	27	80	86	82

	SIC 3254 Steering and Suspension			SIC 3255 Wheel and Brakes			SIC 3256 Plastic Parts		
	1985	1989	1994	1985	1989	1994	1985	1989	1994
1–49	12	24	14	22	30	22	33	38	19
50–199	7	13	14	10	20	21	34	30	27
200+	12	11	14	11	13	10	14	26	20
Total	31	48	42	43	63	53	81	94	66

Table 4.7 (continued)
Canadian Auto Parts Industry, Number of Establishments by Size by SIC Industry, 1985, 1989, and 1994

	SIC 3257 Fabric Accessories			SIC 3259 Other Parts and Accessories			SIC 325 Parts and Accessories		
	1985	1989	1994	1985	1989	1994	1985	1989	1994
1–49	n/a	18	14	124	145	113	253	337	223
50–199	n/a	4	8	31	73	71	140	213	211
200+	5	6	11	37	41	46	105	125	133
Total	20	28	33	192	259	230	498	675	567

Source: Statistics Canada 1997.

Table 4.8
Canadian Auto Industry, Value Added (Production)
by SIC Industry, 1985–1995
(in constant 1986 Can$, millions)

	SIC 3231 Vehicle Assembly	SIC 325 Parts and Accessories	SIC 3251 Engine and Engine Parts	SIC 3252 Wiring Assemblies	SIC 3253 Stampings
1985	4,987.6	6,279.8	1,658.8	143.9	970.2
1986	4,474.0	6,092.0	1,399.5	208.6	1,023.4
1987*					
1988	5,204.0	6,465.7	1,592.9	196.9	996.3
1989	5,131.9	6,775.3	1,743.1	239.6	882.3
1990	4,928.1	6,145.2	1,204.7	216.8	878.6
1991	4,210.1	5,587.6	621.1	184.9	852.6
1992	4,738.9	5,873.3	528.5	190.0	896.3
1993	5,326.3	7,179.3	940.8	384.9	1,181.2
1994	6,611.5	7,866.0	953.4	511.4	1,328.9
1995	6,997.6	8,543.2	1,271.7	444.0	1,435.1

	SIC 3254 Steering and Suspension	SIC 3255 Wheel and Brakes	SIC 3256 Plastic Parts	SIC 3257 Fabric Accessories	SIC 3259 Other Parts and Accessories
1985	360.6	555.1	447.9	396.1	1,747.1
1986	355.8	493.7	576.1	410.1	1,624.9
1987*					
1988	411.8	515.9	616.5	410.5	1,724.8
1989	425.6	527.5	630.6	481.4	1,845.2
1990	388.6	473.3	555.3	498.2	1,929.7
1991	330.2	422.3	487.8	517.8	2,171.0
1992	393.5	475.0	507.0	593.3	2,290.1
1993	511.3	537.2	678.0	613.1	2,332.8
1994	601.1	641.0	754.0	688.0	2,388.0
1995	668.0	653.2	761.1	712.1	2,598.0

Source: Statistics Canada 1997.
* No data were published for 1987.

plants. It was among the smaller establishments (employing fewer than 50 workers) that most of the loss was experienced. The sectors in which the reduction in the number of establishments was most marked were motor vehicle engines and engine parts (SIC 3251), motor vehicle plastic parts (SIC 3256), and motor vehicle wiring assemblies (SIC 3252); each lost between one-third and one-half of its establishments between 1989 and 1991 and saw no significant increase in these numbers after 1991.

The shakeout was followed by a substantial wave of new capital investment, with nearly Can$7 billion invested into Canadian parts plants since 1992 (figure 4.2). Although the number of establishments increased again in some sectors between 1991 and 1995, the overall number remained significantly less than in 1989. Employment in most parts industries has been rising since 1991 in the larger establishments and falling in the smaller plants. As a result, by 1995 production and employment was concentrated into fewer but larger plants. Taken as a whole, SIC 325 experienced a rapid growth in employment during the 1980s, reaching a peak of 96,254 in 1989. Employment then dropped by almost 20,000 during the 1989–1991 shakeout but had recovered by 1995 to 100,673 (table 4.6).

When disaggregated to the four-digit level the data reveal some marked differences in employment performance among subsectors. The engines and engine parts sector experienced the most dramatic change over the 10-year period. With the exception of the ubiquitous "other parts" sector (SIC 3259), engines was the largest auto parts sector in 1985, with 15,450 employees. By 1995 this figure had fallen to 8,367. Motor vehicle stampings (SIC 3253), with 15,947 employees, had become by 1995 the largest of the separately defined parts industries. It was also the most stable parts industry, experiencing only a very modest downturn in employment during the 1989–1991 period and then recording growth of 47 percent between 1991 and 1995. The one parts industry to show sustained employment growth throughout the 1985–1995 period was "other parts" (SIC 3259), which increased by almost 50 percent to 35,461. This industry includes a number of large multiproduct plants owned by large manufacturers such as Magna, Hayes, Dana, Lear, Siemens, Volkswagen, and GM, all of which have experienced strong growth during the 1990s.

These changes in numbers of establishments, employment, and output resulted in some significant changes in productivity as measured by value added per hour paid (in constant 1986 dollars). Productivity in the motor vehicle assembly sector rose by 48.9 percent between 1985 and 1995, with most of the growth coming after 1991 (table 4.9). Growth in the auto parts sector was a much more modest 9.6 percent although once again this overall figure masked some significant differences among the various parts industries. Wiring assemblies (80.9 percent), motor vehicle fabric (53.2 percent), motor vehicle engines (49.8 percent), and plastic parts (24.5 percent) all registered substantial improvements in productivity while the general "other parts" sector, which accounts for over one-third of all the establishments and employment in SIC 325, actually saw labor productivity decline marginally between 1985 and 1995. There was also a substantial difference in levels of labor productivity among the various parts industries (table 4.9). Productivity in 1995 was highest in the engine industry, exceeding even the level in the motor vehicle assembly industry, and lowest in the plastic parts industry where the productivity level was less than half that in the engine industry. These differences reflect the very different levels of labor intensity across the broader auto parts industries.

Given the differences in labor productivity levels among the various industries that make up the automotive sector, it is not surprising that there are also significant variations in wages (table 4.10). In 1995 current dollars, hourly wages ranged from a high of Can$23.89 in the motor vehicle industry to a low of Can$13.40 in the motor vehicle plastic parts industry. Motor vehicle engines and stampings were the only parts sectors with hourly wages of more than Can$18.00. Wiring assemblies and plastic parts were the two lowest-paying industries. In the vehicle assembly industry real hourly wages (expressed in 1987 constant dollars) increased steadily from Can$15.08 in 1985 to Can$17.90 in 1995. By contrast, in the motor vehicle parts sector they fell from Can$12.97 to Can$12.69. At the level of the four-digit SIC parts industries, real wages drifted downward between 1985 and 1995 in many industries except for the wiring assemblies industry, where they rose by almost 25 percent.

In summary,

- The motor vehicle industry (SIC 3231) experienced a stable pattern of employment between 1985 and 1995. Output, value added, and productivity were relatively level from 1985 to 1991 and increased significantly between 1991 and 1995. Wages measured in both current and constant dollars rose steadily throughout the period although they lagged behind the growth in productivity.

- The motor vehicle parts industry (SIC 325) between 1989 and 1991 experienced a significant shakeout of plants, especially among plants employing fewer than 50 people. The period after 1991 saw a wave of major new investment in the sector and a sharp increase in output and employment.

- When the parts industry is disaggregated into its eight constituent industries at the four-digit SIC level, we find considerable variation among industries with regard to their performances over the 1985–1995 period.

- The engine and engine parts industry, the wiring assemblies industry, and the plastic parts industry appear to have been the sectors of the parts industries most affected by the 1989–1991 shakeout. They lost significant numbers of smaller plants and workers but subsequently experienced the strongest growth in productivity between 1991 and 1995.

- There is considerable variation in wage rates across the auto parts industry, with the motor vehicle engines, engine parts, and motor vehicle stampings industries having the highest wages; and the more labor-intensive and lower value-added plastic parts and wiring assemblies industries having the lowest wages.

- By 1995, motor vehicle stampings (SIC 3253) had become the largest of the separately defined parts industries when measured in terms of either employment or value of shipments. The stampings industry was probably the most stable industry, experiencing only a very modest downturn in employment during the 1989–1991 period and then employment growth of 47 percent between 1991 and 1995. The engine and engine parts industry was second largest in terms of value of shipments, but the plastic parts industry was the second largest in terms of employment.

Table 4.9
Canadian Auto Industry Productivity by SIC Industry, 1985–1995
(measured by value added per worker [W] and value added per hour paid [H])

A. Current Can$:

Year	SIC 3231 Vehicle Assembly		SIC 325 Parts and Accessories		SIC 3251 Engine and Engine Parts		SIC 3252 Wiring Assemblies		SIC 3253 Stampings	
	W	H	W	H	W	H	W	H	W	H
1985	106,256	43.9	86,346	39.6	122,392	52.8	41,838	21.6	95,367	44.4
1986	107,556	40.4	84,191	38.3	104,934	46.0	44,279	22.2	96,940	44.1
1987*										
1988	119,809	49.6	79,144	36.5	119,618	49.6	50,562	25.1	97,735	45.5
1989	110,613	47.3	80,237	37.5	124,660	55.3	49,946	24.9	86,316	40.7
1990	106,132	49.4	81,294	38.1	125,758	55.4	48,373	22.9	87,031	41.0
1991	91,686	43.3	82,494	38.9	122,586	57.3	55,655	26.8	91,088	42.5
1992	113,761	52.8	80,439	37.9	103,068	47.7	58,374	27.5	90,803	42.8
1993	138,871	60.7	95,805	44.9	170,191	79.0	91,404	43.4	104,045	48.4
1994	183,227	75.9	103,592	46.9	167,502	72.3	115,259	53.5	114,722	53.1
1995	200,289	86.1	107,503	48.5	203,622	88.3	96,806	43.7	115,059	52.9

Table 4.9 (*continued*)
Canadian Auto Industry Productivity by SIC Industry, 1985–1995
(measured by value added per worker [W] and value added per hour paid [H])

A. Current Can$ (*continued*)

	SIC 3254 Steering and Suspension		SIC 3255 Wheel and Brakes		SIC 3256 Plastic Parts		SIC 3257 Fabric Accessories		SIC 3259 Other Parts and Accessories	
	W	H	W	H	W	H	W	H	W	H
1985	78,939	37.9	96,191	44.3	53,291	24.7	68,494	30.7	83,056	38.5
1986	85,611	39.1	93,292	42.5	59,398	27.6	71,696	32.0	86,033	39.0
1987*										
1988	74,866	34.9	75,327	35.8	54,832	26.4	63,825	28.5	71,078	33.7
1989	73,579	33.5	79,904	39.2	55,555	26.5	68,220	31.2	74,868	35.2
1990	68,752	31.8	79,948	37.7	61,881	29.7	79,518	37.0	78,364	37.4
1991	69,332	32.2	79,300	37.8	58,101	28.1	82,367	39.5	86,101	40.2
1992	70,150	33.6	82,694	39.9	55,981	26.4	92,951	44.0	81,868	38.4
1993	88,635	40.6	90,233	42.6	66,342	31.1	105,031	47.1	89,494	42.7
1994	95,888	41.9	111,700	51.9	75,867	34.5	110,327	51.9	91,713	41.2
1995	101,179	44.4	124,203	57.5	74,592	34.4	114,707	52.5	93,145	41.6

(*continued*)

Table 4.9 (*continued*)
Canadian Auto Industry Productivity by SIC Industry, 1985–1995
(measured by value added per worker [W] and value added per hour paid [H])

B. Constant 1986 Can$:

Year	SIC 3231 Vehicle Assembly		SIC 325 Parts and Accessories		SIC 3251 Engine and Engine Parts		SIC 3252 Wiring Assemblies		SIC 3253 Stampings	
	W	H	W	H	W	H	W	H	W	H
1985	112,440	46.4	88,288	40.5	125,145	54.0	42,779	22.1	97,512	45.4
1986	107,556	40.4	84,191	38.3	104,934	46.0	44,279	22.2	96,940	44.1
1987*										
1988	125,849	52.1	80,513	37.2	121,687	50.5	51,436	25.5	99,425	46.3
1989	116,927	50.0	82,463	38.5	128,119	56.8	51,332	25.6	88,711	41.9
1990	111,483	51.9	84,068	39.4	130,050	57.3	50,024	23.7	90,001	42.4
1991	94,424	44.7	84,436	39.8	125,472	58.6	56,965	27.4	93,232	43.6
1992	108,758	50.5	80,600	38.0	103,275	47.8	58,491	27.6	90,985	42.9
1993	123,004	53.8	93,469	43.8	166,040	77.1	89,175	42.4	101,510	47.2
1994	152,182	63.0	97,820	44.3	158,170	68.2	108,837	50.5	108,331	50.1
1995	160,746	69.1	98,446	44.4	186,467	80.9	88,650	40.0	105,365	48.4

Table 4.9 (*continued*)
Canadian Auto Industry Productivity by SIC Industry, 1985–1995
(measured by value added per worker [W] and value added per hour paid [H])

B. Constant 1986 Can$ (continued)

	SIC 3254 Steering and Suspension		SIC 3255 Wheel and Brakes		SIC 3256 Plastic Parts		SIC 3257 Fabric Accessories		SIC 3259 Other Parts and Accessories	
	W	H	W	H	W	H	W	H	W	H
1985	80,715	38.7	98,354	45.3	54,490	25.3	70,034	31.4	84,924	39.3
1986	85,611	39.1	93,292	42.5	59,398	27.6	71,696	32.0	86,033	39.0
1987*										
1988	76,161	35.5	76,630	36.4	55,780	26.9	64,929	29.0	72,308	34.2
1989	75,620	34.4	82,121	40.3	57,096	27.2	70,113	32.1	76,945	36.2
1990	71,099	32.9	82,676	39.0	63,992	30.7	82,232	38.2	81,038	38.6
1991	70,964	33.0	81,167	38.7	59,469	28.7	84,306	40.4	88,128	41.1
1992	70,291	33.7	82,859	40.0	56,093	26.5	93,138	44.1	82,032	38.5
1993	86,473	39.6	88,032	41.5	64,724	30.3	102,469	46.0	87,311	41.6
1994	90,546	39.6	105,477	49.0	71,640	32.5	104,180	49.0	86,604	38.9
1995	92,655	40.6	113,739	52.7	68,307	31.5	105,043	48.1	85,297.	38.1

Source: Statistics Canada 1997.   * No data were published for 1987.

Table 4.10
Canadian Auto Industry Hourly and Annual Wages by SIC Industry, 1985–1995
(in current Can$ and constant [1986] Can$)

A. Hourly and annual wages in current Can$:

	SIC 3231 Vehicle Assembly		SIC 325 Parts and Accessories		SIC 3251 Engine and Engine Parts		SIC 3252 Wiring Assemblies		SIC 3253 Stampings	
	Hourly	Annual	Hourly	Annual	Hourly	Annual	Hourly	Annual	Hourly	Annual
1985	14.47	35,060	12.45	27,123	16.29	37,759	8.24	15,938	11.74	25,246
1986	14.06	37,404	12.49	27,470	15.78	36,005	8.47	16,897	12.47	27,432
1987*										
1988	17.05	41,189	13.47	29,187	17.13	41,268	8.91	17,942	13.97	30,027
1989	18.14	42,449	13.91	29,767	17.48	39,419	10.25	20,591	14.77	31,299
1990	18.80	40,405	14.45	30,838	19.78	44,931	10.30	21,763	14.58	30,947
1991	20.15	42,616	14.86	31,525	18.80	40,222	11.22	23,328	14.93	31,952
1992	21.11	45,446	15.33	32,507	18.18	39,242	11.39	24,169	15.54	33,002
1993	22.65	51,801	15.86	33,850	18.52	39,905	12.46	26,228	16.31	35,089
1994	23.14	55,855	16.48	36,371	19.18	44,443	13.09	28,219	17.22	37,222
1995	23.89	55,582	16.94	37,579	20.00	46,100	14.27	31,603	18.06	39,288

Table 4.10 (*continued*)
Canadian Auto Industry Hourly and Annual Wages by SIC Industry, 1985–1995
(in current Can$ and constant [1986] Can$)

A. Hourly and annual wages in current Can$ (*continued*)

	SIC 3254 Steering and Suspension		SIC 3255 Wheel and Brakes		SIC 3256 Plastic Parts		SIC 3257 Fabric Accessories		SIC 3259 Other Parts and Accessories	
	Hourly	Annual	Hourly	Annual	Hourly	Annual	Hourly	Annual	Hourly	Annual
1985	13.16	27,440	12.42	26,984	8.89	19,163	13.14	29,349	11.83	25,543
1986	12.86	28,152	12.21	26,814	9.24	19,899	13.36	29,895	12.37	27,289
1987*										
1988	13.14	28,167	13.47	28,313	10.11	21,001	15.12	33,834	12.81	27,052
1989	13.05	28,643	14.06	28,674	10.85	22,761	14.83	32,406	13.38	28,468
1990	13.43	29,052	13.71	29,083	11.51	24,003	15.36	33,042	14.18	29,729
1991	13.58	29,250	13.95	29,272	11.95	24,735	16.60	34,647	15.45	33,087
1992	14.32	29,904	14.28	29,606	12.56	26,602	16.39	34,631	16.25	34,617
1993	16.09	35,143	14.60	30,941	12.94	27,596	16.96	37,807	16.78	35,205
1994	16.37	37,476	15.28	32,862	13.59	29,919	17.97	38,219	17.14	38,152
1995	16.62	37,920	16.44	35,487	13.40	29,088	17.57	38,354	17.48	39,136

(*continued*)

Table 4.10 (continued)
Canadian Auto Industry Hourly and Annual Wages by SIC Industry, 1985–1995
(in current Can$ and constant [1986] Can$)

B. Hourly and annual wages in constant 1986 Can$:

	SIC 3231 Vehicle Assembly		SIC 325 Parts and Accessories		SIC 3251 Engine and Engine Parts		SIC 3252 Wiring Assemblies		SIC 3253 Stampings	
	Hourly	Annual	Hourly	Annual	Hourly	Annual	Hourly	Annual	Hourly	Annual
1985	15.08	36,521	12.97	28,253	16.97	39,333	8.59	16,602	12.23	26,298
1986	14.06	37,404	12.49	27,470	15.78	36,005	8.47	16,897	12.47	27,432
1987*										
1988	15.70	37,927	12.40	26,876	15.77	38,000	8.20	16,521	12.86	27,649
1989	15.91	37,236	12.20	26,111	15.33	34,578	8.99	18,063	12.96	27,455
1990	15.73	33,811	12.10	25,806	16.56	37,600	8.62	18,212	12.20	25,897
1991	15.96	33,768	11.77	24,980	14.90	31,872	8.89	18,485	11.83	25,319
1992	16.48	35,477	11.97	25,376	14.19	30,634	8.90	18,867	12.13	25,763
1993	17.37	39,725	12.16	25,958	14.20	30,602	9.55	20,112	12.50	26,909
1994	17.70	42,735	12.61	27,828	14.67	34,004	10.02	21,591	13.18	28,479
1995	17.90	41,635	12.69	28,149	14.98	34,532	10.69	23,673	13.53	29,429

Table 4.10 (continued)
Canadian Auto Industry Hourly and Annual Wages by SIC Industry, 1985–1995
(in current Can$ and constant [1986] Can$)

B. Hourly and annual wages in constant 1986 Can$ (continued)

	SIC 3254 Steering and Suspension		SIC 3255 Wheel and Brakes		SIC 3256 Plastic Parts		SIC 3257 Fabric Accessories		SIC 3259 Other Parts and Accessories	
	Hourly	Annual	Hourly	Annual	Hourly	Annual	Hourly	Annual	Hourly	Annual
1985	13.71	28,583	12.94	28,109	9.26	19,961	13.69	30,572	12.33	26,608
1986	12.86	28,152	12.22	26,814	9.24	19,899	13.36	29,895	12.37	27,289
1987*										
1988	12.10	25,937	12.40	26,071	9.31	19,338	13.92	31,155	11.80	24,910
1989	11.45	25,125	12.33	25,152	9.51	19,966	13.01	28,426	11.74	24,972
1990	11.24	24,312	11.47	24,337	9.63	20,086	12.85	27,650	11.86	24,878
1991	10.76	23,178	11.05	23,195	9.47	19,600	13.16	27,454	12.24	26,218
1992	11.18	23,344	11.15	23,111	9.81	20,766	12.79	27,034	12.68	27,023
1993	12.34	26,950	11.20	23,728	9.92	21,163	13.00	28,993	12.87	26,998
1994	12.53	28,673	11.69	25,143	10.40	22,892	13.75	29,242	13.11	29,190
1995	12.45	28,404	12.32	26,582	10.04	21,789	13.16	28,729	13.09	29,315

Source: Statistics Canada 1997.   * No data were published for 1987.

Patterns of Trade and Canada's Changing Role within the North American Automotive Industry

This section focuses on recent patterns of Canadian automotive trade, the extent of regional specialization, and the role that Canada plays within the continental industry. The analysis is based on data drawn from the automotive trade database developed by the Automotive Branch of Industry Canada. The database is built from information collected by Statistics Canada and reported on the basis of harmonized commodity codes. However, the trade data on the parts industry are reported by categories that broadly correspond to the four-digit SIC industries.

The existing level of cross-border trade and economic integration in the North American auto industry has been achieved in two broad stages. First, the Auto Pact enabled the Big Three to move rapidly during the late 1960s and early 1970s to rationalize and integrate production between Canada and the United States. Because the auto industry had already operated under a virtual tariff-free trade environment for more than two decades, CUFTA of 1989 had relatively little impact on the geography of the industry or the geography of automotive trade between the two countries although it did affect the Auto Pact in some important ways (Johnson 1993). Second, a radical shift in Mexican state economic and industrial policy at the end of the 1980s signaled that the Mexican auto industry, whose links to the industry in the United States and Canada had been growing throughout the decade as the result of the strategic choices made by a number of transnational automakers, was set on a course to become fully integrated into a truly North American auto industry. Thus the momentum toward full integration of Mexico into the continental auto industry appeared irreversible well before the negotiation of NAFTA.

The first of the following three subsections provides a brief overview of the evolution of the continental trade regime governing the North American auto industry from the Auto Pact to NAFTA; the second documents recent trends in Canada's automotive trade patterns; and the third analyzes Canada's role in the pattern of regional specialization that appears to be emerging in the North American auto industry under NAFTA.

Auto Pact to NAFTA: Canada's Role in the Integrated North American Automobile Industry

Even though the Auto Pact was signed more than 30 years ago, it is still fundamental for understanding the role that Canada plays today in the North American auto industry. Since the Auto Pact came into force in 1966, the Canadian auto industry has been part of a highly integrated North American auto industry. The Auto Pact allowed the Big Three to rationalize vehicle and in-house component production in Canada and fully integrate it with their production units in the United States to form one production and marketing system. The high level of integration and easy access to the largest automotive market in the world led to the rise in Canada of highly efficient world-scale vehicle assembly and components plants that produce high-quality products. For the past three decades each Canadian assembly, engine, and transmission plant has specialized in the production of a limited number of models, and the vast majority of the output from each plant has been exported to the United States. The Big Three have similarly imported a range of vehicles manufactured in the United States to supply the Canadian market and have imported significant proportions of the componentry required to assemble the vehicles sourced from Canadian assembly plants.

Although the Auto Pact created an integrated continental market for automotive products, it also contained safeguards designed to ensure that a certain portion of combined Canadian and U.S. vehicle and parts manufacturing took place in Canada. Each manufacturer was free to supply the Canadian market from either domestic or U.S. production, but the volume of such sales that the manufacturer could make in Canada was linked to the volume of production. Furthermore, a CVA requirement was designed to ensure that Canadian production amounted to more than mere assembly. During the past 15 years the Big Three automakers have exceeded by a wide margin their Auto Pact production–sales ratio and CVA commitments (Industry Canada 1997).

The Auto Pact resulted in duty-free, two-way movement between Canada and the United States of new vehicles and OEM parts although the basis for granting duty-free treatment has been completely different on the two sides of the border. This latter point is important for understanding certain aspects of the contemporary pattern and composition of Canadian automotive trade. To qualify for duty-free treatment under the Auto Pact, new vehicles and OEM parts imported into the United States have to come from Canada and must contain at least 50 percent North American content. Eligibility for duty-free treatment of vehicles and parts entering Canada is based not on the commodities' origin but on the fulfilment by the importing manufacturer of the Auto Pact performance criteria (volume of Canadian production and the CVA requirement). As long as these criteria are

met, it does not matter where the new vehicles or OEM parts originate or where they are shipped from. So, for example, besides the
Can$40.2 billion of automotive imports entering Canada from the
United States under the Auto Pact in 1996, a further Can$4.5
billion entered under the Auto Pact from a number of third
countries, including Mexico (Can$2.8 billion), Japan (Can$597
million), Europe (Can$453 million), and Brazil (Can$152 million).
In fact, fully 77.4 percent of automotive imports into Canada in
1996 entered under the Auto Pact (table 4.11).

The restructured Canadian auto industry that emerged
under the Auto Pact regime was competitive and efficient by
North American standards and enjoyed significant growth and
expansion. The Auto Pact gave Canada a disproportionately
large share of vehicle assembly while research and development,
product engineering, and the production of high-valued parts
such as body stampings and drivetrain components remained
heavily concentrated in the United States. Two consequences
have flowed from this geographical division of labor in the
industry. First, Canada has regularly registered large trade surpluses with the United States in finished vehicles and large trade
deficits in parts and components. Second, given the enormous
difference in the size of the U.S. and Canadian markets, the economic vitality of the auto industry in Canada is highly dependent on the decisions by the Big Three as to which specific
vehicle platforms are to be built in Canadian assembly plants
and on the strength and composition of vehicle demand in the
U.S. market.

Because the rationalized and integrated Canadian and U.S.
auto industries had already operated under a virtual free-trade
environment for close to 25 years, CUFTA had much less immediate impact on the auto industry than it had on many other
Canadian industrial sectors (Holmes 1992). However, it did have
a significant impact on the rules governing the Auto Pact. By
preventing Canada from further granting of Auto Pact status to
new manufacturers and requiring the phasing out of the export-
and production-based duty-remission orders introduced during
the 1980s to entice Asian investment, CUFTA eliminated an
incentive for non–Auto Pact manufacturers (that is, transplant
producers such as Toyota, Honda, and Hyundai) to expand their
Canadian operations or increase their use of Canada-produced
parts. CUFTA thus created two classes of vehicle manufacturers
in Canada: those with Auto Pact status (GM, Ford, Chrysler,
Volvo, and CAMI) and those without (Toyota, Honda, and

Hyundai). The real competitive advantage of Auto Pact status is that it allows the Big Three and CAMI to import vehicles and parts from third countries duty-free as long as they continue to meet the Canadian performance requirements demanded by the Auto Pact.

The automotive provisions of NAFTA facilitate the development of a continentally integrated North American auto industry, but intracontinental automotive trade and investment flows will still be managed, particularly during the 10-year NAFTA phase in, when the Big Three will enjoy preferred status over the transplants. Eden and Molot (1993, 3) observe that

> the NAFTA talks pertaining to the automotive sector centered on the protection of market access and the continued management of auto trade. Industry stakeholders advanced provisions that would strengthen their individual competitive positions as the industry continued to integrate along continental lines. As a result of the NAFTA, the Mexican market will be opened to Canadian and U.S. auto firms, and the two classes of auto producers established under the Canada-U.S. Free Trade Agreement will be extended to include producers in Mexico during the phase-in period.

To Canada's advantage, NAFTA does allow for the continuation of the Auto Pact and Canada's duty-remission orders, which allow companies with Auto Pact status to import vehicles and parts duty-free from third countries. Under NAFTA, however, the North American content requirement for vehicles is set at 62.5 percent for cars, light trucks, and their engines and transmissions and at 60 percent for other vehicles and parts.[3] This is higher than the 50-percent requirement that had been sought by the Canadian negotiators in an effort to protect Canada's attractiveness for new auto industry investment. Furthermore, Toyota and Honda plants in Canada will not be able to export to Mexico during the 10-year transition period because neither had assembly capacity in Mexico at the time that NAFTA was signed.

One of the major benefits of NAFTA is the opening of the Mexican market to imports, and the principal beneficiaries are likely to be the Big Three; because they already had production facilities in Mexico, NAFTA gives them preferential treatment. The benefits to Canada, however, are unlikely to be large in the short run given the limited volume of Canada–Mexico automotive trade and uncertainties regarding future growth in the Mexican market (Eden and Molot 1993).

Table 4.11
Canadian Automotive Imports by Country and Category, 1996
(in thousands of Can$)

Country	Cars	Light-Duty Trucks	Engines	Total Parts	Total
United States total	10,278,598	3,414,990	6,353,251	31,537,696	49,187,392
Auto Pact	8,731,895	3,339,798	5,482,614	26,481,899	40,228,083
Auto Pact as % of total	85.0	97.8	86.3	84.0	81.8
United States as % of total	73.9	94.4	86.1	88.2	85.0
Mexico total	1,463,904	191,534	366,421	1,597,382	3,267,427
Auto Pact	1,125,190	191,534	344,157	1,532,369	3,193,250
Auto Pact as % of total	76.9	100.0	93.9	96.0	97.7
Mexico as % of total	10.5	5.3	5.0	4.5	5.7
Japan total	1,209,949	3,146	525,325	1,366,600	2,858,083
Auto Pact	7,805	0	367,980	588,452	597,380
Auto Pact as % of total	0.6	0.0	70.0	43.0	20.9
Japan as % of total	8.6	0.0	5.0	1.6	4.9

Table 4.11 (*continued*)
Canadian Automotive Imports by Country and Category, 1996
(in thousands of Can$)

Country	Cars	Light-Duty Trucks	Engines	Total Parts	Total
Others total	972,202	9,011	130,504	1,266,816	2,534,783
Auto Pact	227,743	48	41,062	851,574	2,098,340
Auto Pact as % of total	23.4	0.5	31.5	67.2	83.0
Others as % of total	7.0	0.3	1.8	2.4	4.5
Total	13,924,653	3,618,669	7,375,501	35,768,494	57,847,685
Auto Pact	10,092,633	3,531,380	6,235,813	29,454,294	44,772,010
Auto Pact as % of total	72.5	97.6	84.5	82.3	77.4

Source: Industry Canada 1996.

Recent Trends in Canada's Automotive Trade

In its automotive trade with the United States, Canada has traditionally run a deficit in auto parts trade and a surplus in motor vehicles, reflecting Canada's post–Auto Pact role of assembling vehicles for sale in the United States and Canada. Owing to the highly integrated nature of production, there is an almost mechanistic formula that ties levels of parts imports to the number of vehicles being assembled in Canada for export to the United States. Given our earlier observation that the Canadian assembly sector was extremely buoyant during the past decade, it should be no surprise that both the trade surpluses of vehicles and deficits in parts with the United States rose over the 1985–1995 period, the vehicle surplus reaching a record Can$31.67 billion and the parts deficit Can$18.04 billion in 1995.

During the 1980s Canada's trade deficits with Japan in both vehicles and parts increased steadily. The total automotive trade deficit with Japan peaked at approximately Can$4.9 billion (Can$3.4 billion in vehicles, Can$1.3 billion in parts, and Can$0.2 billion in "others") in 1992 and then decreased to Can$2.7 billion (Can$1.1 billion in vehicles, Can$1.4 billion in parts, and Can$0.2 billion in "others") by 1996. This rapid decline was largely due to substituting vehicles produced in North America by the Japanese assembly transplants for vehicles imported from Japan. Automotive trade between Mexico and Canada was minuscule until 1989, but imports from Mexico of both vehicles and parts increased rapidly between 1990 and 1996. The value of vehicles imported from Mexico rose more than twelvefold from Can$133 million to Can$1.7 billion; and in 1996 almost 100,000 Mexico-built cars entered Canada. Over the same period the value of parts imports doubled from Can$0.8 billion to Can$1.6 billion. Although they increased from Can$91 million in 1990 to Can$240 million in 1996, Canadian automotive exports to Mexico remain relatively negligible. As a consequence, the automotive trade deficit with Mexico increased more than fourfold to Can$3.0 billion in 1996, with assembled vehicles and parts contributing almost equally. In 1995 Mexico eclipsed Japan as Canada's second largest supplier of both vehicles and component parts.

While one should not downplay the significance of Canada's automotive trade with Mexico and Japan, it must be emphasized that the overwhelming majority of Canada's total automotive trade continues to be with the United States. The U.S. market in 1996 was the destination for more than 98 percent

Table 4.12
Canadian Automotive Exports by Country and Category, 1996
(in thousands of Can$)

Country	Cars	Light-Duty Trucks	Engines	Total Parts
United States:				
Total United States	34,993,595	8,297,037	3,604,863	14,289,500
United States as % of total	98.3	99.4	98.2	91.4
Mexico:				
Total Mexico	63,303	962	0	175,567
Mexico as % of total	0.2	0.0	0	1.1
Japan:				
Total Japan	112,696	1,272	1,818	40,592
Japan as % of total	0.3	0.0	0.0	0.3
Others:				
Total others	411,984	50,770	65,402	1,134,466
Others as % of total	1.2	0.6	1.8	7.3
Total exports	35,581,578	8,350,041	3,672,083	15,640,125

Source: Industry Canada 1996.

of all Canadian vehicle exports and more than 91 percent of Canadian automotive parts exports (table 4.12). In the same year, Mexico was the destination for a minuscule 1.1 percent of Canadian parts exports and an even smaller percentage of assembled vehicles. The picture for Canadian imports is a little different (table 4.11). Although Canada still relies on the United States for 78 percent of its imported cars and light trucks and 88 percent of its automotive parts imports, imports also come from Mexico, Japan, Europe, and other countries. Between 1991 and 1996, Japan lost ground to both the United States and Mexico as a source for automotive imports entering Canada. Table 4.11 also illustrates the very significant proportions of 1996 imports from the United States (82 percent), Mexico (98 percent), and even Japan (21 percent) that enter Canada under Auto Pact regulations.

Within the broader automotive parts sector, engines (from the United States, Japan, and Mexico), stampings (overwhelmingly from the United States), and electrical systems (from the United States and Mexico) represent the three leading product groups by value with regard to imports. Engines and engine parts, wheel and brake systems, and stampings are the three leading product groups that are exported to the United States. Given the high degree of intra-industry trade in this industry, some complex patterns of specialization and trade begin to emerge as the data are disaggregated. With sufficient time and resources a more detailed analysis of intra-industry trade patterns by harmonized commodity code could be undertaken.

As was the case with production, employment, wages, and productivity discussed in the past section, it is impossible to detect from the available data any significant direct impact of NAFTA on patterns of Canadian automotive trade. Even though the numbers are still very small in comparison with the corresponding numbers for the United States, there is no question that Mexico is becoming an increasingly important source of both cars and automotive parts for Canada; however, this trend was well under way before 1994. Given the relatively small size of the automotive sectors in Canada and Mexico vis-à-vis the United States and the historical development of Canada's role within the North American auto industry, Canada is likely to be much more sensitive than the United States to expanded investment and production in the Mexican auto industry. Mexico has replaced Canada as the continental industry's least-cost production site—a competitive advantage enjoyed by Canada for close to 30 years under the Auto Pact. However, Eden and Molot (1994, 84) argue:

> . . . while the potential exists for competition between Canadian and Mexican parts firms to supply the U.S. market, the fact that many of the exporting plants are almost all subsidiaries of multinational parts manufacturers makes it less likely. Thus, rather than overt competition, we expect continued plant rationalizations and reductions in product lines.

There were some well-publicized instances in the late 1980s and early 1990s of plants that produced such low-technology, labor-intensive parts as wiring harnesses, electrical equipment, and hand-sewn seating cushions relocating from Canada to

Mexico and the United States in search of lower labor costs. The Statistics Canada data certainly point to a significant reduction in the number of plants in particular four-digit segments of the parts industry during the 1989–1993 period (see previous section). Furthermore, an Ontario Ministry of Economic Development list of auto parts plants closed since 1991 contains a total of 62 plants and all but 12 of these closings occurred between 1991 and 1993. However, the full extent and reasons for these closings are not well documented or well understood and deserve further study. Large Canadian parts firms currently operating in Mexico include Magna, Woodbridge, Ventra, and Fleck Manufacturing and, according to the Automotive Parts Manufacturers Association of Canada (APMA 1997, 29), 51 of its member firms have expressed an interest in investing in Mexico.

Executives of Canadian parts manufacturers are more concerned, however, about the potential loss of new investment in parts plants to the United States than to Mexico (APMA 1997). In one press report (Fowlie 1993) it was reported that 50 Canadian parts plants had closed in the past few years, many of them owned by U.S.-based companies that had consolidated their operations in the United States. More recent reports tell of small stamping firms moving from Ontario to Michigan because of more competitive labor costs.

Intra-Industry Trade and Specialization

Weintraub (1997) emphasizes that economic integration is most valuable when it allows countries to specialize *within* the same overall industry or economic sector. Such specialization will be reflected in increased intra-industry trade. Weintraub (1997, 18) succinctly notes:

> One must therefore ask how much specialization NAFTA has induced. Phrased another way, has trade within the same industrial sector—intra-industry trade—increased? Have producers taken advantage of the particular factors that are most favorable for production and marketing in each of the countries such that output can be maximized at the least cost?

In considering intra-industry trade and specialization in the North American auto industry we must remember that the movement toward continental economic integration in this industry dates back to the late 1960s and the Auto Pact. As a consequence, a very high level of intra-industry trade and specialization in automotive products between Canada and the United States has existed for some considerable time. Similar integration is now under way in the auto industry among the United States, Canada, and Mexico. Based on the emerging geography of the integrated North American auto industry—with one major regional production complex centered in the Midwest/ Upper South/Ontario and a second but at present much smaller complex emerging in northern Mexico—and the relative sizes of the three industries and markets, we conjecture that intra-industry trade in the auto industry will likely grow fastest between the United States and Mexico.

The general extent of intra-industry trade in the North American auto industry is reflected in the fact that in 1996 automotive products were five of the top six commodities (Harmonized System, or HS, tariff classification code) by value exported from the United States to Canada and Mexico and three of the top six U.S. imports from those two countries. Five of Canada's six largest commodity imports from the United States were automotive products (motor vehicle parts, motor vehicle bodies, intermediate-size vehicles, compact cars, and engines), and three of its six largest exports were various types of motor vehicles. Canada's top four imports by value (compact cars, wiring sets, engines, and seating parts) from Mexico were automotive products as were three of Canada's top five exports to Mexico ("other" motor vehicle parts, larger vehicles, and gearboxes). The value of each of these imports and exports rose significantly between 1992 and 1996.

Intra-industry trade and specialization is most evident and most easily identified with regard to vehicles and major components such as engines and transmissions. The efficient operating scales for plants producing these commodities are very high: 200,000 for a vehicle assembly plant, 300,000–500,000 for each engine line, and over 1,000,000 for transmissions. We have already documented the fact that there is considerable and increasing intra industry trade in each of these products among the three countries. Individual car and truck models for sale in the combined North American market are produced in, at most, two assembly plants. Canadian assembly plants are the sole source for a number of popular car and truck models. In the case of Mexico and Canada there appears to be a tendency toward specialization in the production of vehicles tied to particular segments of the market. The vast majority of vehicles produced in Mexican assembly plants are subcompact and compact cars. Part of the output from these plants is used to feed the U.S. and Canadian markets for smaller size cars. Canadian assembly plants mainly produce trucks, minivans, and midsize and full-size cars, the vast majority of which are exported for sale in the United States.

There is considerable intra-industry trade and specialization in engine and transmission production. Large quantities of engines and engine parts are exported and imported by each country in order to link specialized engine plants with specialized assembly plants. In 1996 Canada imported more than 1,200,000 engines from the United States and 163,000 from Mexico and exported more than 895,000 engines to the United States; only a few hundred engines are exported from Canada to Mexico. The following specific examples illustrate specialization and intra industry trade in engine production.

The Ford Essex engine plant in Windsor is the sole source for the 3.8-liter engines used in the Windstar, which is assembled only at Ford Oakville; the Cougar and Thunderbird, assembled in Lorain, Ohio; and the Mustang, assembled in Dearborn, Michigan. Ford Oakville imports the smaller 3.0 liter engines for the Windstar from Lima, Ohio; and the larger 4.6-liter engines for the Cougar, Thunderbird, and Mustang are made in the Ford engine plant in Romeo, Michigan. Chrysler assemblies in Windsor and St. Louis, which assemble the popular Caravan and Voyager minivans, sole source 2.4- and 3.3-liter engines from Saltillo, Mexico, and Trenton, Michigan, respectively.

Another major and important category of parts is stampings. There are two types of stamping plants: big, centralized stand-alone plants that supply many assembly facilities; and on-site stamping operations adjacent to or contiguous to an assembly plant. More and more stamping plants are producing parts for specific vehicles and are not dedicated to making only specific types of stampings (e.g., doors, hoods, fenders) for a range of vehicles. As part of this trend there is a continuing move toward more contiguous or on-site stamping plants (in Canada there are on-site stamping operations at GM Oshawa, Chrysler Bramalea, CAMI, Honda Alliston, and Toyota Cambridge), which means a potential reduction in the number of stampings that enter cross-border trade. Countering this, however, is a tendency for stamping plants that make parts for common vehicles to stamp parts for each other. For example, Honda East Liberty makes Civic parts for Alliston, and Alliston stamps some parts for East Liberty; and NUMMI (New United Motor Manufacturing Inc., a GM-Toyota joint venture plant) stamps Corolla parts for Toyota Cambridge, which in turn makes parts for NUMMI.

Table 4.13 records three indexes by which to judge the degree of intra-industry trade and specialization for four-digit SIC automotive industries in Canada during the period 1988–1995. The first measure is total trade for the industry (exports plus imports), which obviously will increase as intra-industry trade increases. The second indicator is exports as a percentage of domestic shipments, and the third measures imports as a percentage of the apparent domestic market (defined as domestic shipments plus imports and minus exports). An increase in the second and third indexes could be interpreted as indicative of more intercountry trade in the industry while a decline may be interpreted as a sign that a greater proportion of domestic production is being directed toward the domestic market where it is substituting for previous imports. A number of trends are evident:

- There was a significant increase in total trade in each sector of the auto industry between 1991 and 1995. The degree to which this growth can be attributed to increased intra-industry specialization and trade that results from continuing economic integration as opposed to the cyclical recovery of the U.S. market is presently an open question.
- With only a very few notable exceptions, all the import and export indexes are very high, suggesting a high degree of intra-industry trade and specialization between Canada and the United States.
- The import and export indexes for the motor vehicle industry (SIC 3231) increased between 1988 and 1995, indicating a trend toward even greater specialization in vehicle assembly.
- While remaining high, the import–export indexes for many parts industries such as wiring assemblies, steering and suspension assemblies, engines, and SIC 3259 (other parts) exhibit a downward trend. This suggests that domestic producers are capturing a larger share of the domestic market for those components, possibly as a result of their improved competitiveness. Industry Canada (1996a) reached a similar conclusion with respect to U.S.-Canada trade in component parts. The export index for wiring harnesses dropped by more than 60 percent between 1992 and 1993.

Table 4.13
Canadian Auto Industry, Measures of Intra-Industry Trade by SIC Industry, 1988–1995
(total trade in millions of current Can$)

	1988	1989	1990	1991	1992	1993	1994	1995
SIC 3231 (Motor Vehicles)								
Total trade	39,779	38,146	37,308	38,132	41,587	50,033	61,934	66,747
Exports (% of domestic shipments)	86.5	86.1	87.9	90.7	92.4	91.7	94.8	93.7
Imports (% of domestic markets)	80.3	79.0	80.2	85.8	86.3	83.1	89.5	86.1
SIC 3251 (Engines)								
Total trade	7,327	6,334	7,131	6,326	7,250	9,314	11,155	11,489
Exports (% of domestic shipments)	85.7	76.6	103.9	155.7	159.3	138.2	130.7	122.8
Imports (% of domestic markets)	88.5	77.2	102.9	127.4	128.3	118.7	113.6	109.4
SIC 3252 (Wiring)								
Total trade	1,280	1,357	1,352	1,313	1,485	1,886	2,290	2,290
Exports (% of domestic shipments)	51.9	51.0	52.0	46.0	49.2	23.1	22.2	19.8
Imports (% of domestic markets)	86.0	82.3	84.1	84.8	85.3	72.5	70.3	69.6

(continued)

Table 4.13 (*continued*)
Canadian Auto Industry, Measures of Intra-Industry Trade by SIC Industry, 1988–1995
(total trade in millions of current Can$)

	1988	1989	1990	1991	1992	1993	1994	1995
SIC 3253 (Stampings)								
Total trade	5,580	5,377	4,754	4,337	4,932	6,018	7,166	7,214
Exports (% of domestic shipments)	45.9	52.9	42.2	38.4	43.2	47.2	50.7	48.0
Imports (% of domestic markets)	78.3	79.7	75.7	72.5	74.5	75.9	77.2	74.8
SIC 3254 (Steering and Suspension)								
Total trade	2,066	1,974	1,877	1,810	2,161	2,774	3,189	3,309
Exports (% of domestic shipments)	81.4	76.6	80.1	84.9	82.0	75.0	69.5	64.7
Imports (% of domestic markets)	89.6	86.3	88.1	92.1	90.5	87.5	83.3	80.3
SIC 3255 (Wheels and Brakes)								
Total trade	2,021	1,951	1,941	1,932	2,412	3,164	3,716	3,961
Exports (% of domestic shipments)	93.1	89.8	99.6	106.6	116.8	123.8	114.7	115.9
Imports (% of domestic markets)	93.4	89.6	99.6	105.9	114.6	117.2	109.9	110.6

Table 4.13 (*continued*)
Canadian Auto Industry, Measures of Intra-Industry Trade by SIC Industry, 1988–1995
(total trade in millions of current Can$)

	1988	1989	1990	1991	1992	1993	1994	1995
SIC 3256 (Plastics)								
Total trade	547	616	276	304	402	561	761	852
Exports (% of domestic shipments)	33.4	35.6	21.1	26.1	32.4	36.3	41.2	45.8
Imports (% of domestic markets)	9.7	10.1	3.9	4.4	5.4	4.9	4.6	5.2
SIC 3257 (Fabric)								
Total trade	578	715	462	414	629	849	1,265	1,088
Exports (% of domestic shipments)	41.4	49.1	23.7	19.1	20.9	23.4	43.0	39.4
Imports (% of domestic markets)	20.7	22.9	15.6	15.6	21.9	27.1	25.7	20.6
SIC 3259 (Other)								
Total trade	9,731	9,133	9,074	8,334	9,659	11,670	13,420	14,446
Exports (% of domestic shipments)	95.8	79.9	83.5	62.6	66.9	71.0	67.6	82.1
Imports (% of domestic markets)	97.4	87.6	88.5	74.5	78.1	82.8	82.1	78.5

Source: Industry Canada, Strategies On-line Database.

- Two industries that stand out as being different are motor vehicle plastic parts and motor vehicle fabric. Imports account for less than 10 percent of the domestic market for plastic parts and approximately 20 percent for fabric. In both industries domestic shipments and exports have increased significantly since 1991, while the value of imports as a percentage of the domestic market has remained stable.

A complex picture begins to emerge from this limited investigation. Convincing evidence shows that there has been a significant increase in intra-industry trade during the past four years. And strong support exists for the idea of an increasing specialization between regions in the production of different types of motor vehicles that are then supplied to all three national markets. Specialization and cross-border trade are also important with regard to major components such as engines, transmissions, and stampings. Some analysis suggests, however, that despite high integration with the industry in the United States the tendencies during the past four years have been for more of the demand for some parts by Canadian assembly plants to be met from Canada-based parts manufacturers and a relative (though slight) decline in the importance of imports and exports.

Effects of Industry Restructuring on Labor

The Canadian automobile industry has been undergoing significant restructuring since the early to mid-1980s, creating both threats and opportunities for labor. The process of restructuring has entailed both the expansion of production and investment in new plants by foreign manufacturers as well as large-scale rationalization and modernization of plant facilities and equipment by the Big Three and parts producers. The restructuring has been shaped by four dynamics:

- Currency fluctuations, in particular the rise of Japanese yen against the U.S. dollar in the mid-1980s that led Japanese manufacturers to set up plants in Canada and the United States; and also the decline in the value of the Canadian dollar in relation to the U.S. currency since 1990, which has bolstered Canada's competitive position;

- Internationalization of production, due in large part to the competitive pressures from Japanese automakers;
- Changing consumer preferences toward more fuel-efficient, high-quality cars, minivans, and sport-utility vehicles, resulting in a steady decline in the market share of the Big Three and the rising proportion of imports and/or transplant sales; and
- Growing momentum toward greater continental integration of the industry, spurred by the new trade and investment policy regime under CUFTA in 1989 and further strengthened by NAFTA in 1993.

The nature and scope of this restructuring of production and management systems, aimed to achieve greater efficiencies and operational flexibilities as well as improvements in product quality, have been particularly significant at the Big Three. During the past 10 years, the three companies have invested close to $15 billion in modernization and rationalization of their plant facilities and equipment. The key initiatives pursued by management have included

- A product mix significantly altered toward midsize and intermediate-size passenger cars, minivans, and pickup trucks to meet the growing demand for these products in the U.S. market;
- Adoption of lean production methods with emphasis on new technology, just-in-time inventory systems, reduction in subassembly processes, and indirect labor to increase value added;
- Greater outsourcing of component parts, materials, and services, and a new supply-chain management philosophy that favors consolidating the number of suppliers and increasing their involvement in product design and development to ensure cost efficiencies and better component-parts quality;
- Greater capacity utilization through alternative work arrangements; and
- Downsizing of the workforce and instituting a new system of work organization, including management delayering and reducing supervisor–worker ratios, increased employee involvement in shop-floor administration, greater information sharing with the union, enhanced training and skill formation, and wherever possible introduction of

performance-related compensation and union involvement or "partnership" in continuous improvement and product quality matters.

This restructuring, in particular the emphasis on outsourcing and consolidation of supply-chain management, has stimulated a similar process of change in the independent auto parts sector. New capital spending in the parts industry has almost tripled over the past 5 years. The surge in new investment in plant and equipment has been particularly noteworthy in large firms that aspire to become Tier One and Tier Two suppliers.

Because the workforce, especially at the Big Three, is highly unionized, the restructuring process has been largely shaped by the union response. The CAW, the primary union representing workers at the Big Three and major independent parts producers, has viewed the restructuring strategy of the companies with skepticism and concern. The union is apprehensive of the narrow economic interest and the underlying motives behind the change process, especially in the case of the adoption and diffusion of lean production and work reorganization. While reaffirming its commitment to "an efficient and productive workplace producing quality products" and recognizing "the potential benefits of new technology and new work processes to workers," the CAW has been vehement in its opposition to the introduction of Japanese-style management techniques. It regards lean production as a potential source of job losses, deskilling, work intensification, job stress and repetitive injuries, and increased management control. The union is not only concerned over loss of worker autonomy and control but is also fearful of the erosion of the independent workplace role of the union under lean production. Citing divergent interests of labor and management and the unequal power between the two parties, the union has opposed management initiatives for "jointness" and "partnership" in shop-floor administration and performance-related contingent compensation in lieu of standard wage increases; these two issues were the predominant reasons behind the CAW's 1985 breakaway from the UAW that, largely to save jobs, had accepted them in its agreements with the Big Three in the United States. Instead the CAW has promoted a "close working relationship with the employers" and negotiated change based on concrete needs and mutual priorities.

In an effort to make the lean production system more responsive to workers' needs, the CAW has articulated an independent and distinctive agenda. The agenda is both defensive and proactive, reflecting the union's culture of ideological resistance and negotiated change. It encompasses elements of both continuity and change: *continuity* that preserves the fundamental elements of the system of industrial relations that have evolved over the past 50 years and have been a source of stability and progress in the industry; and *change* to meet the changing needs and priorities of both workers and employers. The purpose of the union agenda is to make the production system more human centered, preserve and expand jobs, make work more comfortable, ensure a safe and healthy work environment, and enhance worker skills and capacities as well as provide employers with the needed flexibility to meet their efficiency and product quality goals and remain competitive.

The union stresses the need for significant improvements in four key areas to humanize the lean production system: work pace and production standards; training; job design; and union input into production decisions. The agenda calls for

- training committees to assess training needs and develop joint programs to increase both the extent and content of both technical and social training through negotiated guarantees of training time;
- ergonomics committees to improve the design of jobs and work stations;
- technology committees that focus on the design, implementation, and effects of new technology; and
- environmental committees to discuss environmentally sound products and production methods (CAW 1996b).

In the area of work reorganization, while the CAW opposes the kinds of formal employee involvement programs and team concept structures that have been endorsed by the UAW in the United States, it supports informal and incremental changes that use "workers' experience, knowledge and skills to produce good quality products in well designed workplaces." The union is also not averse to participating in group work structures as long as they not involve workers taking responsibility for functions that have traditionally been exercised by management. In a similar vein, the union has supported changes in work schedules and work arrangements that increase capacity utilization and either preserve or increase bargaining unit jobs.

The militant union response has led to significant modifications in the adoption and implementation of lean production methods and associated workplace changes in Big Three assembly plants and major independent parts facilities in Canada. For example, our recent case studies of Big Three assembly plants have found that, despite the union's ideological resistance to lean production, in almost all plants there is a tremendous emphasis and drive to further standardize work and reduce non-value-added time, redesign work stations to reduce operator travel distance and floor space, organize production around one-piece flow by eliminating off-line subassembly work and reducing work-in-progress, develop just-in-time systems both within the plant and between outside suppliers and the assembly plant, and incorporate quality-monitoring and continuous-improvement methods into the production process (Kumar and Holmes 1997). In the area of work reorganization, the traditional postwar wage-setting formula of cost-of-living allowance and annual improvement factor as well as uniform pattern bargaining continue to prevail across all of Canada's unionized (as well as non-unionized) plants. Contrary to U.S. practice, none of the Big Three Canadian plants has contingent compensation schemes such as lump sum bonuses, profit sharing, or pay-for-knowledge schemes. The Big Three in Canada have also not succeeded in achieving any significant reduction in the number of job classifications or in eroding the strict use of the seniority system with regard to either the assignment of workers to jobs or the assignment of overtime. The union's insistence on strict adherence to the seniority system has prevented management from either introducing formal job rotation systems or restricting workers' traditional job bidding practices.

Significant changes have occurred, however, in work scheduling, work arrangements, and training provisions. The Canadian plants have also been able to introduce work groups on an informal and/or experimental basis although these groups primarily focus on product quality matters and rarely, if ever, address productivity or continuous-improvement (*kaizen*) issues. Most of these changes have benefited both management and the union. Through the informal work groups, management has been able to reduce the number of firstline supervisors and non-value-added time, thus achieving cost efficiencies. The union has been able to empower workers around the issue of quality improvement while it maintains the integrity of the bargaining unit and avoids the blurring of the relationship between management and workers. It is also noteworthy that workplace changes remain diverse, and there is more variety among plants than among companies.

The conclusions of our case study research are consistent with the findings of a survey of Big Three assembly plants in Canada conducted by Pil and MacDuffie (1996) as part of their worldwide survey of auto assembly plants under the auspices of the Massachusetts Institute of Technology-based International Motor Vehicle Program (IMVP). The IMVP survey found that compared with the United States the Canadian plants are "quite lean in terms of incoming and in-process inventory . . . and in the area of automation closely resemble their U.S. counterparts," they have been "slower than the U.S. auto industry in adopting high involvement/performance work and HR practices." The survey results (Pil and MacDuffie 1996, 16) show that

> Indeed, with the exception of the quality responsibilities of workers on the line, there are virtually no work practices associated with lean production in place at Big Three plants in Canada.

A comparison of Big Three U.S. and Canadian plants (see table 4.2) with the IMVP survey results reveals that "despite the fairly traditional Fordist work arrangements found on the Canadian assembly lines, the Canadian [plants] do have remarkably good productivity as well as quality performance." Pil and MacDuffie (1996, 15) conclude:

> Indeed, at a little under 20 hours per vehicle, the Canadian plants are 15% more productive than their U.S. counterparts. . . . [O]ne aspect of the Canadian performance that is quite remarkable is the low percent of the workforce in indirect and salaried activities in relation to the workforce in direct activities. In terms of quality, the Canadian plants have dramatically improved their quality over the last six years, and their quality levels are similar to those of the transplants.

In addition to high productivity and quality ratings, the Big Three have also been successful in their quest for increased operational flexibility. As Katz and Meltz (1989) discovered in their comprehensive survey of auto assembly plants belonging to General Motors, even though the Canadian plants do not have formal team concepts or employee involvement programs, management has been able to increase considerably the flexibility in work rules. (See Kumar and Meltz [1992] for details.) Moreover, there have been relatively few interruptions to production in Big Three Canadian plants compared with the United States, where flexibility issues have become a constant source of struggle between management and the UAW locals.

In Canada, union–management relations appear more stable and the changes more mutually beneficial to the companies and to workers' issues. Management for its part has achieved significant cost efficiencies through impressive gains in productivity, product quality, and operational flexibility. Workers have benefited in securing greater job and income security, improved health and safety provisions, enhanced social and technical training, and increased protection and representation as a result of the stronger and more independent role of the union at the workplace level. The positive working relationship between management and labor, despite their divergent perspectives on lean production and work reorganization, has been cited as one of the key reasons behind the increased investment and improved economic performance of the Canadian auto industry during the 1980s and 1990s.

The following sections briefly present the impact of restructuring on productivity and product quality, employment, wages, hours of work, working conditions and the work environment, and human resource and labor relations policies and practices. Presented also is a review of key challenges facing labor as a result of the increasing continental integration of the automobile industry.

Productivity and Product Quality

The modernization of plant equipment, application of new technologies, and implementation of lean production techniques have led to significant cost efficiencies and improvements in productivity and product quality. Productivity gains have been impressive in both vehicle assembly operations and, since 1991, parts and accessories manufacturing. Almost all segments of the parts industry have recorded significant increases in productivity. The gains have been particularly large during the five years 1991–1995, partly because of the cyclical increase in production and partly as a result of efficiencies and higher capacity utilization. Productivity improvements due to efficiencies have been particularly high in vehicle assembly, wiring assemblies manufacturing, and stampings. Estimates provided by Harbour and

Associates (1997) further confirm the steady increase in productivity performance of vehicle assembly plants over the period
1989–1996. Eden, Husbands, and Molot (1996, 4) similarly conclude that "Canadian parts producers have become much more
efficient in recent years."

Employment

Recall that, although the overall industry employment has
remained stable over the past decade at approximately 150,000,
the pattern of growth has varied markedly among the individual
components of the industry. Employment in vehicle assembly,
for example, has shown a slight but steady decline from nearly
57,000 in 1985 to a little over 54,000 in 1995, but the total employment in the parts industry has been increasing, albeit in a cyclical pattern. Employment in parts and accessories manufacturing
averaged 84,374 in 1985. It rose to 96,254 in 1989 following a
strong recovery in parts shipments, plummeted to 78,264
between 1989 and 1991 as a result of the recession, but rose again
to a record level of 100,673 by 1995 in tandem with export-led
recovery.

The employment effects of industry rationalization are also
evident in the pattern of employment growth by the size of
establishment in the parts industry. Between 1985 and 1995,
although overall employment in the parts industry was up by 10
percent, employment declined by nearly 15 percent in small
establishments (employing 1–49 workers) and by about 2 percent in large establishments (with 200 and more workers).
Meanwhile, employment in medium-size establishments (50–
199 workers) increased 68 percent. The employment declines in
small establishments can be attributed to a growing trend
toward consolidation of the supplier base, leading to mergers,
acquisitions, and the closure of smaller, less profitable plants,
particularly since 1989 (there were only 223 small establishments
in 1994 compared with 337 in 1989). Employment stagnation in
large establishments reflects the modernization of facilities, including the gradual adoption of lean production in response to
pressures from the Big Three. Employment declines in these
establishments are in sharp contrast to a significant increase in
the value of shipments and value added per worker. The medium-size establishments appear to be growing on the strength
of subcontracting by larger parts and vehicle manufacturers.

Value of shipments (in constant dollars) in this size category has more than doubled during the past decade, from Can$1.6 billion in 1985 to Can$3.9 billion in 1994. Value added by manufacturing per worker, a measure of productivity, has similarly increased by 8 percent. As a result of modernization and restructuring, there has been a shift toward a higher proportion of skilled workers in the parts sector.

The adverse employment effects of rationalization are most pronounced at the Big Three. All three companies have been engaged during the past decade in a vigorous downsizing of their hourly and salaried workforce and a consolidation of their in-house component parts facilities as a part of their lean production strategy. Employment at the Big Three was less than 63,000 in 1995, compared with 77,000 10 years earlier. The downsizing has been most noticeable at General Motors of Canada, where total employment has declined by nearly 28 percent from 48,100 in 1985 to 34,877 in 1995. Ford has reduced its employment from 15,500 to 14,000 over the same period, while Chrysler's employment has increased slightly from 13,100 to 14,071 owing to the introduction of the three-shift operation at the minivan plant in Windsor. Employment mix is also changing as a result of restructuring. The growing emphasis on value added has led all vehicle and parts producers to cut their administrative and related indirect employment. The Big Three have substantially reduced their salaried nonproduction workforce.

Wages

While all segments of the industry have recorded productivity gains in varying degrees, the effects of restructuring on real wages have been mixed. Although theoretically real wages depend on productivity performance, in practice unionization or the threat of unionization and size of establishment have had a more pronounced effect on real wage behavior. Real wage gains are consequently most evident in vehicle assembly and the captive parts sector where levels of unionization are very high. Real average hourly earnings as well as average annual earnings at the Big Three have been rising steadily owing to hard union bargaining on productivity sharing (collective agreements among the three companies typically include a cost-of-living allowance and an average annual increase of 2-3 percent as a reward for long-term productivity growth in the industry). Real-wage movements in other parts of the industry vary with the degree of unionization (it is difficult to estimate the precise differences owing to lack of separate data on earnings of workers and rates of unionization in the independent parts industry). Statistics Canada estimates show that real hourly earnings were up 19 percent between 1985 and 1995 in the vehicle assembly industry but were stagnant in the parts and accessories industry. Among the various segments of the parts industry, real hourly earnings have shown a slight decline in engine and related parts manu-facturing, steering and suspension parts production, and the wheel and brake manufacturing industry, but were either stable or rising in wiring assemblies, stampings, plastic products, and motor vehicle fabric industries. By size of establishment, real wages have increased in small establishments but have been stagnant or have increased only marginally in large and medium-size establishments. Note that

- productivity growth in large establishments during the period 1985–1995 has averaged nearly 40 percent com-pared with 5 percent in medium-size and 12 percent in small establishments, and
- despite a 19 percent rise in real wages between 1985 and 1995, small establishments still pay only 56 percent of the average wage paid to workers in large establishments.

Hours of Work

Average hours worked in the industry have been stable at approximately 42 hours a week during the 1985–1995 period (the average standard work week in Canada is 40 hours) although they are subject to cyclical fluctuations. Average hours showed a decline from 42 hours a week in 1985 to 39 hours a week in 1991. Since 1991 there has been an upward trend in hours worked in both the vehicle assembly and the parts industries, reflecting the growing use of overtime to meet the rising volume of produc-tion. In the vehicle assembly industry, weekly hours averaged 43.8 in 1985, declined steadily to 40 hours a week between 1985 and 1991, and were up again to 42.3 hours a week in 1995. In the auto parts industry the fluctuations in weekly hours has been less pronounced, varying between 40.7 in 1985, 38.3 in 1991, and 40.9 in 1995. It is also noteworthy that average hours worked in both assembly and the parts industry in Canada are significantly lower than in the United States, and the gap is growing over time. In the vehicle assembly industry, for example, hours per week (including overtime) averaged 44 in both countries in 1985. During the past decade, hours of work in Canada declined to less than 40 hours by 1991 and subsequently increased to 42 by 1995. In the United States, hours of work declined for only a short period between 1985 and 1988 and have been rising steadily since then, reaching over 47 hours a week in 1994.

Working Conditions and Work Environment

There are no published official data on working conditions and/ or work environment in the industry. Anecdotal evidence indicates that working conditions and the overall work environment, including the level of protection afforded to workers against cyclical layoffs and technological change, are generally better in highly unionized Big Three and large independent parts producers than in small and medium-size parts manufacturing, where levels of unionization are low and the only protections are those provided by employment standards legislation.

Recent studies show, however, that working conditions in both the assembly and the parts manufacturing industries are deteriorating as a result of restructuring and rationalization of the industry and, in particular, as a result of the increasing diffusion of lean production practices into the plants. A detailed survey conducted in 1995 of a random sample of 1,677 workers in a cross section of 16 independent auto parts plants (with the workforce ranging from 131 to 830) found that in comparison with traditional plants workers in lean companies reported heavier and faster workloads, an increased pace of work, and more frequent health and safety problems.

Workers in the lean companies also reported a loss of control and autonomy and a decline in training and skills development opportunities (Lewchuk and Robertson 1997; CAW 1995). The survey report found a wide gap between workers and management officials in their perceptions of working conditions and work environment. While management officials claimed that changes to the equipment and work organization have made work more worker friendly and that there is more employee involvement in shop-floor decisions, workers reported increased management control and authority, faster paced work, and fewer opportunities to learn.

Similar conclusions were reached in a second survey of 3,000 workers employed in Big Three assembly and component parts plants conducted by the same two authors (Lewchuk and

Robertson 1997; also CAW 1996b). Although there was considerable variation in the working conditions and the work environment across plants, the survey found evidence of deterioration in working conditions, heavier work loads, and high levels of health and safety risks. Among the three companies, the quality of work life appeared worse in the GM and CAMI plants where management was most aggressive in introducing lean production methods and reorganizing the work process. Workers in the two companies "reported high work loads, but little potential for modifying working conditions or controlling the rhythm of work." The authors of the report (Lewchuk and Robertson 1997) concluded that "workers in lean plants have less, not more control over the quality of their work life."

Human Resource Management and Labor Relations Practices

Up until 1985, because of the high level of integration between Canadian and U.S. operations of the Big Three, the terms and conditions of employment as well as the pattern of human resource policies and practices were almost uniform. This uniformity, dating back to the mid-1970s when wage parity became reality across Big Three plants in Canada and the United States, is generally attributed to coordinated bargaining between the Big Three and a single union, the UAW, representing auto workers in both countries. This continued until 1985, when there was a split in the union on the issue of forging a "partnership with management" in shop-floor decisionmaking and the use of contingent compensation in the form of lump sum payments and profit sharing in lieu of standard wage increases. The UAW in the United States supported these initiatives in an effort to save jobs while the Canadian section opposed them, fearing an erosion of hard-won gains and perceiving a threat to the independence of the union and the long-term interests of the workers. The sharp divisions led to a split in the union and the formation of the CAW in Canada.

Since 1985, there has been a growing divergence between the two countries in such areas as base wages and new-hire rates, hours of work, paid leave and vacation entitlements, employment and income security provisions, work practices, work organization, and the nature of union–management relations (Kumar and Holmes 1996, 1997; Holmes 1992, 1996; Holmes and Kumar 1995; Kumar and Meltz 1992; Pil and MacDuffie 1996;

and table 4.2). Although Canadian plants have become more productive than the Big Three plants in the United States during the past decade, human resource management and labor relations practices have diverged markedly (Pil and MacDuffie 1996). For example, compared with plants in the United States, Canadian plants have more job classifications and greater job-control focus, less teamwork, different training arrangements, and no contingent compensation, job rotation, or any form of jointness or partnership with management. However, the incidence of information sharing, consultation, and informal employee involvement in product quality and technology use remains high. The union in Canada is also stronger than the UAW in terms of its organizational strength and internal solidarity in both assembly and parts manufacturing. (The UAW in the United States has suffered a substantial loss in membership, particularly in the independent auto parts industry, and is riddled with internal factions.) The divergent responses of the two unions to industry restructuring and the organizational weakness of the UAW in the auto parts sector have significant implications for labor in the face of the growing continental integration of the industry under NAFTA. Although leaders of unions in both countries recognize the need for a coordinated cross-national approach to bargaining and organizing, this may prove very difficult to achieve in practice.

Challenges Facing Labor

Workers and their unions face several difficult challenges from the increasing continental integration of the Canadian automobile industry. The key challenges include the growing trend toward the outsourcing and subcontracting of parts, materials, and services to achieve cost efficiencies, the increasing adoption and diffusion of lean production practices to reduce costs and enhance management flexibility, and the aging of the workforce and its implications for training and skills development.

Increased outsourcing of parts, materials, and services by the Big Three—and the subsequent subcontracting by large auto producers to independent enterprises to achieve cost efficiencies—is the biggest challenge facing workers and their unions. The importance of this issue was highlighted by the 1996 bargaining round involving General Motors and the CAW. The company wanted to sell two of its component parts facilities and contract out several hundred jobs to reduce costs. The union, hoping to ensure that existing wages and benefits would be maintained if an in-house components plant were to be sold to the independent parts sector, demanded protection against the outsourcing of jobs by having successor rights incorporated into the collective agreement. The dispute led to a six-week work stoppage. Although the union succeeded in getting protection through successor-rights clauses as well as a commitment that the company would not outsource any major operations during the life of the new agreement, the issue created serious tensions within the labor movement and emphasized the vulnerabilities of labor on the outsourcing issue.

Outsourcing and subcontracting are particularly threatening to organized labor in view of the low levels of unionization in the independent auto parts industry and the large differentials in wages and benefits between unionized and non-unionized workplaces as well as between large and small establishments. According to one estimate (APMA 1997), workers in Big Three in-house parts plants are paid nearly Can$42 per hour in wages and benefits compared with Can$23–$28 per hour to workers in the independent parts sector. This differential acts as a penalty against those assemblers such as General Motors that are most vertically integrated. Thus the average labor cost per vehicle is approximately Can$600 higher at GM, which relies heavily on the in-house sourcing of parts, than at Ford and Chrysler who outsource the majority of their components from the independent parts sector. Unless the union is able to organize fully the independent parts sector, the growing incidence of outsourcing at the Big Three—particularly at GM—will continue to be a contentious issue for labor and could lead to lower wages and benefits and worsening labor conditions in the industry.

The CAW response to outsourcing calls for an accelerated drive to organize non-union plants, increase collective bargaining coordination within subsectors such as stamping and plastics or among plants belonging to specific companies to raise overall standards, explore the potential for satellite bargaining (i.e., work outsourced by a company would be treated as satellite work and the union would bargain with the company and the supplier as if they were part of the same company), and negotiate an employer code of conduct. The code of conduct would include a commitment to encourage unionization on the part of the company outsourcing jobs, a commitment to recognize basic worker rights on the part of any supplier to a CAW plant, and a commitment to include automatic successor-rights provisions when CAW-organized companies buy or sell a plant.

In view of the high level of North American integration in the industry, a union outsourcing strategy also must include close cooperation among auto unions in Canada, the United States, and Mexico. Such cooperation may initially involve information sharing, exchange of ideas and experiences, and technical and financial assistance to weaker unions but ultimately may also include coordinated North American bargaining strategies. Although elements of this cooperative strategy are currently in place between the UAW and the CAW and have produced some positive results, such as outsourcing protections and the framework for the employer code of conduct, Mexican unions are excluded owing to the fragmented nature of the Mexican labor movement and the domination of the official Confederación de Trabajadores de México (CTM)-affiliated unions by the traditional ruling party, the Institutional Revolutionary Party (PRI). For a coordination strategy to be successful, unions in the three countries will have to develop a framework for cooperation based on mutual needs and priorities.

The second major challenge relates to the impact of lean production on the pace of work, worker control and autonomy, health and safety risks, and work organization. The increasing diffusion of lean production in auto plants has brought the issues of work load, health and safety, and overtime into the limelight. Over the past two years there has been a growing number of work stoppages around these issues, particularly in the United States. In Canada the CAW, which is opposed to the ideology of lean production and continually monitors its effects on workers and work environment, has articulated a proactive agenda that includes negotiating production standards and relief staff, more paid time off including more time for breaks during shifts, better job designs, more resources for health and safety/ergonomics training, and greater input into production decisions through joint committees. Although the union has achieved some success in negotiating expanded funds for training and joint committees, the progress on production standards and relief time has been very limited. Lean production–related work organization issues such as teamwork, multiskilling, and job rotation also loom large as a crucial area where labor and management have to find a compromise.

A third key challenge facing labor in the auto industry is the aging of the workforce and its implications for training and skills development. The average age of workers in Canadian vehicle and parts plants is between 45 and 50, and nearly one-quarter of the workforce is older than 55. The industry needs not only effective, consensus-based successor planning to deal with the aging workforce but also an integrated strategy for training and retraining workers. Modernization and the growing use of new technology, resulting in a shortage of skills in many segments of the parts industry, have accentuated the need for developing mechanisms for effective evaluation of training needs and for allocating appropriate resources for training.

Although the Big Three have taken some initiatives in consultation with their unions and are devoting increased resources for training, auto parts employers have been reluctant to make training a priority. In 1994, the union and the industry, with government support and funding, started an innovative training program to develop generic transferable skills under the Auto Parts Sectoral Training Council. While the sectoral training program was highly valued by both workers and companies, it was discontinued in 1996 owing to the lack of "hard commitment" by employers. Two key reasons are cited for this lack of commitment: the low status of nonmandatory training on companies' lists of priorities, especially generic training and training for production workers; and the union involvement (APSTC 1996). A consultant's report (Paget Consulting Group 1996) prepared after the demise of the program indicated that small parts producers did not have the desired resources and even large companies, especially the non-unionized, were not prepared to commit resources toward mandated generic training partly because they perceived the training agenda to be union dominated and they feared that workers from different companies would make unfavorable wage and working-condition comparisons. Despite the demise of the Auto Parts Council program, however, training continues to be a major issue, a prerequisite for the successful restructuring and rationalization of the industry. Many executives of large Canadian parts producers have voiced serious concerns recently over the availability of skilled labor. There is a growing belief that, without a coordinated strategy, there will be an even greater skills shortage in the future (APMA 1997).

Summary and Conclusions

The most significant and distinctive factor that has shaped the Canadian automobile industry over the past three decades is its high level of integration with its counterpart in the United States. This integration dates to 1965 when the two countries signed the Auto Pact, which provided for duty-free trade in vehicle and original equipment parts subject to certain safeguards for Canadian production and employment. The rationalization of production and trade triggered by the Auto Pact led to full integration of the production of both parts and assembled vehicles into *one industry* that supplies the combined U.S. and Canadian market. As a result, assembly plants located in both the United States and Canada use parts and materials manufactured in both countries to build vehicles for sale across the continent. An overwhelming proportion of vehicles assembled in Canada are sold in the United States and, similarly, a significant proportion of vehicles sold in Canada are assembled in the United States. Indeed, most vehicles produced in Canada are the sole source for sales of that model in the U.S. market. The production of engines, transmissions, and major stampings, which require very large volumes for efficient production, was also rationalized by the Big Three under the Auto Pact. Canadian plants producing these key components are highly specialized and often feed cross-border assembly plants in the United States, while Canadian assembly plants import engines and transmissions from both the United States and Mexico. Restructuring of the Big Three's operations in the 1980s, in response to competitive pressures from Japanese producers, and the signing of CUFTA in 1989 led to a further rationalization of vehicle and parts production and a deepening of integration between the United States and Canada.

The integration of the industry following the commencement of the Auto Pact in 1965 and the program of restructuring in the 1980s generated positive results for both Canada and the United States. Canada gained substantially through increased production and investment, expanded trade, significant productivity growth, and attainment of a greater share of high-wage North American automotive employment. Overall, the industry has contributed significantly to Canada's economic performance during the past three decades because of the multiplier effects of its input–output linkages with numerous sectors of the economy. The benefits to the United States have been equally important. The integration has enabled the U.S. auto companies to remain competitive and to serve the needs of U.S. consumers more efficiently and effectively. Their Canadian operations, compared with plants in the United States, have been generally profitable and cost efficient because of higher productivity and product quality and lower labor costs. This has provided significant savings to assemblers and large parts producers.

The industry is presently at a crossroads, facing difficult challenges of further rationalization and restructuring as a result of the impending full integration of Mexico into the North American auto industry under NAFTA and the continued implementation of lean production techniques. The empirical evidence presented here demonstrates that the trade in automotive products is increasing among Canada, the United States, and Mexico. While the momentum toward Mexico's integration into the continental auto industry was well under way before the signing of NAFTA in 1993, the principal challenge facing the Canadian industry is whether it will be able to retain its current share of the U.S. market in the face of increased levels of vehicle and parts exports from Mexico to the United States. Automotive imports from Mexico are also making inroads into the Canadian market; in 1996 automotive imports from Mexico totaled Can$3.3 billion, more than one-half of all Canadian imports from Mexico. The ratio of imports to exports is rising rapidly and stood at 14:1 in 1996. The automotive trade deficit with Mexico (which stood at Can$3.0 billion in 1996 and constituted nearly two-thirds of Canada's total trade deficit with Mexico) has almost doubled since 1992. It now exceeds the deficit with Japan and is nearly five times the automotive trade deficit with the whole of Europe. Although NAFTA requires that an automotive product must contain 62.5 percent North American content by value to qualify for duty-free treatment, there are no national content requirements. Although the Auto Pact still applies to automotive products manufactured or assembled in Mexico by the Big Three, other large Mexico-based exporters (such as Volkswagen and Nissan) can sell to Canada duty-free under NAFTA with no obligation to create Canadian jobs. If this happens, the Big Three share of the Canadian market could slip further, discouraging them from further new investment in plants and facilities.

Industry Canada (1996a; see also Eden 1994) reports:

Canadian parts production is challenged by Mexican and offshore production in products of less complexity requiring lower technological sophistication and labor skills. At the high end, the market is dominated by U.S., Japanese and European multi-national firms. The Canadian share has largely been in the middle range. . . . [T]he challenge for the Canadian parts industry is to carve out as much business as possible from this middle ground and to move into the higher end of systems subassembly work.

Changing buyer–supplier relationships, particularly the pressures put by assemblers on parts producers to cut costs and the increasingly frequent vehicle platform and model changes, are also a source of major uncertainty for the Canadian parts industry.

Finally, what does the limited amount of empirical evidence assembled for this chapter tell us about both the integration of the North American auto industry under NAFTA and the present state and future prospects for the industry in Canada?

First, there is strong evidence of a significant increase in intra-industry trade over the past four years. This is manifested in increased volumes of automotive exports and imports between Canada and the United States and between the United States and Mexico. Although still relatively small in absolute numbers, the volume of Mexican automotive exports to Canada is also increasing very rapidly; Canadian exports to Mexico are growing much more slowly, especially when compared with U.S. automotive exports to Mexico.

Second, there is strong support for the idea of an increasing specialization among the regions *within* North America with regard to the production of different types of motor vehicles and major components such as engines and transmissions. There is also evidence, however, that assemblers may be moving to regionalize networks of suppliers around their major assembly complexes. For example, our data show a tendency toward a larger proportion of the demand for parts by Canadian assembly plants being met by Canada-based parts manufacturers. Given sufficient time and resources, it would be both useful and instructive to conduct further analysis of intra-industry trade and regional specialization at both the four-digit SIC level and at the harmonized commodity code level. Such analyses could also be supplemented by more detailed case studies of the actual component sourcing patterns and supply chains associated with individual assembly plants.

Third, the Canadian auto industry has exhibited considerable strength during the 1990s. The motor vehicle industry experienced a stable pattern of employment and an impressive increase in output, productivity, and value-added between 1985 and 1995. After a significant shakeout of smaller plants at the turn of the decade, output and employment in the Canadian motor vehicle parts industry grew rapidly between 1991 and 1996. With the two caveats that at best we have two full years of data since NAFTA came into force in 1994 and that it is difficult if not impossible to factor out the very positive impact of the strong recovery of the U.S. domestic market during this same period, there is no evidence that NAFTA has had any negative impact on the Canadian auto industry in the short term. The rationalization and restructuring of the parts sector and especially the consolidation of the supplier base through acquisitions and mergers seem to have been driven much more by the continued introduction of lean production and just-in-time methods than by NAFTA per se.

The fourth and, notwithstanding the present robustness of the Canadian industry, the most important challenge for the industry for the next decade will be the retention of its present share of North American production, value added, and employment as Mexican production is fully rationalized and integrated into the rest of the continental auto industry. Viewed as a whole, however, the automotive industry will probably remain both a significant and a technologically sophisticated branch of Canadian manufacturing and a mainstay of the Ontario economy.

Appendix
Key Indicators of the Canadian Automobile Industry, 1975–1996

Automotive Trade (in millions of Can$)

Year	Exports		Imports		Trade Balance			
	Vehicles	Parts	Vehicles	Parts	Vehicles Total	Vehicles with U.S.	Parts Total	Parts with U.S.
1975	4,211	2,225	3,535	4,631	676	665	-2,406	-2,380
1976	5,296	3,173	3,714	5,644	1,392	1,487	-2,591	-2,531
1977	6,588	3,956	4,566	7,043	2,066	2,044	-3,167	-3,127
1978	7,942	5,015	5,071	8,407	2,505	2,688	-3,287	-3,339
1979	7,436	4,854	6,257	9,111	841	1,010	-4,097	-4,177
1980	7,304	3,825	5,764	7,955	1,540	2,065	-4,130	-4,195
1981	9,886	4,493	5,713	9,786	2,287	3,230	-4,865	-5,079
1982	12,529	5,281	4,188	10,080	6,395	7,368	-4,749	-4,774
1983	15,034	7,669	6,296	11,618	6,052	7,395	-4,657	-4,303
1984	21,141	11,615	8,470	15,726	9,011	10,841	-6,207	-5,159
1985	23,281	11,819	14,243	18,897	9,038	10,563	-7,078	-5,926
1986	22,464	11,995	15,406	19,396	7,058	10,780	-7,401	-6,058
1987	20,530	11,961	16,053	18,228	4,477	8,370	-6,267	-4,818
1988	23,992	12,098	15,617	21,586	8,375	12,008	-9,488	-8,204
1989	23,882	11,805	14,866	19,867	9,016	12,659	-8,062	-6,021

Appendix (*continued*)
Key Indicators of the Canadian Automobile Industry, 1975–1996

Automotive Trade (in millions of Can$) (*continued*)

Year	Exports		Imports		Trade Balance			
	Vehicles	Parts	Vehicles	Parts	Vehicles		Parts	
					Total	with U.S.	Total	with U.S.
1990	24,395	10,480	13,785	19,175	10,610	14,532	-8,695	-6,263
1991	24,273	9,136	14,886	18,471	9,387	14,116	-9,335	-6,647
1992	27,956	10,391	14,842	21,696	13,114	17,841	-11,305	-8,397
1993	35,782	13,078	15,926	27,881	19,856	23,496	-14,803	-11,800
1994	43,845	14,789	19,105	33,423	24,740	27,803	-18,634	-14,592
1995	47,404	14,809	19,685	35,034	27,719	30,553	-20,225	-18,222
1996	47,590	15,640	20,079	35,678	27,511	31,006	-20,038	-17,248

Source: Industry Canada, *Statistical Review of the Canadian Automotive Industry* (annual).

(*continued*)

Appendix (*continued*)
Key Indicators of the Canadian Automobile Industry, 1975–1996

Investment, Productivity, and Employment Data

Year	New Investment (in millions of Can$)		Labor Productivity/Output per Hour (1986=100)		Employment (in thousands)		Average Hourly Earnings (Can$)		Average Weekly Hours	
	Vehicles	Parts	Vehicles	Parts	Vehicles	Parts	Vehicles	Parts	Vehicles	Parts
1975	61	81	109.5	66.6	39.8	61.4	6.0	5.6	39.4	38.7
1976	60	63	104.9	75.9	42.7	68.8	6.7	6.4	40.6	40.8
1977	153	110	98.7	77.9	46.6	72.5	7.5	7.1	40.9	40.8
1978	84	204	91.0	80.9	48.2	76.2	8.1	7.7	40.6	40.6
1979	111	331	93.7	76.4	48.6	73.4	8.6	8.1	40.0	39.6
1980	136	781	68.5	64.7	40.8	59.0	9.6	8.8	38.9	37.8
1981	273	667	71.2	71.5	40.0	63.9	10.7	10.0	39.9	39.8
1982	203	189	81.1	80.5	39.5	58.8	11.6	10.8	39.6	39.3
1983	463	141	100.8	97.0	42.0	60.5	13.4	11.5	41.5	41.2
1984	256	171	103.6	104.6	46.9	70.5	14.2	12.1	41.7	40.7
1985	714	332	99.1	107.1	48.0	76.1	15.0	12.5	43.8	40.6
1986	1,897	403	100.0	100.0	48.0	81.0	16.0	12.9	42.5	39.9

Appendix (*continued*)
Key Indicators of the Canadian Automobile Industry, 1975–1996

Investment, Productivity, and Employment Data (*continued*)

Year	New Investment (in millions of Can$)		Labor Productivity/ Output per Hour (1986=100)		Employment (in thousands)		Average Hourly Earnings (Can$)		Average Weekly Hours	
	Vehicles	Parts	Vehicles	Parts	Vehicles	Parts	Vehicles	Parts	Vehicles	Parts
1987	1,584	755	92.3	93.3	48.6	85.3	16.8	13.3	41.6	40.1
1988	1,917	646	121.2	102.9	49.0	89.6	17.9	14.0	42.0	40.5
1989	1,438	584	116.6	111.7	52.1	92.3	18.5	14.5	40.6	39.7
1990	787	457	110.9	115.8	50.3	86.8	19.3	15.1	40.5	39.5
1991	1,305	553	109.0	115.2	50.6	74.3	20.3	16.0	40.0	38.3
1992	1,628	588	113.9	110.2	49.9	72.1	21.3	16.3	41.4	39.9
1993	1,960	680	126.1	117.5	52.0	77.5	22.6	16.9	42.5	41.1
1994	1,342	1,774	134.4	125.1	52.9	83.8	24.1	17.7	43.2	41.7
1995	1,608	1,656	140.8	123.5	52.8	88.1	24.9	17.7	42.3	40.9
1996	2,741	917	132.2	121.7	54.3	92.2	25.0	17.8	42.3	40.8

Sources: Industry Canada, *Statistical Review of the Canadian Automotive Industry* (annual) for the new investment data; unpublished estimates from Statistics Canada for other data.

(*continued*)

Appendix (continued)
Key Indicators of the Canadian Automobile Industry, 1975–1996

Canadian Vehicle Sales (thousands of units)

Year	Total	% of N.A. Market	North American-Built			Distribution of Total Sales		Imports			% of Total Sales
			Total	Cars	Trucks	% Share of Big Three	% Share of Transplants	Total	Cars	Trucks	
1975	1,317	10.3	1,146	836	310	86.5	0.5	171	154	17	13.0
1976	1,291	8.7	1,124	793	331	86.4	0.7	167	153	14	12.9
1977	1,345	8.2	1,136	798	338	84.3	0.1	210	194	16	15.6
1978	1366	8.0	1,180	816	364	85.6	0.8	186	173	13	13.6
1979	1396	8.7	1,244	863	381	87.0	2.1	152	140	12	10.9
1980	1,266	9.6	1,053	741	312	81.0	2.2	213	191	22	16.8
1981	1,191	9.5	898	647	251	72.8	2.6	293	257	36	24.6
1982	920	7.7	656	489	167	69.0	2.3	264	224	40	28.7
1983	1,081	7.9	817	625	193	70.4	5.3	263	218	45	24.3
1984	1,284	8.0	999	725	274	75.5	2.3	285	246	39	22.2
1985	1,530	8.6	1,140	795	345	72.2	2.3	390	342	48	25.2
1986	1,510	8.3	1,130	762	368	72.1	2.7	380	329	51	25.2
1987	1,528	9.0	1,113	701	412	70.6	2.2	415	364	51	27.2
1988	1,566	8.8	1,185	725	460	72.9	2.8	381	332	49	24.3

Appendix (*continued*)
Key Indicators of the Canadian Automobile Industry, 1975–1996

Canadian Vehicle Sales (thousands of units) (*continued*)

Year	Total	% of N.A. Market	North American-Built			Distribution of Total Sales		Imports			% of Total Sales
			Total	Cars	Trucks	% Share of Big Three	% Share of Transplants	Total	Cars	Trucks	
1989	1,483	8.8	1,196	674	422	69.3	4.6	387	319	68	26.1
1990	1,318	8.4	941	580	361	65.7	5.7	377	305	72	28.6
1991	1,288	9.0	921	573	348	64.1	7.4	367	300	67	28.5
1992	1,227	8.3	877	507	370	64.4	7.1	350	291	59	28.5
1993	1,193	7.6	896	494	402	69.2	5.9	297	245	52	24.9
1994	1,259	7.4	1,048	573	475	73.1	10.1	211	175	36	16.8
1995	1,165	7.1	1,022	553	469	75.6	12.1	143	116	27	12.3
1996	1,205	7.2	1,091	573	518	75.4	15.1	114	88	26	9.5

Sources: Industry Canada, *Statistical Review of the Canadian Automotive Industry* (annual); *Ward's Automotive Year Book* (annual).

(*continued*)

Appendix (*continued*)
Key Indicators of the Canadian Automobile Industry, 1975–1996

Value of Shipments and Production Data

| Year | Value of Shipments (in millions of Can$) | | Total Vehicle Production (thousands of units) | | | | | |
	Vehicles	Parts	Cars	Trucks	Total	% Share of Big Three	% Share of Transplants	Total as % of N.A. Market
1975	6,024	2,552	1,055	387	1,442	94.0	6.0	13.4
1976	7,276	3,418	1,146	501	1,647	95.9	4.1	12.2
1977	8,610	4,139	1,162	602	1,764	95.6	4.4	12.0
1978	10,070	5,120	1,162	656	1,818	97.3	2.7	12.0
1979	10,724	4,897	997	635	1,632	97.7	2.3	12.0
1980	10,071	5,877	847	527	1,374	96.3	3.7	13.9
1981	11,403	8,358	784	497	1,281	98.1	1.9	13.0
1982	12,344	11,494	788	448	1,236	94.4	5.6	14.2
1983	15,591	12,923	955	547	1,502	95.9	4.1	13.6
1984	21,263	12,922	1,023	812	1,835	95.3	4.7	14.0
1985	24,599	12,739	1,078	856	1,934	96.8	3.2	13.8
1986	25,094	25,094	1,062	793	1,855	95.9	4.1	13.8
1987	22,154	12,739	810	838	1,648	95.7	4.3	12.7
1988	26,866	14,471	1,028	950	1,978	95.8	4.2	14.4
1989	28,059	1,4718	1,002	938	1,940	94.5	5.5	14.5

Appendix (continued)
Key Indicators of the Canadian Automobile Industry, 1975–1996

Value of Shipments and Production Data (*continued*)

Year	Value of Shipments (in millions of Can$)		Total Vehicle Production (thousands of units)					
	Vehicles	Parts	Cars	Trucks	Total	% Share of Big Three	% Share of Transplants	Total as % of N.A. Market
1990	27,239	13,902	1,098	850	1,948	85.0	15.0	15.5
1991	26,017	12,707	1,060	827	1,887	82.3	17.7	16.1
1992	29,564	14,099	1,020	938	1,958	84.1	15.9	15.4
1993	37,657	16,311	1,353	893	2,246	84.2	15.8	15.8
1994	43,632	18,391	1,216	1,106	2,322	83.8	16.2	14.8
1995	49,474	22,333	1,337	1,077	2,414	83.5	16.5	15.8
1996	50,473	22,771	1,280	1,117	2,397	84.3	15.7	15.4

Source: Industry Canada, *Statistical Review of the Canadian Automotive Industry* (annual); Ward's Communications 1997.

Notes

Funding for this research was provided by the Center for Strategic and International Studies, Washington, D.C., and the Social Science and Humanities Research Council of Canada. We acknowledge Mike Marshall (Industry Canada Automotive Branch) for his help with the data and the able research assistance provided by Robert Holmes and Mark Tabachnick. We thank Sidney Weintraub and Christopher Sands for their helpful comments on a preliminary draft of the chapter. The authors are solely responsible for the interpretations and opinions expressed in the chapter.

1. Our analysis and most of the data presented in this chapter are for the period since 1985. To provide a slightly longer historical perspective, we include an appendix of annual key indicators of the Canadian automobile industry from 1975 to 1996.

2. The fewer the hours or workers per vehicle, the higher the productivity.

3. It is important to emphasize the differences in the content requirements of the various agreements. The content provisions of the Auto Pact define content requirements in *national* terms, that is, Canadian value added (CVA). Under CUFTA and, subsequently, NAFTA, content is defined as *regional* (North American) content, set at 50 percent in CUFTA and 62.5 percent or 60 percent in NAFTA. Thus, under NAFTA per se there is no requirement for the Big Three and CAMI to make parts in Canada or to purchase parts from Canadian parts producers. To maintain their preferred Auto Pact status, however, these producers must continue to meet the CVA requirements of the Auto Pact. This provides some measure of continued protection to Canadian parts producers.

Bibliography

Automobile Parts Manufacturers' Association of Canada (APMA). 1997. *Automotive Components: June 1997 Industry Outlook.* Toronto: Automobile Parts Manufacturers' Association of Canada.

Automotive Parts Sectoral Training Council (APSTC). 1996. *Report to the APSTC Executive Committee on Viability Research Project.* Markham, Ontario: Automotive Parts Sectoral Training Council.

Booz, Allen, Hamilton Inc. 1990. *A Comparative Study of the Cost Competitiveness of the Automobile Parts Manufacturing Industry in North America.* Toronto: Automotive Parts Manufacturers' Association of Canada.

Canadian Auto Workers (CAW). 1995. *Auto Parts Working Conditions: Benchmark Study.* North York, Ontario: Canadian Auto Workers.

————. 1996a. *CAW 1996 Big 3 Bargaining: Facts and Figures.* North York, Ontario: Canadian Auto Workers.

————. 1996b. *Working Conditions Study: Benchmarking Auto Assembly Plants.* North York, Ontario: Canadian Auto Workers.

Eden, Lorraine. 1994. Who Does What after NAFTA? Location Strategies of U.S. Multinationals. In *Multinationals in North America,* edited by Lorraine Eden. Calgary: University of Calgary Press.

Eden, Lorraine, Kaye Husbands, and Maureen Appel Molot. 1996. *Competing in a Lean World: How the Auto Parts Industries in Canada and Mexico Are Responding to the Pressures of Free trade and Lean Production.* Cambridge, Mass.: MIT International Motor Vehicle Program.

Eden, Lorraine, and Maureen Appel Molot. 1993. *The NAFTA's Automotive Provisions: The Next Stage of Managed Trade.* C. D. Howe Institute Commentary, no. 53. Toronto: C. D. Howe Institute.

————. 1994. The Challenge of NAFTA: Canada's Role in the North American Auto Industry. In *NAFTA's Impact on the North American Automobile Industry.* Washington, D.C.: National Planning Association.

Fowlie, Laura. 1993. Auto Parts Industry Thrives Under Free Trade, GST: Study. *Financial Post,* July 2, 1993.

Harbour and Associates. 1997. *The Harbour Report 1997: North America.* Troy, Mich.: Harbour and Associates.

Holmes, John. 1992. The Continental Integration of the North American Auto Industry: From the Auto Pact to the FTA and Beyond. *Environment and Planning A* 24 (1): 95 - 119.

————. 1996. Restructuring in a Continental Production System. In *Canada and the Global Economy,* edited by J. N. H. Britton. Kingston, Ontario: McGill-Queen's University Press.

Holmes, John, and Pradeep Kumar. 1995. Harmonization and Diversity? North American Economic Integration and Industrial Relations in the Automobile Industry. In *Human Resources and Industrial Spaces: A Perspective on Globalization and Localization,* edited by Bert van der Knapp and Richard Le Heron. New York: John Wiley & Sons.

Industry Canada. 1992. *The Canadian Automobile Industry: Issues and Options.* Report of the Automotive Advisory Committee. Ottawa: Industry Canada.

————. 1996a. *Automotive Industry: Part 1—Overview and Prospects.* Ottawa: Industry Canada.

————. 1996b. *Automotive Trade 1996*. Ottawa: Industry Canada, Automotive Branch.

————. 1997. *Statistical Review of the Canadian Automotive Industry*. Ottawa: Industry Canada. (Published annually.)

Johnson, John R. 1993. The Effect of the Canada-U.S. Free Trade Agreement on the Auto Pact. In *Driving Continentally*, edited by Maureen Appel Molot. Ottawa: Carlton University Press.

Katz, H. C. and N. Meltz. 1989. Changing Work Practices and Productivity in the Auto Industry: A U.S.-Canda Comparison. In *Proceedings of the Twenty-Sixth Conference of the Canadian Industrial Relations Association*, edited by M. Grant. Quebec City: Canadian Industrial Relations Association.

KPMG. 1996. *A Comparison of Business Costs in Canada and the United States*. Ottawa: Department of Foreign Affairs and International Trade, USA Trade and Investment Division.

Kumar, Pradeep, and John Holmes. 1996. Change, But in What Direction? Divergent Union Responses to Work Restructuring in the Integrated North American Auto Industry. In *Social Reconstructions of the World Automobile Industry*, edited by Frederick C. Deyo. New York: St. Martin's Press.

————. 1997. Continuity and Change: Evolving Human Resource Policies and Practices in the Canadian Automobile Industry. In *Evolving Employment Practices in the World Auto Industry*, edited by Thomas Kochan, John Paul MacDuffie, and Russell Lansbury. Ithaca, N.Y.: Cornell University Press.

Kumar, Pradeep, and Noah Meltz. 1992. Industrial Relations in the Canadian Automobile Industry. In *Industrial Relations in Canadian Industry*, edited by Richard Chaykowski and Anil Verma. Toronto: Dryden.

Lewchuk, Wayne, and David Robertson. 1997. Work Organization and the Quality of Working Life in the Canadian Automobile Industry: Assembly and Component Manufacturing Plants. Paper presented at the International Research Conference on Working Lean: Labour in the North American Auto Industry, at Benémerita Universidad Autónoma de Puebla, April 28–30, 1997, in Puebla, Mexico.

Paget Consulting Group. 1996. *Capitalizing on the Curriculum: The Viability and Long-Term Plan for the Automotive Parts Sectoral Training Council*. Ottawa: Paget Consulting Group Inc., F. J. Durdan and Associates.

Pil, Frits K., and John Paul MacDuffie. 1996. Canada at the Cross-Roads: A Comparative Analysis of the Canadian Auto

Industry. Paper presented at the Canadian Workplace Research Network Conference, October 1996, in Vancouver.

Statistics Canada. 1997. *Manufacturing Industries of Canada: National and Provincial Areas, 1996.* Statistics Canada Catalog Number 31-203. Ottawa: Government of Canada.

Ward's Communications. 1996. *Ward's Automotive Year Book 1996.* 58th ed. Southfield, Mich.: Ward's Communications.

———. 1997. *Ward's Automotive Year Book 1997.* 59th ed. Southfield, Mich.: Ward's Communications.

Weintraub, Sidney. 1997. *NAFTA at Three: A Progress Report.* Washington D.C.: Center for Strategic and International Studies.

5

The Impact of Environmental Regulation on the North American Auto Industry since NAFTA

John Kirton

This chapter examines how environmental policy and regulation as shaped by the North America Free Trade Agreement (NAFTA) regime of rules and institutions is affecting automotive trade, investment, and production in North America and is creating broad economic implications for the North American automotive industry, including its consumers and other stakeholders.[1] It aims at identifying specific policy measures that move toward more optimal outcomes and areas where further research is warranted.

This study argues that three broad forces affect the environmental regulation and performance of the North American automotive industry in the NAFTA era.[2] The first is an intensification of the move toward a full-scale rationalization and integration of the industry on a regional rather than a national basis, with a corresponding production incentive to have a uniform set of relevant environmental standards in all three countries and across all their subfederal jurisdictions.

The second is a new wave of high-level regulatory harmonization as NAFTA's consciousness raising, institutions, dispute settlement mechanisms, and incentives have prevented any regulatory race to the bottom but instead have inspired a push to the top, driven and guided largely by the anticipatory and voluntary efforts of industry and its stakeholders.

The third is the rapid spread of this push to high-level harmonization from the assembly to the original-equipment-manufacturer (OEM) parts and then aftermarket sectors; and from manufacturing standards to fuel standards and then inspection, maintenance, and other operating standards.

NAFTA is, first, leading to the full integration and rationalization of the North American auto industry on a regional rather than a national basis by absorbing the historically protected Mexican market into the long-integrated U.S.-Canada production system and by drawing the latter ever more tightly together.

One leading analyst (Weintraub 1997, 41) put it: "It is now appropriate to talk of a North American auto market."[3] Although delayed by the 1995 peso crisis in Mexico and the paucity of new investment in Mexico by the Big Three U.S. automakers during NAFTA's first three and one-half years, it is clear this process of full rationalization is proceeding. With it, and with moves to just-in-time inventory and tiering of the parts chain, comes an increasing interconnection and rationalization that will lead industry to seek and secure from governments—and itself implement in management and industry practice—higher and regionally harmonized environmental standards.[4]

Second, NAFTA and its accompanying environmental consciousness and protection have unleashed a new wave of high-level harmonization of environmental and safety regulations. NAFTA is creating—beyond industry—an emerging North American community whose citizens are looking toward the best practices in the partner countries as models and calling for more open, environmentally responsible practices from actors in all three countries. Canada, as well as Mexico, is rapidly moving up to the U.S. and even the pathfinder California level of environmental consciousness. In contrast with fears that NAFTA would bring a regulatory race to the bottom, there is instead a push to the top. Citizen, corporate, and regulator demands for the latest generation of automotive emission, fuel technology, inspection, and maintenance standards are becoming widespread.

Third, this high-level environmental harmonization will increase in the coming years and will extend from OEM assemblers and parts producers to the fuels and aftermarket sectors. Public opinion in all three countries shows that the desire for environmentalism remains strong, especially as the health effects and monetary costs of poor environmental performance become better known. A total systems approach to environmental protection requires action on fuels, inspection and maintenance, pollution prevention, and international cooperation. The centrality of the automotive industry to the core environmental challenges of the future is clear.

Cars and trucks are the single leading source of air pollution on the North American continent (Marchi 1997). In densely populated and industrialized areas such as southern Ontario, Canada's heartland, auto emissions account for up to 80 percent of benzene, 60 percent of nitrogen oxides, 55 percent of volatile organic compounds, and 4 percent of sulphur oxides released into the air. In Canada as a whole, a full 80 percent of this automotive pollution comes from only 20 percent of the vehicles—the older, poorly maintained ones—because each such car or truck produces the same amount of pollution as 25 new vehicles.

National Automotive Environmental Regulatory Systems before NAFTA

Before the passage of NAFTA, the United States, Canada, and Mexico possessed a largely integrated automotive industry (for assemblers and OEM parts producers) but a substantially varied set of environmental regulations and enforcement patterns. The result was that the larger U.S.-based and -owned manufacturers generally applied the higher U.S.-level standards in Canada and Mexico in their ongoing industrial practices; and they sought and often secured from these governments a common set of standards based on standards prevailing in the much larger U.S. market. But the different standards-setting systems in the three countries, production in Mexico for the domestic Mexican market, separate California standards in the United States, and the move toward additional special state and provincial systems created an inconvenient and prospectively expanding and more costly differentiation.

The Foundation of Regulatory Uniformity

Before NAFTA there was a substantial foundation of regulatory uniformity across the United States, Canada, and Mexico. Proximity, openness, a common geography (relative to Europe and other regions), the sheer size of the U.S. market, and policy instruments such as the 1965 Canada-U.S. Automotive Pact, the 1982 U.S.-Mexico La Paz Agreement, and the 1990 Canada-U.S. Air Quality Agreement had produced a substantial degree of environmental convergence relevant to the automotive industry. Although most advanced in the case of the highly contiguous and long-time highly integrated Canada-U.S. relationship, this process developed quickly between the United States and Mexico as Mexico opened to trade during the 1980s and saw automotive products replace oil as its dominant trade item with the United States.

In practice, the great size and integrated nature of the automotive industry led to a high degree of environmental management and international convergence on the part of the major assemblers and parts manufacturers. In both their demands on government and their adoption of internal environmental management systems and pollution control equipment and technology, these large firms sought and largely secured uniform high standards. They did so not only as a matter of corporate conviction but also in response to customer demands, concerns about corporate reputation, consideration of insurance and liability, public pressures, and anticipated regulatory developments in all three countries. This was especially true in Canada; led by Ontario, Canada sent 85 percent of its automotive production to the United States and hosted almost 20 percent of continental automotive assembly activity.[5] Of the 20 leading commodities exported by the United States to Mexico in 1995, 2 were auto parts and internal combustion engines, while 4 of the 20 leading U.S. imports from Mexico came from the automotive sector (Weintraub 1997, 34–35).[6] Because the auto industry also dominated the three trading and transborder investment relationships in the region and because these links were growing before passage of NAFTA, the pressures for regulatory convergence in policy and practice steadily strengthened. This process was reinforced as parts of lightly populated Canada (in the lower Fraser Valley and southern Ontario) began to acquire visible environmental problems similar to those in demographically and industrially dense parts of the United States.[7]

Differing Systems and Standards

Yet there remained important differences, not only in regulatory levels and particular standards but, more important, in constitutional and legal approaches to regulation, federal-subfederal divisions of responsibility, and testing and certification procedures. In Mexico, the power of environmental regulation is concentrated heavily in the federal government, based on a statist regulatory model often applied to national monopoly industry suppliers that produce for a highly protected national market, and is unalleviated by voluntary, private sector–driven standards that involve environmental nongovernmental organizations (NGOs) and other stakeholders. In the United States there prevails a litigation-based regulatory enforcement approach, with power shared between federal and state governments, and a heavy reliance on voluntary standards setting by thousands of associations outside government (such as the American National Standards Institute). In Canada, where an estimated 70 percent of responsibility for environmental regulation lies with provincial governments, there flourished an administrative-consensus approach with minimum litigation, based in part on consensus-oriented standards setting among multistakeholders centered in the five major quasi-public umbrella, standards-setting organizations (operating under the auspices of the Standards Council of Canada).

Beyond differences in government systems, there were three broad, economy-based exceptions to the prevailing pattern of high-level, harmonized industry performance. The first was in the substantially protected Mexican segment of the industry, which was still among the smaller parts and aftermarket producers in Canada and the United States who faced the additional challenge of integrating into increasingly outsourced but multitiered supplier systems. The second exception came from the fuels sectors, whose products were becoming more consequential to the ability of assemblers with fuel-sensitive electronic diagnostic systems to meet higher emissions standards but who wielded greater relative size, influence, regional power, and monopoly claims and less modern capacity in Canada and Mexico than in the United States. The third exception came in operating standards—not manufacturing standards—where local differences and responsibilities were greater and the temptation to make ad hoc adjustments for protectionist and political purposes more intense.

The Separated Mexican Parts Sector

The largest initial challenge came in the parts and aftermarket sector. Here the unbalanced capabilities across the three countries made it difficult for many firms, especially in Mexico, to match the rising levels of expected environmental performance, even with assistance from the larger firms they supplied.[8] In particular, Mexican parts producers, which represented almost half the Mexican auto industry, were relatively small in size and lagged in technology.[9]

To survive in an era of NAFTA-intensified regionalization and increased globalized production, these Mexican auto parts firms needed economies of scale, technological infusions, and total quality and environmental management systems. As the NAFTA process started, they were moving to get them. Many received government credits and sought to forge strategic alliances with foreign firms.

Among the 100 largest and most dynamic Mexican firms, in particular, the process of NAFTA-inspired modernization began in earnest. Led by the export-oriented engine plants established largely by the Big Five assemblers in northern Mexico in the early 1980s, the parts industry became more export oriented. The 750 *maquiladoras* producing auto parts in Mexico, many U.S.-owned and associated with assemblers, expanded their operations. In 1993 there were approximately 100 joint ventures in auto parts, bringing in badly needed foreign capital and technology.[10] In the four years preceding 1993, many Mexican suppliers received awards for reaching international quality standards.[11] But there remained much room for this segment of the auto industry to increase its exports to the U.S. market, and thus competitively move the prevailing environmental standards, because only 10 percent of Mexican parts production in 1992 was exported, primarily to the United States.

The New NAFTA Regime

The advent of the NAFTA regime brought a strong move toward such export-oriented behavior, more stringent and expanded environmental regulation and enforcement, and regulatory convergence. NAFTA brought the prospect of the full incorporation of Mexico into the more integrated U.S.-Canada production system, new rules with targets and timetables for improved environmental performance, new trilateral institutions for ongoing dialogue and expanding cooperative action, and an enhanced consciousness of the need for improved environmental enhancement throughout the North American region.

To understand the significant breadth, depth, and impact of NAFTA, it is important to recall that NAFTA was no mere trade agreement but, instead, a full-fledged economic and political regime with five consequential dimensions for the auto industry.[12]

The NAFTA Debate

The first element was the NAFTA debate and the negotiation that took place from 1990 to 1994. They had the effects of alerting smaller firms and new entrants to the economic opportunities in the other countries' markets; acquainting firms, regulators, and publics with the prevailing environmental standards and systems in the prospective partners; and catalyzing several actions, particularly in Mexico, to assist NAFTA's passage by showing that companies were rapidly and visibly moving to meet U.S. levels and modus operandi. A flurry of inspections and temporary shutdowns of U.S.-owned automotive and other plants in Mexico; a major increase in Mexico's environmental standards, certification and testing procedures, and environmental inspectors (under the Mexican attorney general for environmental protection, or PROFEPA); and the emergence of Mexican environmental NGOs (such as the Mexican Center for Environmental Law) and trilateral associations (such as the North American Trilateral Standardization Forum) were among the most notable results.

NAFTA Rules

A second element was the extensive rule changes NAFTA brought. Those economic rules affecting the automotive industry are well described elsewhere.[13] Moreover, the core NAFTA text and its accompanying North American Agreement on Environmental Co-operation (NAAEC) contained provisions that made NAFTA the most environmentally friendly and advanced free trade regime in existence.[14] Most important, while NAFTA allowed each country the freedom to establish its own environmental standards (subject to some restrictions on scientific risk assessment procedures), it declared NAFTA's overall purpose to be the promotion of environmentally sustainable development, gave precedence to the major global environmental agreements (including that on stratospheric ozone), restricted international investment migrating to "pollution havens" to escape stringent regulations in the home country, and called for an upward harmonization of environmental regulations across the three participating countries.

Some of NAFTA's rules that dealt with the automotive industry specifically also had a direct bearing on its environmental performance. By allowing 75 percent of U.S. parts exports to enter Mexico duty-free by 1998 and 100 percent by 2003, NAFTA provided an enormous incentive—as Mexico's emissions and environmental standards rose—for competing Mexican parts producers to upgrade their environmental performance to retain their domestic market share with U.S.-owned assemblers and others. NAFTA's establishment of regional rules of origin of 62.5 percent North American value added for autos, light trucks, engines, and transmissions; 60 percent for other vehicles and parts; and the net-cost tracing method for 69 parts made it more likely that North America–produced emission control equipment would be used throughout the region and, thus, that common, regionwide standards related to this equipment would be adopted.[15] Further incentives for convergence flowed from the rule that allowed producers in 1997 to designate whether Mexican and Canadian production is domestic or foreign for corporate average fuel economy (CAFE) purposes of 27.5 miles per gallon average fuel economy and that designated all Mexican auto products as domestic by 2004.[16]

NAFTA Institutions

A third element of the NAFTA regime was the array of 50 or more intergovernmental bodies created or inspired by the agreements and designed to implement, interpret, and extend their provisions. The most directly relevant to the automotive industry's environmental performance are two components of the Committee on Standards-Related Measures: the Land Transportation Subcommittee (LTS) and the Automotive Standards Council (ASC).[17] Together these bodies have a NAFTA requirement to produce work plans to harmonize standards for dangerous-goods transport within six years and for automotive emissions within three years and a NAFTA permissive mandate to address emissions from off-road vehicles.

NAFTA's Dispute Settlement Mechanisms

The fourth element of the NAFTA regime were the three economic and two environmental dispute settlement mechanisms it created.[18] The economic mechanisms are those for antidumping and countervail (Chapter 19), general problems (Chapter 20), and—innovatively—for investment (Chapter 11). The environmental mechanisms, flowing from the NAAEC, are for scientific study (Article 13) and persistent nonenforcement of national environmental laws (Articles 14 and 15).

NAFTA's Incentives for Policy Harmonization

The final element was the incentives NAFTA contained for further policy harmonization. These include provisions that inhibit the reimposition of border barriers to meet balance-of-payments difficulties; this inspires alternative solutions and further cooperation in cases such as the peso crisis of December 1994. These incentives also include an impetus for cooperation among sub-federal officials and other societal actors. NAFTA further created an incentive for the three national governments to band together as a North American consultative group in broader multilateral forums.

NAFTA's Economic Impact

Taken together, these provisions have strongly increased the integration of the North American automotive industry since NAFTA took effect, although the impulse toward rationalization through new U.S. foreign direct investment (FDI) in and resulting intracorporate trade with Mexico has been rather restrained. Total vehicle and parts trade between the United States and Mexico doubled between 1991 and 1995 to $25 billion. From 1993 to 1996 U.S. exports of vehicles and parts to Mexico increased 11 percent. U.S. exports of vehicles alone increased more than 500 percent. President Clinton's July 1997 report (USTR 1997, 48) on NAFTA's impact concluded: ". . . with the growth in U.S.-made vehicle sales to Mexico, the opportunities for sales of U.S. aftermarket parts in Mexico should rise." Consistent with this view is the fact that U.S. exports of parts were 25 percent higher in the first quarter of 1997 than in the first quarter of 1993. The U.S. share of Mexico's parts imports rose steadily from 66.3 percent in 1993 to 71.7 percent in 1996.

During the same period, U.S. imports of vehicles and parts from Mexico doubled.[19] Because U.S. imports of Mexican-assembled vehicles contain more than 50 percent U.S.-made parts (a figure that is rising under NAFTA), what is clearly taking place is a trade-induced integration that will intensify as NAFTA eliminates the previous requirement to use Mexican-made parts. U.S. imports of Mexican parts rose 58.4 percent from 1993 to 1996. The result is a strong, NAFTA-produced incentive for parts manufacturers in both the United States and Mexico to meet the highest environmental standards that their customers and eventual assemblers demand.

Trade specialization has not yet extended in a major way to increased FDI. There has thus far been a paucity of new FDI into Mexico, in part because major companies have been wary of providing evidence to support the "giant sucking sound" argument featured so prominently in the initial NAFTA debate in the United States. In the three years following adoption of NAFTA, the Big Three automakers have invested $39.1 billion in plant and equipment in the United States but less than one-tenth of that amount ($3 billion) in Mexico. However, even increased U.S. investment is assisting the process of rationalization and the regionwide uniformity in environmental performance that it brings.[20]

Post-NAFTA National Rule Changes

During its first three and one-half years, the NAFTA era has seen a rapid and often explicit upward Canadian and Mexican environmental harmonization based on U.S. standards for automotive emissions and fuel use, the adoption of U.S.-like inspection and maintenance programs at the subfederal level, and the spread of U.S.-pioneered pollution prevention programs to the NAFTA neighbors.[21] This process is most readily apparent in the already highly integrated but uniquely interdependent U.S.-Canada relationship but is also evident in the U.S.-Mexico case. Yet to date there have been very limited moves toward direct Canada-Mexico harmonization or fully trilateral (as opposed to U.S.-centric hub-and-spoke) convergence or harmonization. Moreover, the role of the NAFTA institutions and the dispute settlement mechanism in the convergence process has thus far been secondary in the core manufacturing and fuels areas that are of central interest to the automotive industry.

United States

Air pollution and air quality are central to the environmental performance of the North American automotive industry. In the United States, the primary relevant regulatory framework is set by the Clean Air Act that specifically regulates six elements central to atmospheric pollution: ozone, particulate matter, nitrogen dioxide, carbon monoxide, sulphur dioxide, and lead.[22] Revisions to the standards take place every five years to account for evolving scientific information. The next revision is due in 1999.

Despite the enhanced competitive pressures brought by NAFTA and the election in the 1994 midterm elections of a Republican majority opposed to stringent environmental regulations, the United States has continued to upgrade its environmental standards.[23] In November 1996, the U.S. Environmental Protection Agency (EPA) proposed new National Ambient Air Quality Standards (NAAQS) for ground-level ozone and particulate matter, based on epidemiological and human toxicological data. Despite considerable criticism, the standards were adopted in June 1997. The ozone standard will thus rise in 2000 from .12 parts per million measured over one hour to .08 parts per million measured over eight hours; full compliance will come several years later.[24] Particulate-matter standards will remain for larger particles (PM-10) and be imposed on smaller particles (2.5 micrometers or smaller), with plans to meet such standards required by 2002. The new standards will push the number of nonattainment areas in the United States from 106 counties to approximately 250 counties, with many of the additions coming from the Canada-U.S. Great Lakes border.[25]

Increasing U.S. air quality standards are also affecting the U.S. automotive industry more directly. The EPA will move in 1998 to Tier Two emission and diagnostic standards and then will define the next level to be in force by 2003. The states of Massachusetts and New York are currently before the courts seeking to join California in having the right to set their own, higher vehicle emission standards.

The move to an integrated, total systems approach has also been an impetus for an increase in fuel standards. One sign of the upward trend is the unwillingness of 15 U.S. petroleum producers and the state of California to take advantage of a recent administrative-law ruling allowing the use of the gas additive MMT, which EPA banned 17 years ago and California still outlaws. U.S. petroleum producers who represent more than 80 percent of the market are refusing to use it while EPA tests its health effects.

Although rollback in fuel standards has been avoided, forward movement has been more difficult. The U.S. automotive and petroleum industries have combined in a joint study to assess standards for low-sulphur gasoline that, like MMT, threatens major damage to on-board diagnostic systems and, thus, emissions on vehicles. Although the automotive industry is calling for a low-sulphur-fuels standard that it knows is compatible with the diagnostic and emissions technology it currently has, with the standards it must meet, and with the capacity of petroleum refiners, it has agreed to the petroleum industry's request to determine whether new automotive technologies might permit a less stringent low-sulphur standard to be imposed.

The integrated approach to pollution control is also propelling a spread and rise in automotive inspections and maintenance systems, pioneered by California several years ago. In the face of rising frustration from motorists who yo-yo between state inspection stations that find them noncompliant and service centers that conduct inadequate repairs, a consensus has emerged that the solution lies in enhanced certification and training for those who conduct the repairs. The primary bottleneck at present, amid a booming economy like California's, is the lack of well-trained and well-paid technicians (Moore 1997). Yet the spread of such systems to other states also raises costs to consumers and some aftermarket producers.[26]

If an integrated approach to automotive emission control requires a lateral link to fuel standards and a forward link to inspection and maintenance, it has also inspired a backward link to pollution prevention in the plants and processes that assemble the vehicles and produce their parts. In September 1991, EPA, the U.S. Motor Vehicle Manufacturing Association (MVMA), and the state of Michigan initiated the Auto Industry Pollution Prevention Project (Auto Project) that led to a program for reducing the release of persistent toxic substances into the Great Lakes. This effort built on the work of individual companies following the pollution prevention strategy prepared by the U.S. President's Commission on Environmental Quality (Neblett 1992).

Canada

As NAFTA took effect, Canada also moved to higher-level environmental standards and a tighter integration with the U.S. policy, regulatory, and industry system. Since 1993, Canada has raised its automotive emission standards and a few fuel standards to U.S. levels by explicitly adopting evolving U.S. regulations as the new Canadian standards. It has also assisted the spread of U.S.-pioneered inspection and maintenance and pollution prevention programs.

In spring 1996, Sergio Marchi, Canada's new environment minister (later the international trade minister), announced that a priority for his portfolio was the introduction of "new car emission standards, new fuel efficiency rules and new encouragement for alternative fuels" (Marchi 1996). He also promised to follow the call of the Canadian Council of Ministers of the Environment (CCME) for Canada to harmonize with anticipated U.S. standards for low-emission vehicles or for moving independently if the United States did not proceed.[27] On March 3, 1997, Marchi announced that the federal government was tightening emission standards for cars and trucks by harmonizing in 1998 its regulations with those of the federal government in the United States. This would reduce emissions of hydrocarbons by 30 percent and of nitrogen oxide by 60 percent.[28]

Canada would also require that manufacturers equip new vehicles in the 1998 model year with diagnostic systems that can monitor emissions; and Canada would bring emissions regulations to new types of vehicles (such as motorcycles), fuels (such as methanol, liquefied petroleum gas, and natural gas), and processes (including exhaust, evaporative, and refueling emissions).

Marchi further urged the provinces, which have responsibility for cars once they are on the road, to follow British Columbia's Aircare program of mandatory car and truck inspection and repair. Such a move would reduce by half the pollutants emitted into congested southern Ontario. Finally, Marchi pointed to one of the inescapable physical incentives for environmental regulatory harmonization by noting that half the smog in Canada's core, the Windsor-Quebec corridor, is produced in the United States.[29] He thus called for the 1990 Canada-U.S. Air Quality Agreement on acid rain to be expanded to regulate smog, air toxins, and inhalable particulate matter, with a goal of reducing imported pollution by 50 percent by the year 2010.[30]

Because high-level controls on auto emissions require similar controls on fuel quality, Canadian action and the pressures of high-level harmonization moved seamlessly to fuel standards and thus the petroleum industry. In Canada, however, even compared with the United States, progress has been slower, industry resistance greater, and NAFTA—through its investment provisions—a prospective initial obstacle rather than an aid to forward movement. Yet the functional need for a total systems approach to meet the higher emission control standards should soon lead to continental and ultimate regional harmonization in Canada as well.

The first post-NAFTA case of Canadian harmonization on prevailing U.S. fuel standards was the Canadian federal government's move in 1996 to ban international and interprovincial trade in MMT.[31] This substance was first introduced in 1977 to replace lead as an octane enhancer in gasoline (Vogel and Rugman 1997). In an early sign that pressures for convergence are arising in the third (i.e., Canada-Mexico) leg of the NAFTA triangle, the Canadian move led Mexico, where MMT is still legal, to initiate an evaluation of its effects.

The ban on MMT is being followed by a similar move to reduce the level of or remove sulphur in Canadian gasoline.[32] In early 1997, the cabinet in Canada passed new diesel fuel regulations requiring, as of January 1, 1998, all on-road vehicles to use diesel fuel no more than .05 percent by weight of sulphur (the current Mexican standard).[33] Marchi also said he planned to "come forward with a plan and a timetable to reduce the sulphur content of gasoline."[34]

The emerging total systems approach to automotive environmentalism involves, as its third component, enhanced mandatory inspection and maintenance programs. Here the impact of NAFTA's informal pressures toward high-level harmonization is also evident. States and provinces have begun to cooperate to adopt similar programs and create transnational, subgovernmental coalitions for more advanced measures such as quotas for zero-emission vehicles. The available evidence indicates that the immediate pre- and post-NAFTA period has seen extensive U.S.-Canada, state-provincial cooperation on environmental, emissions, and automotive standards (including cooperation on the introduction of zero-emission vehicles) but that trilateral, subfederal cooperation has been slower to develop and is strongest in operating transportation standards.[35]

The movement is clearly evident in Ontario, a jurisdiction whose current government is generally averse to environmental regulation but is nonetheless now considering the adoption of a variant of the Aircare program pioneered in British Columbia a few years ago.[36] The Canadian assembly industry naturally prefers a uniform system across Canada and the continent, one that is consistent and has a central repository for test data that the assemblers can challenge in regard to warranty claims. Such a system (INM 240) could steer the bulk of the work to the OEM dealerships.[37] The Ontario government currently seems inclined to adopt a more decentralized, "repair grade" model, under which any properly licensed, equipped, and trained service station could perform the inspection.

Canada has also moved aggressively on pollution prevention. This effort, paralleling that of the United States, began in May 1992 when an agreement among the federal and provincial governments and the Canadian MVMA (which created the Canadian Automotive Pollution Prevention Project) made the automotive industry the first to enter a voluntary pollution prevention agreement (Task Force 1996). Almost from its inception, discussions were held with its U.S. counterpart.[38] The two task forces quickly committed to biannual meetings to coordinate their activities and formalize communication. In December 1994 they hosted a joint suppliers forum, the North American Auto Supplier Environmental Workshop. The joint program, which reinforced the significant achievements secured in each country, was reexamined in the summer of 1996. Neither the Commission for Environmental Cooperation (CEC) nor other NAFTA institution was involved in the venture. Nor was there any move to extend the cooperative activity to include Mexico.

Mexico

The pattern of upward high-level harmonization is also visible in Mexico, where transportation is the leading cause of CO_2 emissions from fossil fuel consumption (accounting for 37 percent of the total) and a major contributor of atmospheric pollution overall. Current projections (Sheinbaum and Viqueria 1996) indicate that Mexican CO_2 emissions in the year 2005 will be 40 percent higher than their 1990 level. Tentative evidence further suggests that from 1987 to 1993 the acidity (pH) of rain in Mexico City from mobile and stationary emissions has been rising (SEDESOL 1994).

Mexico acquired its first federal laws and regulations governing emissions of atmospheric, fluid, and solid wastes and noise in 1972. In 1993 it set standards (NOM-CCA-001-ECOL/ 193 [DOF 1993]) regulating water quality, including wastewater discharges from industrial facilities such as automotive plants. As of 1997 it has not established any standards for maximum levels of soil pollutants but informally follows what are largely European standards covering organic compounds such as hydrocarbons and inorganic compounds such as mercury and lead.

In contrast, Mexico has moved rapidly to set and raise standards for air quality. At the outset of 1994 its Ministry of Health published air quality standards relating to concentrations of atmospheric pollutants.[39] At present, eight Mexican cities as well as Mexico City have air quality monitoring programs that focus on total suspended particulates and (in the case of Mexico City and Tijuana) ozone.[40] The primary ozone precursors are automobile exhausts, industrial smokestacks, and electrical generating facilities.

In 1994 Mexico set its first standard on fossil fuel quality used by mobile and stationary sources to enhance the environment. In December 1994 its National Ecology Institute (INE) published NOM-ECOL-086-1994 on maximum emission levels for sulphur dioxide and nitrogen oxides from fuels. These covered the maximum levels of lead, vapor, sulphur, benzine, olefin, and ash in gasoline, diesel, natural gas, and fuel oil. Improved fuels, such as the super-unleaded premium gasoline, were quickly introduced into various regional markets. Driven by such policies, and by the Ministry of Energy's integrated fuels policy, unleaded gasoline jumped from 10 percent of total gas consumption in 1991 to 58 percent in 1997. High-sulphur diesel fuel, which represented 79 percent of consumption in 1991, was eliminated in 1993. Low-sulphur diesel (0.05 percent) currently represents 76 percent of consumption. The integrated fuels policy seeks further investment in desulphurization and the establishment of environmental standards in other critical zones and areas of the country.

Mexico has also moved to cooperate with the United States for monitoring and controlling air emission standards at the border. In May 1996, the two countries' foreign ministers extended the 1982 La Paz Agreement to designate the El Paso-Juarez Valley as a common airshed, the International Air Quality Management District (IAQMD). Although it respects each country's existing legal and regulatory regimes, such an agreement envisages the integration of air quality monitoring networks and the reporting of air quality pollution indexes; the exchange of information, training, and technology; public education and outreach; modeling to identify abatement strategies; and emissions trading programs. In addition, the U.S.-Mexico Border 11 Program, with nine working groups, is seeking to reduce emissions from vehicles that idle at border crossings, tracking transboundary hazardous wastes, reducing risks of chemical accidents, and reducing solid wastes from *maquiladoras*.

Role of the NAFTA Institutions

Thus far these moves to high-level harmonization have come largely from industry and national political pressure instead of from the direct work of NAFTA's institutions.[41] This is somewhat of a puzzle, given the explicit responsibilities assigned the ASC in the NAFTA text to move rapidly to stringent, regionwide automotive emission standards. Slow progress here is further highlighted by the progress of the ASC's companion body, the LTS, regarding the transportation of dangerous goods.

The LTS has done much to promote high-level trilateral harmonization of regulations for the transportation of dangerous goods. It has already produced a single emergency response guide giving the three NAFTA countries identical procedures to deal with emergencies caused by an accident during the transport of a dangerous substance. It has assisted Mexico in upgrading its relevant standards. And it is moving rapidly to address such difficult issues as bulk packaging, halogenated organic chlorides (HOCs), and manifests for hazardous waste. With a mandate to make the parties' standards for the transportation of dangerous goods compatible by the year 2000 and based on broader United Nations standards, it has taken as its vision the development of single North American dangerous goods code.

Elsewhere the LTS has been less effective. It has done little to meet its NAFTA obligation to implement a work program within three years of NAFTA coming into effect and to render compatible the parties' vehicle standards, including emissions, environmental, and pollution standards not covered by the work program of the ASC. Nor has its companion body, the ASC, which lacks any NAFTA-imposed deadline for action, done much more.[42] The ASC also has not taken up its NAFTA authority to address emissions from on-road and nonroad mobile sources, even though off-road vehicles might account for up to 30 percent of all transportation emissions. Yet the ASC's initial consultations with industry identified a list of 17 priority issues that included the full array of emissions, fuels, pollution prevention, and operating standards. The list of such issues that involved all three NAFTA countries included emission and emission test procedures (especially California emission regulations adopted by British Columbia and, prospectively, the New England states), alleged Mexican nonenforcement of emission regulations, the safety of MMT in gasoline, the nonavailability of low-sulphur fuel in Canada, and different noise standards in the three countries. None of these problems, however, appeared to have a clear, trade-inhibiting effect.

Compliance and Enforcement in Principle and Practice

Higher-level environmental action and international cooperation and convergence are also evident in the areas of compliance, inspection, and enforcement. Here again it is the broader NAFTA regime rather than the NAFTA institutions or dispute settlement mechanisms directly that are propelling the process. The pre- and post-NAFTA need to demonstrate NAFTA's environmental effectiveness to U.S. publics had led to a major increase in inspection and enforcement action in Mexico, while the larger need to secure and maintain the open NAFTA market has led the larger firms to comply readily, often on a voluntary and anticipatory basis.

NAFTA's Dispute Settlement Mechanisms in Action

One striking trend during NAFTA's first years has been the exceptional record of compliance with NAFTA's environmental and overall obligations. There have been relatively few cases taken to NAFTA's three trade and investment dispute settlement panels because the very credibility of the NAFTA dispute settlement process appears to have deterred unfair actions from occurring in the first place. Moreover, the wider array of NAFTA institutions have avoided, managed, or settled politically most disputes before they have had to go to the so-called NAFTA court.[43] Of the 30 or more cases thus far before the Chapter 19 mechanism, none has involved the auto industry. Automotive-related disputes have been similarly absent from Chapter 20 cases. They are tangentially involved through the one Chapter 11 case thus far—on MMT. Nor has any of the 10 cases taken to the CEC under NAAEC's Article 14-15 process nor either of the two cases under Article 13 involved the automotive industry.[44] Given the industry's dominant size and share within North America in both economic and environmental terms, this is a striking finding.

The one automotive-related dispute of some significance is the pending Chapter 11 case on MMT. The sole North American producer and Canadian supplier of MMT, Ethyl Corp. of Virginia, has charged the Canadian government under NAFTA's Chapter 11 dispute settlement mechanism with treating the Canadian distributor Ethyl owns less favorably than potential Canadian producers of MMT.[45] It further charges de facto expropriation and a violation of NAFTA's performance requirements.[46]

The case is a test of whether the NAFTA investment dispute settlement mechanism will take full account of environmental concerns and scientific evidence in making its judgement. It also underscores the need for the NAFTA institutions, from the ASC onward, to develop the competence and financial capacity to undertake scientifically credible evaluations and resolutions of such disputes.[47]

Patterns of National-Level Inspection and Enforcement

As governments in all three countries have moved aggressively to address serious fiscal deficits, the resources available for environmental inspection and enforcement at the national and sub-federal levels have been challenged by severe budgetary cutbacks to environmental agencies. Such moves have curtailed the available capacity in Canada and the United States. Yet in Mexico, despite the particularly severe shocks brought by the 1994 peso crisis, the record of environmental inspection and enforcement and compliance has improved markedly.

Since NAFTA took effect, Mexico has done much to augment its capacity for environmental enforcement (USTR 1997, 112, 125).[48] It has created an environmental crime unit in its attorney general's office. It has increased the number and quality of its environmental inspectors, especially in important fields such as the transboundary shipment of hazardous waste. Since 1992 Mexico has trained more than 660 environmental inspectors, including 460 from border states. EPA trained 230 inspectors in 1995 and 220 in 1996 from both the United States and Mexico.[49] Mexico has also expanded the number of enforcement actions.

The results of these actions are evident in the record of the *maquiladoras*, where many automotive parts operations are clustered. From 1992 to 1996 Mexico conducted 12,347 inspections and compliance verification visits in the border area, fined 9,884 facilities, and partially or completely closed 548 facilities. From 1993 to 1996 there has been a 43 percent increase in the number of *maquiladoras* in complete environmental compliance and a 72 percent reduction in serious environmental violations in the *maquiladoras*.[50]

Since 1992, Mexico has promoted voluntary compliance—in addition to its government enforcement—through a new environmental auditing program. In 1996, 274 operations joined the program. By April 1997, 617 facilities had completed environmental audits. More than 400 had adopted compliance action plans that generated more than $800 million in new environmental investments.

To these trends can be added the absence of any known cases of industries migrating to Mexico to take advantage of Mexico's allegedly weak pattern of environmental enforcement.[51] Together they suggest that, with continued U.S. assistance, there are adequate technical and financial resources for enforcement, especially as Mexican growth is now being vibrantly restored. The record further suggests that Mexico's initial pre-NAFTA increase in environmental inspection, fines, and shutdowns as part of the NAFTA debate has been joined by a deep-seated and sustained desire to maintain a high level of environmental enforcement as a matter of national policy. It is also possible that NAAEC's ultimate power to reimpose tariffs in the event of a persistent pattern of environmental nonenforcement and the increasing value of liberalized NAFTA trade to Mexico's economy have conditioned Mexico's authorities to maintain high standards or economywide environmental enforcement, especially in the visible border area.

Nor do the costs of compliance appear to have placed an undue burden on Mexican- or foreign-owned firms in Mexico. The Mexican government gave smaller firms a grace period for compliance when the peso crisis left them unable to meet their legal obligations for environmental improvements. The relatively small amount (3 percent) that pollution control equipment commands in the overall costs of U.S. industry has been overwhelmed as a cost factor by massive exchange rate, growth, demand, interest rate, and inflation rate changes in the Mexican economy, even as the general trend toward greater environmental regulation in the United States temporarily abated after the midterm congressional elections in 1994. The absence of large-scale U.S. automotive investment in Mexico since 1993 is consistent with this pattern of higher Mexican enforcement and a reduced rise in U.S. costs, but the causes of the investment trend lie primarily in calculations of broad politics rather than in specific environmentally related costs.

Economic Implications of Environmental Policy for the Auto Industry

Although NAFTA's automotive institutions have begun work relating to manufacturing emissions standards, fuel standards, operating standards, and enforcement as potential agenda items, it is industry forums for international dialogue and pressure on national governments, together with strong public environmental consciousness, that are driving the process of higher-level, regionwide harmonization. There have thus been minimal costs and substantial benefits to industry in the area of manufacturing standards, as they have largely shaped the regulatory process and reaped the rewards of rapid and pioneering pollution prevention action. Nor have compliance and enforcement proved to be major burdens to most firms. The major challenges and potential costs to the industry come from the prospective proliferation of different standards in increasingly smaller state and provincial jurisdictions; in the difficulty of reaching consensus with the petroleum industry on U.S. and, thus, Canadian and, eventually, Mexican fuel standards; and in the diversity of subfederal inspection and maintenance systems.

Benefits of a Single Regional Regulatory System

In general, the prevailing trends of regional integration and rationalization and high-level continental and eventual regionwide environmental regulatory harmonization are of major benefit to the industry. They make all three NAFTA markets more open to the products and services of the other countries.[52] Regionwide uniformity in industry practice and government regulation will be of particular advantage to those smaller and weaker producers that lack the capacity to absorb the transaction costs to produce separate products and services for segmented markets.[53] The move to harmonize Canadian emissions and diagnostic standards with those of the United States in 1998 has thus been strongly and wisely supported by the integrated automotive industry in both countries, which have long recognized the value of "one standard, one test, one mark."[54]

Despite this ideal, there are some remaining consequential challenges across the U.S.-Canadian border. Although Canada will adopt the U.S. 1998 emissions standards, effective September 1997, the industry in both countries is being harmed by the current uncertainty about what the U.S. and thus the Canadian regulations for the year 2001 will be. The confidence in 1996 that the projected 2001 standards would go forward in the United States and, therefore, Canada has largely evaporated, given the current dispute over whether the 2001 standards should include a mandatory fuel requirement for sulphur levels of 30 parts per million on average and 80 parts per million maximum. The auto industry favors such a standard but is participating in a joint auto–oil study to determine what the appropriate level might be if new technologies for catalysts that are more tolerant of sulfur come on stream. Current technologies are known to work at 30/80 and the refining technology has long been available to take the sulphur out.[55]

Similar issues arise with regard to the current dispute over MMT, which some regard as a precursor of the larger political struggle to come over sulphur and other fuel standards. The MMT issue raises the important questions of whether the required technology will become available to allow the continued use of MMT and who will incur the costs of developing the technology required for enhanced pollution control. Will it be the refiners, or the OEMs, or parts makers, or governments?[56] Will it require aftermarket parts producers to engage in equally expensive product upgrades or to open new markets for their advanced products?

The current uncertainty points to the advantages that government regulation can have over the voluntary standardization that industry properly generally prefers and strongly relies on. Despite its success in the national low-emission vehicle (NLEV) program and pollution prevention programs and in maintaining the floor in the case of MMT, voluntary regimes are always vulnerable to the danger of defection and thus offer less certainty, especially in focusing on future targets and timetables, than mandatory government regulation. The prospects of defection are increased when solutions involve not only the highly concentrated automotive industry but also the more diffuse set of actors from the petroleum industry who might seek allies (the Pemex monopoly in Mexico and the relatively powerful petroleum industry in Canada) in NAFTA partner countries.[57]

Challenge of Subfederal Differentiation

The greatest challenge and potential cost, however, flow from the threat of further subfederal differentiation and the adoption of different and higher standards in increasingly smaller jurisdictions and markets. These trends threaten to impose significant additional costs on the automotive industry (which already incorporates approximately $2,000 worth of environmental equipment into each car) and weaken its ability to compete internationally (especially with European Union rivals) in the rapidly emerging era of the global car. Even in the core area of automotive manufacturing emissions standards, Massachusetts and New York are currently before the courts seeking permission to follow California in setting their own local standards. Their success would destroy a system in which the United States maintained only two standards (federal and California) and encourage the legally more powerful Canadian provinces led by British Columbia to reproduce this proliferation in Canada. An increasing array of issues, such as requirements for a minimum percentage of zero-emission vehicles, could become the subject of such subfederal regulatory proliferation.

If allowed to develop, such a trend could impose major costs on industry, especially because the additional state and provincial jurisdictions increasingly lack the market size of California. Moreover the smaller Canadian and Mexican vehicle and parts producers in particular lack the ability to economically produce for these segmented markets. Thus far the industry response has been to initiate voluntary, preventive action through its new NLEV program. In the usual pattern, the U.S. auto industry developed the program, its Canadian counterpart joined and is urging its government to harmonize on the EPA's U.S.-wide 1998 level. Such continental collaboration, and related work to develop precompetitive technology for a new generation of vehicles, has as yet not fully involved Mexican industry nor made use of the resources of the NAFTA regime and the CEC.

The threat of subfederal regulatory proliferation is also acute in regard to inspection and maintenance programs, especially as the trendsetting California model is encountering problems and is in a state of flux. From an aftermarket industry perspective, it will be important to ensure that the North American norm for such programs emphasizes replacement and upgrade, with appropriate warranty programs, instead of the early scrapping of vehicles. Scrapping programs should be combined with a move to the disposable-reusable vehicle to open up a major new segment of the aftermarket industry as it has in Europe.

The case of industry would be strengthened, and its economic and environmental strength enhanced, with further moves to expand the well-developed pattern of U.S.-Canadian collaboration to Mexico. The low levels of U.S. and Canadian FDI in the Mexican automotive industry in the post-NAFTA period have meant a restricted flow of new environmental technology and management systems through corporate practices and industry diffusion. There is a particular need in Mexico, especially in the wake of the peso crisis and its temporary regulatory relaxations, to diffuse environmentally state-of-the-art practices and technology downward from the largest assemblers into the smallest tier of Mexican parts and aftermarket firms. Nor has industry itself moved to deal on a trilateral basis, in an anticipatory and preventive fashion, with issues such as pollution prevention, NLEV, fuels standards, and next-generation vehicles.

Conclusions and Recommendations

Thus far NAFTA has imposed few environmental burdens on the automotive industry while it has opened important new economic opportunities for it. NAFTA has brought no discernable additional environmental costs to the automotive industry. Yet its economic provisions have led to regionwide integration and rationalization and an upward-level harmonization of environmental practices and standards that have benefited producers and citizens in all three countries. The policy challenge of the present and future is thus to build on this foundation; more precisely, it is to harness the NAFTA regime to prevent emerging environmental regulatory backsliding (MMT), uncertainty (2001 emissions and sulphur fuel standards), and differentiation (emissions and also inspection and maintenance programs) within and between the United States and Canada by involving Mexico and the NAFTA institutions more directly in the largely informal U.S.-Canada processes that have prevailed to date. This challenge has acquired some urgency: Canada and Mexico already are enjoying free-trade agreements with promising South American partners, the Free Trade Area of the Americas (FTAA) deadline of hemispheric free trade by 2005 is approaching, and the Asia-Pacific Economic Cooperation (APEC) process of free trade by 2010/2020 promises a down payment of liberalization in environmental products and services.

Analytical Conclusions

North America–wide automotive industry integration and rationalization, higher-level harmonization of environmental regulation, and public pressure for higher environmental standards and performance are the dominant trends of the NAFTA era. But the process remains uneven. Within the United States and Canada, regulatory proliferation is strengthening at the subfederal level even though there is a place for states and provinces within NAFTA's environmental institutions and regime. As the case of MMT shows, the threat exists of an economically and environmentally costly backsliding with 17-year-old fuel standards and NAFTA's dispute settlement mechanism a potential accomplice in the unraveling. Even in the United States and thus Canada, where industry cooperation and regulatory harmonization come easily, there is a harmful uncertainty over emission and fuel standards even though the NAFTA text instructed its premier automotive institutions, the ASC and LTS, to have in place by the start of 1997 a work plan to harmonize automotive emission standards. And in ongoing industry processes such as the diffusion of technology through FDI and multistakeholder pollution prevention programs, Mexico often remains outside the Canada-U.S. loop.

It is thus clear that the intergovernmental, trilateral institutions and processes created by NAFTA are not performing up to their potential and are thus not adequately assisting the automotive industry with the environmental regulatory challenges it faces. In broad terms, the directions the NAFTA regime should follow to support the needs of the industry are clear:

- Prevent a further differentiation of regulations among the NAFTA countries and their subfederal jurisdictions so that the common upward progression can be maintained and the costs of a regulatory patchwork avoided.
- Legitimize an integrated, total systems–based approach to environmental regulation so that the costly conflicts between the automotive and petroleum industries can be minimized.
- Foster a genuine trilateral process that engages Mexico as a full equal.
- Strengthen the role of science, technical cooperation, and policy advice to governments seeking harmonized regulations, in ways that broaden the base of involved stakeholders and thus the legitimacy the NAFTA regime commands.
- Equip North American industry to prevail in the competition for the markets of the hemisphere and beyond.

Recommendations

Within these broad guidelines, what might feasibly be done at present within and alongside the NAFTA regime? Although several steps are feasible, five at a minimum are both actionable and urgently required. Although modest in themselves, they have the potential to move the overall NAFTA regime in the direction identified above.

1. Assign the ASC, working with the CEC, the task of conducting, through a scientifically based process involving the automotive and petroleum industries in all three NAFTA countries, a scientific study of the environmental and health effects of MMT. Such a mandate would require expanding, perhaps on an ad hoc basis, the already strained resources of the CEC. It would also involve ensuring that the CEC is involved in any potential Chapter 11 proceeding on MMT to guarantee that the results of scientifically credible evidence of environmental effects are fully factored into any decision. Such moves would prevent the threat of environmental regulatory backsliding (for a small immediate economic reward) and establish a precedent that could ease the process of defining the new fuel standards (for sulphur and benzine) that will soon be required.

2. Encourage the ASC to move promptly to define and complete an ambitious work plan to harmonize automotive emission standards throughout the region. Such action would assist in providing the regulatory certainty and integration industry badly needs and contain burgeoning pressures toward subfederal regulatory differentiation. This requires creating ASC working groups on a trilateral rather than national basis and opening them up to a broader array of stakeholders.

3. Invite the ASC, working with the CEC, to activate its NAFTA mandate to develop and harmonize standards for off-road vehicle emissions. Evidence indicates that such emissions may cause up to 30 percent of air pollution in some locations, and even in Canada a common federal regime for such vehicles remains underdeveloped.

4. Establish a forum, perhaps using NAFTA and CEC support, for a regionwide discussion and eventual convergence of inspection and maintenance regimes. Such a regime would take into account the different levels of economic development of the various subfederal jurisdictions by defining a graduated approach. It should

begin by sharing information on best practices and establishing common standards, training, and certification for emissions inspection and maintenance technicians (a single North American Aircare regime). Such a system might secure, under the NAFTA provisions for the mobility of designated professional personnel, a right for any certified technician to work in any NAFTA jurisdiction. Such an extension would increase technical capacity and diffusion and assist jurisdictions currently facing shortages of trained personnel.

5. Ask NAFTA's trade and environment ministers, assisted by their officials, jointly and directly to consider how NAFTA's environmental regulations affecting the automotive industry might be strengthened and further harmonized to enable the industries of the three countries to better penetrate the high-growth markets of the Americas and the Asia-Pacific region. With the industry already focused on forging single standards for these broader regions and the world as a whole, it is important that the NAFTA community be as equipped as its European Union rivals for the regulatory and standards-setting discussions yet to come.

Suggestions for Further Research

Several additional initiatives, although promising in appearance, require further research:

- Explore how accelerated tariff reductions under NAFTA—immediately reducing to zero all tariffs and other barriers on all environmentally enhancing components of vehicles—could assist the spread of environmental technology. Such policy measures might also be used to privilege fuel-efficient vehicles, which are currently being challenged by the popularity of fuel-intensive sport-utility vehicles.
- Define a common NAFTA regime for environmentally enhancing subsidies. Such a regime could assist those who conduct research into environmentally enhancing and economically efficient practices and regulatory mixes and those who convert to the production of environmentally enhancing fuels.
- Conduct a common, detailed survey of the automotive and environmental regulations prevailing in the Chilean

market and other promising markets of the Americas, with a view toward identifying what common North American standards would best permit market penetration and allow for the incorporation of the Americas into an eventual single regime. Such a study would also explore how Canada and Mexico might use their existing free-trade and environmental cooperation agreements with Chile to move toward the desired objective.

Notes

1. The North American automotive industry is taken to mean primarily the original-equipment assemblers and parts manufacturers producing in the United States, Canada, and Mexico. Yet, given the pervasive economic and environmental interdependencies, attention extends where necessary to the automotive aftermarket and fuel suppliers. The aftermarket includes "that part of the industry concerned with the manufacturing, re-manufacturing, distribution and retailing of all vehicle parts, tools, equipment, accessories and services, except those products that are used as original equipment to manufacture new vehicles." (Automotive Industries Association of Canada 1993).

2. In assessing NAFTA's effects on the automotive industry and relevant environmental regulations, it is important to recall that NAFTA is but one of many forces shaping the regulatory environment for the industry, there was extensive preexisting integration and harmonization, it is in many cases still too soon to assess NAFTA's effect, and most change at the moment is being felt in the economically smaller and less integrated Mexican partner.

3. He continues: "Integration with Mexico is still not an overwhelming factor in the U.S. automotive industry. But it may well be one day, just as integration with Canada is today." This view that NAFTA will lead in the long term to complete trilateral regional integration to a level enjoyed by the United States and Canada today is accepted by Studer (1994).

4. Although this process has been delayed somewhat by the peso crisis and the lack of new large-scale U.S. automotive investment in Mexico, the additional profitability that integration brings will increase the affordability of high-level environmental performance, while the transfer of technology and training through integration production systems provides an additional incentive.

5. The Mexican industry was also substantially integrated with that of the United States. The automotive industry was and is the single most important sector in two-way U.S.-Mexico trade. Indeed, most of the overall U.S.-Mexico trade comes from intracorporate shipments by the Big Three automakers and U.S. parts producers.

6. In 1995 the United States exported $394 million in vehicles and $6.7 billion in parts to Mexico, while it imported $7.8 billion in vehicles and $10.5 billion in parts (U.S. Department of Commerce 1995; USTR 1997, 48).

7. On the deep and pervasive consensus behind high environmental performance in Canada, see Kirton (1994).

8. The United States began the NAFTA era with 30,000 auto parts producers with $100 billion in annual sales who serviced 15 million vehicles; Canadian firms produced $12 billion worth of parts for approximately 2 million vehicles. In contrast, Mexico had only 680 parts manufacturers who sold $6.5 billion worth of parts for 1 million vehicles (Studer 1994, 45).

9. They accounted for 48 percent of the sector's gross domestic product (GDP). Approximately 500 were Mexican-owned, producing in family-controlled labor-intensive firms low-value-added and low-technology parts largely for the local market and particularly for the aftermarket. These firms accounted for 40 percent of Mexican parts production and 60 percent of employment in the industry (Studer 1994, 25).

10. These enjoyed high technology, value added, and economies of scale. They accounted for 40 percent of auto industry employment and more than half of auto parts exports from Mexico. With Mexico's 1994 removal of all remaining foreign direct investment (FDI) restrictions in the industry, their ranks were clear to expand.

11. Twenty suppliers received Chrysler's Penstar award, 37 more Nissan's Hyoka award during 1991–1992, and 77 Ford's Quality Q-1 certification (Studer 1994, 55).

12. For details see Rugman, Kirton, and Soloway (1997a); Kirton and Soloway (1996); Kirton et al. (1996); and Rugman (1994).

13. See Studer (1994). See also Womack (1994) and Molot (1993).

14. See Munton and Kirton (1994), Johnson and Beaulieu (1996), and Rugman and Kirton (1998).

15. This is compared with 50 percent in the Canada-U.S. Free Trade Agreement (CUFTA). There were also grace periods of eight years (for existing firms) and five years (for new firms) to reach these higher levels and a new, net-cost method tracing test that covered 69 parts. This rule was likely to create trade diversion, even though the amount of such diversion was limited by the average post–Uruguay Round most-favored-nation (MFN) nonagricultural tariff level of 3 percent for the United States and 10 percent for Mexico.

16. CAFE was designed to prevent the Big Three from moving production of their smaller, more fuel-efficient cars abroad but has in practice impeded rationalization of production in North America (Hufbauer and Schott 1992).

17. For details see Kirton and Fernandez de Castro (1997). Also a new transportation consultative group has since emerged. Apart from the methylcyclopentadienyl manganese tricarbonyl (MMT) case discussed below, no auto-related cases of consequence have been taken before NAFTA's three dispute settlement mechanisms. Among the NAFTA institutions, the Free Trade Commission managed the trucking dispute and the Commission for

Environmental Cooperation (CEC) has dealt with broad processes affecting the industry, but they have devoted most of their specific attention to other sectors.

18. There were additional mechanisms for such purposes as labor disputes, the private settlement of agricultural disputes, and commercial arbitration.

19. U.S. imports went from U.S.$11.1 to U.S.$22.9 billion, partly owing to U.S. tariff reductions on light-truck imports from Mexico.

20. There has been some rationalization. For example, Ford has stopped producing Thunderbirds and Cougars in Mexico and has concentrated its production at Lorain, Ohio.

21. The 1997 generation of studies on NAFTA effects, centered on the president's report of July 1997 (USTR 1997), point to extensive economic benefits and environmental disappointments but generally do not address the impact of regulatory changes and convergence. For the main studies see USTR (1997); Heritage Foundation (Sweeney 1997); Center for Strategic and International Studies (Weintraub 1997); Federal Reserve Bank of Chicago (Kouparitsas 1997); Brookings Institution (Lustig 1997); and *The Economist* (When Neighbours Embrace 1997). Those critical of the agreement include the Council on Hemispheric Affairs (1997) and the Economic Policy Institute (1997). The environmental disappointments relate to the absence of a NAFTA development fund to support needed scientific research and environmental enhancement, the low level of environmental enforcement action, and the limited access that environmental groups have to the environmental dispute settlement system instead of to the alleged downward harmonization of environmental rules or the pollution-haven-seeking industry migration that featured so prominently in the initial NAFTA debate.

22. For a full account of the relevant pre-NAFTA U.S. regulatory framework affecting the automotive industry, see Gayle (1993, 181–208). For a comprehensive and detailed review of U.S. and Canadian air and other environmental quality levels and pressures, see DeWiel et al. (1997).

23. This is in part because many freshmen Republican members of the House of Representatives soon discovered that their constituents were strongly committed to high levels of environmental protection.

24. The equivalent 1994 Mexican standard is .11 parts per million over one hour per year.

25. Municipal authorities in Detroit, in particular, are claiming they are unable to meet such standards without severe economic cost.

26. For example, the regulatory climate and environmental issues were two factors that led Sears to abandon full-service automotive operations in favor of a concentration on tires and batteries only (Baffico 1997).

27. The CCME estimated that cleaner air from cleaner vehicles and fuels would produce health benefits of up to C$31 billion or C$1 billion per year (Marchi 1997). Marchi was not alone, for his provincial counterparts, who control an estimated three-quarters of the jurisdiction for environmental protection in Canada, have also been moving. British Columbia had introduced its Aircare program and joined a network of states and provinces exploring the advent of zero-emission vehicles (Munton and Kirton 1996b).

28. According to the minister, each of the more than 14 million automobiles on the road in Canada generates four to five tons of pollutants every year.

29. Canada thus has a clear interest in having U.S. national environmental regulations move strongly and rapidly upward. Canada shares this ecological interdependence with distant Mexico, whose airborne pesticides and pollutants are, for example, arriving in the Great lakes.

30. In April 1996 the current U.S. standard of 120 parts per billion for ozone was well above Canada's objective of 82 parts per billion (Marchi 1996). Marchi also sought to amend the U.S. Clean Air Act, which is up for review in 1999.

31. The Canadian government believes that MMT impedes new pollution control systems in automobiles, produces a neurotoxin in emissions that harms children, and that a ban would bring more health benefits than costs to oil refiners and lead to harmonized, high-level fuel standards and fuel and emission control standards between the United States and Canada. Although MMT reduces nitrous oxide in vehicle emissions, it is thought to increase the discharge of smog-creating volatile organic compounds and, like lead, create symptoms akin to Parkinson's disease. The Canadian government estimated a one-time capital cost of C$115 million and yearly operating costs of C$50 for refiners but yearly health cost savings of C$1.5 billion. Canada's 21 motor vehicle manufacturers, represented by the MVMA, and Canada's auto dealers agree, believing MMT-created malfunctioning pollution control devices would bring major warranty repair and re-engineering costs and lead them to petition the Canadian government for relief from the existing and anticipated 1998 emissions standards. Canadian environmental groups also favor the ban, while the refiners through the Canadian Petroleum Producers Institute (CPPI) stand opposed.

32. At present, Canada's average level of sulphur content of gasoline is 360 parts per million; this is compared with the proposed European level of 150 parts per million—a level slightly lower than that expected in the United States—and a current standard of 30 in California (the trendsetter for automotive-emission regulations). In 1996 the Canadian government created a committee of federal, provincial, and industry officials to examine emissions of sulphur, a natural component of crude oil. Representatives from industry, government, and the environmental community have begun to meet to consider reducing or removing gasoline sulphur emissions.

33. Sulphur generates particulate matters and ground-level ozone precursors that lead to smog. Although diesel trucks make up only 10 percent of the vehicles on the road, they produce a large share of vehicular emissions. The new regulations would reduce emissions of affected vehicles by 23 percent for particulates, 30 percent for sulphur dioxide, 10 percent for volatile organic compounds, and 10 percent for carbon monoxide. The health benefits were estimated at C$4–C$11 billion by the year 2020.

34. The Committee's draft reports of April 1997 indicated that reducing to the California level would save 118 lives a year by 2001 (if the rule were imposed that year) and 192 by 2020, and prevent thousands of respiratory illnesses. However 16 of Canada's 17 refineries would have to spend nearly $1.8 billion to upgrade and C$119 million in annual operating costs to meet the California standard. Adding a reduction in diesel fuel (a less likely step) would require another C$1.2 billion in capital costs. Final reports were expected at the end of May. The auto industry prefers a regulatory rather than a voluntary approach, recalling an earlier case in which a voluntary approach allowed the oil industry to defect in ways that imperiled the sales of three truck manufacturers. CCME ministers also sought a national regulation to curb benzine—a known human carcinogen declared toxic by the Canadian Energy Pipeline Association—in gasoline. Marchi promised to produce in spring 1997 a regulation to halve the benzine content of gasoline to 1 percent by volume, one of the most stringent levels in the world and one that would reduce annual benzine emissions by 3,000 tons by 1999. An estimated 56 percent (this figure is higher in urban areas) of Canadian benzine emissions come from gas-powered vehicles.

35. See Munton and Kirton (1995); Munton and Kirton (1996a); Munton and Kirton (1996b); and Kirton and Munton (1996).

36. British Columbia's Aircare program of mandatory inspection and maintenance, introduced into Vancouver and the Lower Fraser Valley in 1992, tests more than 1 million cars and light trucks for emissions every year and requires repairs to pollution control equipment to meet emission requirements.

37. Existing OEM warranties already accept EPA's test results; and the manufacturers have extended this acceptance to British Columbia's Aircare program, which is deemed to meet EPA levels.

38. Canada also has its equivalent of the U.S. car program to develop precompetitive technology that would generate a threefold increase in fuel efficiency, to 80 miles per gallon, through the use of advanced materials that might not be recyclable and, perhaps, hydrogen fuel cells that might threaten the existing oil industry.

39. The standards, published by the Department of Finance (DOF) on January 18, 1994, covered ozone, carbon monoxide, nitrogen dioxide, sulphur dioxide, total suspended particulates, PM10, and lead. These cover the same six substances specified in the U.S. Clean Air Act and add carbon monoxide.

40. The cities are Mexico, D.F.; Monterrey; Guadalajara; Minatitlan; Ciudad Juarez; Chihuahua; Tijuana; Mexicali; and Torreon.

41. The relevant activity has come from NAFTA's economic institutions. The CEC has not dealt directly with the automotive industry although as of 1997 it has projects on such related areas as environmental laboratories standards, transportation and standards, climate change, ISO 14000, pollution prevention, voluntary compliance, and air monitoring.

42. The Automotive Standards Council, or ASC, is assisted in Canada by the Automotive Advisory Council (AAC), an industry advisory group.

Industry is now aiming at standards that are not necessarily harmonized or identical but that are consistent and accommodating and allow functional equivalency. It also wants standards that are not regionally specific but globally compatible.

43. The one major case of U.S. noncompliance has come over safety concerns in the trucking industry—the December 1995 U.S. decision to postpone indefinitely the implementation of a NAFTA deadline to allow Mexican trucks to circulate in the U.S. Southwest. Although safety was the issue, the president was driven by pressure from the unions, environmental groups, and antidrug crusaders.

44. During its first three years, one of the two Article 13 cases concerned continental pollutant pathways for air pollutants.

45. NAFTA allowed companies to sue directly rather than having to convince their home governments, in this U.S. case the USTR, to take up cases on their behalfs. Although Ethyl employs only 40 individuals at its one mixing plant near Sarnia, the dispute is thought to be a harbinger of the emerging multilateral agreement on investment, which would extend NAFTA's high-level investment guarantees and dispute settlement provisions to the 29 members of the Organization for Economic Co-operation and Development (OECD).

46. The bill banning MMT (Bill C-29) passed the Senate on April 9, 1997. Ethyl Corp. filed its claim for Can$350 million in damages with the Justice Department on April 14, 1997. Its suit claimed that Canada's action had caused other countries such as New Zealand to review their MMT use.

47. Such a move would lead to economic as well as environmental benefits. Canadian auto manufacturers currently fuel all vehicles coming off their assembly lines with MMT-free fuel to meet initial emission inspection requirements. Some oil companies such as Chevron also produce MMT-free fuel in the lower Fraser Valley.

48. Although these data about Mexico do not apply to all firms, the large share of automotive plants in the Mexican economy and particularly in the border regions means the data provide an accurate if rough reflection of patterns prevailing in this industry.

49. The CEC of Canada has been active in the area of enforcement; its secretariat has mounted a major program of cooperation of officials from the three countries.

50. Because NAFTA gives to all of Mexico the trade policy advantages historically enjoyed by the *maquiladoras,* its long-term effect is to lessen both the concentration of industry at the border and the environmental stresses that stem from such concentration.

51. The failures or weaknesses of Mexico's environmental enforcement were largely absent from the 1997 studies reviewing and criticizing NAFTA's effects, a notable contrast with the prominence this issue possessed in the initial NAFTA debate. The few cases cited did not involve the auto industry and represented a temporary response to the peso crisis, not a persistent pattern of nonenforcement.

52. Although currently of greatest value to the smaller NAFTA partners, this will become of increasing benefit to the United States. The percentage of U.S. GDP accounted for by trade is rising: from 10 percent in 1970, to 25 percent at present, to an estimated 33 percent by 2010. In the first five months of 1997, Canada and Mexico alone accounted for more than half (53 percent) of the increase in U.S. exports. The 1993–1996 increase in U.S. trade with its NAFTA partners is more than the level of U.S. trade with all countries except Canada, Mexico, and Japan, making the NAFTA increase alone America's fourth largest trading partner.

53. Although such environmental standards should respect local peculiarities in geography and in environmental stresses, supports, and absorptive capacity, common standards can be constructed in a way that makes allowance for such variations; for example, specifying varying allowable emissions levels measured at different altitudes throughout the NAFTA region or requiring more stringent inspection and maintenance in local hot spots. The classic sovereignty-based demand for the right to regulatory localism in response to distinct political preferences should dissipate as knowledge of health effects becomes more widely known and a sense of a common North American community develops (through, for example, expanded flows of people).

54. Even though existing pollution control equipment adds an estimated $2,000 to the cost of each car, the real issue is less the level or even the type of standard than is its application in law and practice across the entire region in ways that all players, from North America and outside, are obliged to respect.

55. For example, in Canada, Shell already provides such low-sulphur fuel.

56. The auto industry has the option of forcing the issue and the adjustment onto fuel makers by moving from advisory to mandatory its warning in existing warranties that the use of MMT-free fuel is advised.

57. Canada's recent experience with low-sulphur diesel standards provides an example as the petroleum industry's defection from an auto–oil consensus threatened the bankruptcy of some Canadian truck firms and forced the auto industry to seek from government a secure regulatory relief from the new standards.

Bibliography

Automotive Industries Association of Canada. 1993. *Automotive Aftermarket Industry: Outlook Study.* Ottawa: Automotive Industries Association of Canada. July.

Baffico, Paul. 1997. A Retailer's Perspective on the Changing Aftermarket. Address to 23rd Annual Strategic Automotive Aftermarket Conference, July, at Frost and Sullivan, Chicago. July.

Commission for Environmental Co-operation. 1997. *Independent Review of the North American Agreement for Environmental Co-operation*, Montreal: Commission for Environmental Co-operation.

Council on Hemispheric Affairs. 1997. *NAFTA's Failure to Deliver.* Washington, D.C.: Council on Hemispheric Affairs. June 27–29.

DeWiel, Boris, Steve Hayward, Laura Jones, and M. Danielle Smith. 1997. *Environmental Indicators for Canada and the United States.* Vancouver: The Fraser Institute's Fraser Forum. March.

Economic Policy Institute. 1997. *The Failed Experiment: NAFTA at Three Years.* Washington, D.C.: The Economic Policy Institute. June 26.

Eden, Lorraine, and Maureen Appel Molot. 1994. The Challenge of NAFTA: Canada's Role in the North American Auto Industry. *North American Outlook* 5 (November): 56–92.

Gayle, Dennis. 1993. Regulating the American Automobile Industry: Sources and Consequences of U.S. Automobile Air Pollution Standards. In *Driving Continentally,* edited by Maureen Molot. Ottawa: Carleton University Press.

Hufbauer, Gary, and Jeffrey Schott. 1992. *North American Free Trade: Issues and Recommendations.* Washington, D.C.: Institute for International Economics.

Johnson, Pierre Marc, and Andre Beaulieu. 1996. *The Environment and NAFTA: Understanding and Implementing the New Continental Law.* Washington, D.C.: Island Press.

Kirton, John. 1994. *Sustainable Development as a Focus for Canadian Foreign Policy.* Working Paper 25. Ottawa: National Round-table on the Environment and the Economy. September.

———. 1997. NAFTA's Commission for Environmental Co-operation and Canada-U.S. Environmental Relations, *American Review of Canadian Studies* 27 (3): 459–486.

Kirton, John, and Raphael Fernandez de Castro. 1997. *NAFTA's Institutions: Their Environmental Performance and Potential.* Montreal: Commission for Environmental Co-operation.

Kirton, John, and Don Munton. 1996. Subfederal Linkages and the NAFTA Community: The Societal Dimension. Paper prepared for Conference of the Association of Canadian Studies in the U.S., November 8–9, Toronto.

Kirton, John, and Julie Soloway. 1996. *Assessing NAFTA's Environmental Effects: Dimensions of a Framework and the NAFTA*

Regime. NAFTA Effects Working Paper Series 1. Montreal: Commission for Environmental Co-operation. April.

Kirton, John et al. 1996. *Building a Framework for Assessing NAFTA's Environmental Effects.* Trade and Environment Series 4. Montreal: Commission for Environmental Co-operation.

Kouparitsas, Michael A. 1997. A Dynamic Macroeconomic Analysis of NAFTA. *Economic Perspectives.* January.

Lustig, Nora. 1997. *Setting the Record Straight.* Policy Brief 20. Washington, D.C.: Brookings Institution. June.

Marchi, Sergio. 1996. Speech before the Transportation, Air Quality and Human Health Conference. York University, April 25, Toronto.

———. 1997. Speech before the Pollution Probe National Workshop on Vehicle Inspection and Maintenance. Meeting of Environment Canada, March 3, Toronto.

Molot, Maureen, ed. 1993. *Driving Continentally: National Policies and the North American Auto Industry.* Ottawa: Carleton University Press.

Moore, Larry. 1997. California's Environmental Frustrations. Paper prepared for 23d Annual Strategic Automotive Aftermarket Conference, July, Frost and Sullivan, Chicago.

Munton, Don, and John Kirton. 1994. North American Environmental Co-operation: Bilateral, Trilateral, Multilateral. *North American Outlook* 4:161–177.

———. 1995. Province-State Interaction in the NAFTA Era: A Preliminary Report. Paper for the Commission for Environmental Co-operation, Montreal, December.

———. 1996a. Beyond and Beneath the Nation State. Paper presented at International Studies Association Annual Meeting, April 29–30, San Diego, Calif.

———. 1996b. Province-State Interactions in the 1990s: A Preliminary Report. Report for the Department of Foreign Affairs and International Trade, Ottawa. March.

Neblett, Andrew. 1992. Eleven Major Companies Take Quality Environmental Management Initiatives within President's Commission. *Total Quality Environmental Management* 2 (Autumn):17–25.

Rugman, Alan. 1994. *Foreign Investment and NAFTA.* Columbia, S.C.: University of South Carolina Press.

Rugman, Alan, and John Kirton. 1998. *Trade and Environment: Legal, Economic and Policy Perspectives.* Cheltenham, U.K.: Edward Elgar.

Rugman, Alan, John Kirton, and Julie Soloway. 1997a. Canadian
    Corporate Strategy in a North American Region. *American
    Review of Canadian Studies* 27 (2): 199–220.
————. 1997b. NAFTA, Environmental Regulations and Cana-
    dian Competitiveness. *Journal of World Trade* 31, no. 4.
    August.
SEDESOL. 1994. *Informe de la situacion general en materia de equi-
    librio ecologico y proteccion al ambiente, 1993-94.* Mexico D.F.,
    Secretaria de Desarollo Social, Instituto Nacional de Ecolo-
    gia.
Sheinbaum, Claudia, and Louis Rodriquez Viqueira. 1996. *Inven-
    tory of Greenhouse Gas Emissions Associated with Energy Use in
    Mexico.* Instituto de Ingenieria-UNAM, Mexico City, May.
Studer, Isabel. 1994. The Impact of NAFTA on the Mexican Auto
    Industry. *North American Outlook* 5 (November):20–55.
Sweeney, John. 1997. *NAFTA's Three-Year Report Card: A "A" for
    North America's Economy.* Roe Backgrounder, no. 1117. Wash-
    ington, D.C.: Heritage Foundation. May 16.
Task Force of the Canadian Automotive Manufacturing Pollu-
    tion Prevention Project (CVMA Project). 1996. *Fourth Progress
    Report.* June. Toronto.
U.S. Department of Commerce. 1995. *Impact of the North Ameri-
    can Free Trade Agreement on U.S. Automotive Exports to Mexico.*
    Report to Congress prepared by International Trade Admin-
    istration. Washington, D.C.: GPO.
U.S. Trade Representative (USTR). 1997. *Study on the Operation
    and Effect of the North American Free Trade Agreement.* Wash-
    ington, D.C.: GPO. July 1.
Vogel, David, and Alan Rugman. 1997. Environmentally-Related
    Trade Disputes between the United States and Canada.
    American Review of Canadian Studies. October.
Weintraub, Sidney. 1997. *NAFTA at Three: A Progress Report.*
    Washington, D.C.: Center for Strategic and International
    Studies.
When Neighbours Embrace. 1997. *The Economist.* July 5–11.
Womack, James. 1994. The North American Auto Industry Un-
    der NAFTA: Making the Positive Sum Solution Happen.
    North American Outlook 5:3–19.

6

Incomes and Productivity in the Auto Industry in North America

Sidney Weintraub

The integration of U.S.-Canada automotive production took a big leap forward with the entry into effect in 1965 of the Auto Pact between the two countries. The Mexican automotive industry remained largely outside this integration until the entry into effect of the North American Free Trade Agreement at the start of 1994, although some rationalization of production between the United States and Mexico had been introduced by the Big Three. The protection that typified the Mexican industry, and the limits on foreign ownership of parts producers, are being reduced gradually under the agreement. In fashioning the rules of origin for NAFTA, the auto industry was given special protection. Within the United States, the Department of Commerce must provide regular reports to the Congress on this industry because of the great interest that exists.

It is only a moderate overstatement to say that as the auto industry fares in the combined North American area, both assembly and parts, so goes the future of NAFTA. The literature on the industry as it exists in North America is vast. The purpose of this essay is to examine some limited aspects relating to the size of the workforce, the degree of unionization, wages, and labor productivity in the industry in the three countries. Sufficient data will be provided on production, sales, and trade in order to set the context for the main discussion.

Production, Sales, and Trade Data

Table 6.1 shows production of passenger cars and light trucks in the three North American countries from 1992 through 1997. Several features of this table should be highlighted. One is the importance of both passenger cars and light trucks in Canada—2.6 million vehicles produced in 1997. This was 21 percent of the number of vehicles produced in the United States that year. When comparing the U.S. and Canadian economies, a common

Table 6.1
Production of Passenger Cars and Light Trucks in Canada, Mexico, and the United States, 1992–1997
(units)

	Canada	Mexico	United States
Passenger cars:			
1992	1,034,197	778,413	5,659,323
1993	1,348,350	835,079	5,988,534
1994	1,211,428	839,939	6,609,523
1995	1,338,517	698,028	6,326,700
1996	1,288,676	797,680	6,055,939
1997	1,375,814	854,809	5,922,205
Light trucks:			
1992	935,505	274,994	4,116,642
1993	890,517	219,901	4,901,548
1994	1,069,244	240,818	5,707,176
1995	1,091,803	231,866	5,577,515
1996	1,109,034	413,615	5,658,812
1997	1,205,828	483,193	6,129,982

Source: Automotive News 1998 Market Data Book 1998.

rule of thumb is the 10-to-1 relationship—the Canadian economy is about 10 percent the size of the U.S. economy. By this form of reckoning, Canada gets more than its proportionate share of auto production. In addition, the mandate determined by the Big Three automakers for Canadian production has been for larger cars and vans (categorized as light trucks), which have represented the fastest-growing portion of the North American market in recent years. About 96 percent of the vehicles produced in Canada in 1996 were exported to the United States. Of the 1.2 million vehicles sold in Canada in 1996, nearly two-thirds were imported from the United States (Kumar and Holmes, chapter 4 in this volume).

Table 6.2
Sales of Passenger Cars and Light Trucks
in Canada, Mexico, and the United States,
1992–1997
(units)

	Canada	Mexico	United States
Passenger cars:			
1992	797,922	445,311	8,210,627
1993	739,051	398,744	8,519,573
1994	748,697	415,650	8,991,347
1995	671,818	115,091	8,635,557
1996	660,765	200,561	8,529,124
1997	739,926	303,577	8,289,413
Light trucks*:			
1992	412,226	258,870	4,674,589
1993	431,837	258,870	5,398,491
1994	483,548	212,078	6,097,787
1995	465,176	68,715	6,130,411
1996	518,939	133,361	6,611,099
1997	654,310	184,882	6,871,093

Source: Automotive News 1998 Market Data Book 1998.
* Canada figures include some heavy trucks; Mexico figures include tractor trailers and buses.

Vehicle production was rising steadily in Mexico in the 1990s until the 1995 crash of the economy. Vehicle production declined only marginally that year, by 14 percent, compared with domestic vehicle sales in Mexico, which fell by 70 percent (*Automotive News* 1998). The saving grace for Mexico was the ability to maintain production by increasing vehicle shipments to the United States, which rose in dollar terms in 1995 over 1994 by 36 percent (Ramírez de la O, chapter 3 in this volume). Exports of auto parts also increased in 1995, but more modestly than vehicles

Table 6.3
U.S. Motor Vehicle and Parts Trade with
Canada and Mexico, 1991–1996
(millions of $)

	Exports			
Year	Total, of which:	Passenger vehicles and light trucks	Medium and heavy trucks	Parts
Trade with Canada:				
1991	9,136	6,559	2,198	13,575
1992	8,299	5,992	1,886	15,282
1993	9,254	6,412	2,442	18,282
1994	11,423	7,534	3,461	20,097
1995	11,559	7,263	3,748	21,823
1996	12,319	7,798	3,796	22,228
Trade with Mexico:				
1991	299	143	76	5,103
1992	278	80	87	6,515
1993	195	90	24	7,317
1994	683	569	48	7,663
1995	394	290	57	6,737
1996	1,265	835	361	7,078

mainly because the Mexican industry already was exporting a large proportion of its parts production to the United States.

The Mexican economy recovered in 1996, but the increase in domestic vehicle sales was modest. By contrast, vehicle production in Mexico increased by 30 percent in 1996 over 1995. The explanation for this is an increase in U.S. vehicle imports from Mexico from $7.8 billion in 1995 to $11.3 billion in 1996 (see table 6.3, below). Mexico's overall economic recovery continued in 1997 at a 7 percent rate and vehicle sales were 32 percent ahead of 1996.[1]

Table 6.2 gives data on sales of passenger cars and light trucks in the three North American countries from 1992 through 1997. The most salient feature of this table is the dominance of

Table 6.3 (*continued*)
U.S. Motor Vehicle and Parts Trade with
Canada and Mexico, 1991–1996
(millions of $)

	Imports			
Year	Total, of which:	Passenger vehicles and light trucks	Medium and heavy trucks	Parts
Trade with Canada:				
1991	20,638	14,068	6,069	7,973
1992	22,543	14,402	7,674	8,996
1993	26,769	18,267	7,991	10,301
1994	30,959	22,516	7,759	11,324
1995	33,371	24,638	8,072	11,184
1996	33,714	25,256	7,574	12,639
Trade with Mexico:				
1991	2,842	2,578	198	4,890
1992	3,109	2,591	442	6,203
1993	3,727	3,084	543	7,354
1994	4,787	3,943	643	9,702
1995	7,830	5,815	1,773	10,501
1996	11,305	7,899	3,055	11,645

Source: U.S. Department of Commerce, Office of Automotive Affairs.

the U.S. market, which in 1997 accounted for 89 percent of passenger car sales and 89 percent of the light truck sales in the three countries. The United States is the lynchpin of the auto market in North America.

Table 6.3 shows data on U.S. trade with Canada and Mexico from 1991 through 1996 in vehicles and parts. (The data are all from U.S. sources in order to maintain consistency.) U.S.-Canada trade has been rising consistently in both directions over that period and shows a steady bilateral surplus in Canada's favor. U.S.-Mexico trade has not been as extensive. U.S. automotive exports fell sharply in 1995 because of the Mexican economic decline that year, but then picked up smartly in 1996 when the Mexican economy recovered. Mexico's exports to the

United States, by contrast, rose consistently over the 1992–1996 period; this increase began at least 10 years earlier. The export increase to the United States was particularly sharp in 1995 and 1996 (because domestic consumer demand had not yet fully recovered in the latter year). The rate of Mexico's automotive export growth slowed in 1997 because of the recovery in the domestic market (Bancomer 1997).

Mexico now has a substantial surplus in its automotive trade with the United States, both in vehicles and in parts. It is interesting to note that U.S. parts imports from Mexico are now almost equal to parts imports from Canada—$12.6 billion from Canada in 1996 and $11.6 billion from Mexico that year. It is likely that the bilateral trade balance will continue to be in Mexico's favor in light of the investments being made for production of vehicles and parts; but, in the future, the balance also will be an artifact of a number of additional considerations—relative rates of growth in gross domestic product, exchange-rate relationships, relative wage rates, relative rates of growth in productivity, and product mandates for production in various locations in North America.

This last point regarding the relationship between production and trade among the NAFTA countries deserves special mention. The theoretical argument in favor of economic integration is that it promotes specialization by facilitating investment in optimally sized plants in particular locations from which goods can be shipped without tariffs or other border barriers to any other place in the integrated area. Because of modern lean-production techniques in the auto industry, the specialization gives a premium to geographically proximate locations, such as the Detroit-Windsor area for Canada-U.S. production and along the border with the United States for parts production in Mexican *maquiladora* plants. One would therefore expect an increase in intra-industry trade, particularly for parts, and considerable intra-firm trade because the Big Three U.S. auto companies operate in all three countries. The rule of origin in NAFTA for vehicles (rising gradually to 62.5 percent for production in North America to qualify for free trade) and other components (rising gradually to 60 percent) is designed to encourage the use of regional production (and, of course, to benefit the U.S. vehicle producers that already have facilities in the three countries). The export to the United States of the bulk of the vehicles produced in Canada, and the counterpart Canadian import of U.S.-produced vehicles, is one form of specialization. So is the increasing use of Mexico as the locus of small-car production for the U.S. market and for parts production.

Ramírez de la O (1998, chapter 3 in this volume) finds that intra-industry trade in vehicles between Mexico and the United States has been variable because of the relatively low level of trade and the special circumstances that existed in 1995, the second year of NAFTA, when Mexican vehicle imports declined and exports expanded; but he finds increasing intra-industry trade in parts. It is, in fact, in parts that one would expect the major increase in intra-industry trade because free trade encourages specialization in components. In 1994, before the collapse of the economy, Mexican parts imports made up 88 percent by value of all of Mexico's automotive imports, while parts made up 46 percent of Mexico's automotive exports. In 1996, U.S. parts imports from Mexico were $11.6 billion compared with vehicle imports of $11.3 billion.

Table 6.4 provides data on the value of parts production in Canada, Mexico, and the United States.

Productivity, Workforce, Unionization, and Wage Data

The previous data and discussion were designed to set the background for the workforce and productivity data in the automotive industry in North America.

Table 6.5 gives data on changes in labor productivity in the automotive industry in the United States, Canada, and Mexico. Although the data are not directly comparable, they do provide a broad picture of recent developments in this industry in the three countries. The base years are not the same for all three countries, but the picture of change varies little if all changes are measured from the same base year. The U.S. data refer specifically to motor vehicles and equipment, whereas Statistics Canada provides data on transportation equipment—a broader but not markedly different category.[2]

The Kumar-Holmes data show substantial increase in labor productivity in vehicle production in Canada since about 1991, but it has been impossible to verify this from official data from Statistics Canada. Productivity performance in the automotive industry as a whole in the other two countries does not appear to have been outstanding in recent years. The Mexican data show no real growth in productivity from 1987 through 1995, and then a sharp increase in 1996. The data were constructed by Ramírez de la O by setting 1983 at 100 and dividing the index of

Table 6.4
Production (Shipments) of Auto Parts and Accessories
in Canada, Mexico, and the United States, 1985–1996
(billions of $)

Year	Canada	Mexico	United States
1985	9.7	N/A	N/A
1986	9.3	N/A	N/A
1987	N/A	N/A	60.7
1988	12.0	N/A	N/A
1989	13.4	N/A	65.7
1990	12.3	5.8	64.9
1991	11.4	6.4	63.6
1992	11.7	6.4	75.1
1993	12.8	6.0	85.2
1994	13.8	6.2	98.0
1995	14.9	5.0	104.8
1996	N/A	6.3	N/A

Sources: Statistics Canada, Census of Manufacturing; Industria Nacional de Autopartes; U.S. Department of Commerce, Office of Automotive Affairs, Annual Survey of Manufacturers, Census of Manufacturers.

output by the index of employment, in both cases for vehicles and parts. The data should be considered approximate. U.S.-Canada official comparative data show greater labor productivity growth in Canada than in the United States from 1961 to 1992, but higher productivity growth in the United States from 1985 through 1992 (Statistics Canada 1994). Canadian productivity performance may have improved since then (Kumar and Holmes 1998, chapter 4 in this volume).

The former data deal with productivity growth over time. A study undertaken by a European scholar with the help of Statistics Canada calculated that the gross value added per employee in the motor vehicle and equipment industry in Canada was between 72 percent (at U.S. prices) and 74 percent (at Canadian prices) of that in the United States in 1987 (de Jong 1996). De

Table 6.5
Labor Productivity in the Auto Industry, 1983–1996

	Canada			Mexico	United States
	Statistics Canada	Kumar and Holmes			
Year	Transp. Equip.	Vehicles	Parts		
1983	96.6	100.8	97.0	1.0000	86.8
1984	100.1	103.6	104.6	1.1555	91.1
1985	101.2	99.1	107.1	1.2608	95.3
1986	100.0	100.0	100.0	1.1374	95.1
1987	98.4	92.3	93.3	1.1172	100.0
1988	100.0	121.2	102.9	0.7052	103.2
1989	100.5	116.6	111.7	0.7121	103.3
1990	99.0	110.9	115.8	0.7493	102.4
1991	98.3	109.0	115.2	0.9412	96.7
1992	97.6	113.9	110.2	0.8243	104.3
1993	N/A	126.1	117.5	0.8780	105.4
1994	N/A	134.4	125.1	0.9223	107.3
1995	N/A	140.8	123.5	0.9182	104.4
1996	N/A	132.2	121.7	1.1582	N/A

Sources: Statistics Canada; Statistics Canada (as cited by Kumar and Holmes, chapter 4 in this volume); Bank of Mexico, Indicadores Economicos, National Institute of Statistics, Geography, and Information (INEGI) (as cited by Ramírez de la O, chapter 3 in this volume); U.S. Bureau of Labor Statistics.

Jong further calculated that gross value added per actual hour worked in the machinery and transport industry was 85.08 in Canada in 1990, with the United States at 100. (In 1984, the Canadian comparative figure had been 109.32.) The gross value added per person employed in the machinery and transport industry in Canada, according to de Jong's calculations, was 82.35 in 1990, once again with the United States at 100. (The 1984 Canadian figure for this measurement was 107.60.)[3]

Canadian productivity growth lagged that in the United States in practically all manufacturing industries from 1985 to 1992. Indeed, for most years, the Canadian productivity change was negative, and substantially so, by an annual average of -0.6 percent in transportation equipment industries; U.S. productivity also apparently declined in transportation manufacturing industries over those years but, at -0.2, by less than in Canada (Statistics Canada 1994). Both Canada and the United States had a sharp decline in productivity growth generally after 1973 for reasons that are not entirely clear. Salgado (1997) attributes this to the slowdown in capital accumulation relative to labor-force growth and intersectoral shifts. Salgado's comparative data on labor productivity and total factor productivity in the goods sectors of both countries show markedly better performance in the United States from 1981 to 1992.

I have been unable to find reliable information comparing current labor productivity in Mexico with that in the United States in the automotive industry generally, other than on a plant-by-plant basis in the terminal sector and for engine production. (Harbour and Associates 1994). In the vehicle segment of the industry, if one compares the production of vehicles, divided by the level of employment in the three countries in 1996, the ratio is lowest for Mexico, next for the United States, and highest for Canada. This is hardly a sufficient measure of productivity in the vehicle sector, but it conforms with the expectation of lowest productivity in Mexico and is consistent with the Kumar-Holmes data on Canadian productivity.[4]

Table 6.6 shows the size of the workforces in the motor vehicle industries in the three countries. The figures in the first part of the table are aggregated; the second part of the table separates out employment in the parts segment of the industry. The data do not separate production from administrative workers, nor do they give any indication of the indirect employment spawned by this industry.

Total employment in the automotive industry in the United States has actually increased since NAFTA went into effect on January 1, 1994, from 836,600 in 1993 to 971,900 in 1997 (Bureau of Labor Statistics). It is impossible to say whether the increase would have been greater without NAFTA or whether the automotive production inherent in the integration of the Mexican industry into the North American pattern will have deleterious effects on U.S. employment in the future. Employment in the motor vehicle sector in the United States (as opposed to the parts

Table 6.6
Employment in the Motor Vehicle and Equipment Industry in Canada, Mexico, and the United States, 1988–1996/97

Year	Canada	Mexico	United States

Employment in the motor vehicle and equipment industry (aggregated), 1988–1997:

Year	Canada	Mexico	United States
1988	138,600	218,107	856,400
1989	144,400	265,499	858,500
1990	137,100	295,150	812,100
1991	124,900	286,240	788,800
1992	122,000	345,373	812,500
1993	129,500	313,157	836,600
1994	136,700	305,242	909,300
1995	140,900	262,508	970,800
1996	146,500	276,896	962,500
1997	N/A	N/A	971,900*

Employment in the auto parts and accessories industry, 1988–1996:

Year	Canada	Mexico	United States
1988	89,600	177,099	406,000
1989	92,300	217,321	417,000
1990	86,800	237,480	401,000
1991	74,300	225,728	398,000
1992	72,100	285,415	417,000
1993	77,500	258,213	430,000
1994	83,800	255,505	467,000
1995	88,100	214,460	483,000
1996	92,200	226,214	505,000

Sources: Statistics Canada (as cited by Kumar and Holmes, chapter 4 in this volume); Mexican Association of Automotive Industry (AMIA) and the National Institute of Statistics, Geography, and Information (INEGI) (as cited by Ramírez de la O, chapter 3 in this volume); U.S. Bureau of Labor Statistics.

* Preliminary figure

and equipment sector) was 488,000 in 1995, or 50 percent of employment in the industry as a whole that year.[5]

Of the 146,500 employment figure for Canada in 1996 shown in table 6.6, 63 percent was in the parts industry; for Mexico, parts production captured almost 82 percent of total automotive employment. It is evident that Mexico—or the industry in its choice of location—has given greater emphasis to parts than to vehicle production, at least in terms of employment.

Mexican employment data present a number of problems. The American Automobile Manufacturers Association (AAMA) provides higher figures for Mexican employment (Card 1997) than does Ramírez de la O. The AAMA gives as its sources the Mexican Secretariat of Commerce and Industrial Development (SECOFI) and Mexico's national accounts. Ramírez de la O's sources are the Mexican Association of Automotive Industry (AMIA) and the National Institute of Statistics, Geography, and Information (INEGI), the main statistical agency of the country. I am reluctant to vouch for either source as being more accurate.

In any event, total employment in the Mexican automotive industry, using the INEGI-AMIA figures, was 29 percent of the level of employment in the U.S. industry in 1996 and 189 percent the level of Canadian automotive employment that year. Both these percentages—particularly the Canadian comparison—are far higher than the proportions of output in the automotive industry in Mexico compared with the other two countries.

Table 6.7 shows data on unionization in the automotive industry. As has been evident throughout the discussion in this chapter, the most complete information comes from the United States (Bureau of Labor Statistics, or BLS), then from Canada (Statistics Canada, which has not always calculated automotive industry data), and the least satisfactory from Mexico. The Mexican unionization data, in fact, as noted on the table, come from John Tuman of Texas Tech University.

Data from the U.S. Bureau of Labor Statistics indicate that of the 1,295,000 people employed in the U.S. motor vehicle and equipment industry in 1996 (the figure is higher than the 962,500 shown in table 6.6, which may be because this classification is broader than the one shown there), 581,000, or almost 50 percent of the total, were members of unions. Slightly more, 593,000, were represented by unions. This is a high proportion in the U.S. context: private-sector unionization as a whole was only 10 percent of those employed in 1996; and in manufacturing, the percentage of union members was 14.1 percent of those

Table 6.7
Unionization of the Motor Vehicle and Equipment
Industry in Canada, Mexico, and the United States,
1989–1997

Year	Union Members	Employees	Unionization (%)
Canada, 1989–1997:			
1989	111,591	259,851	43%
1990	104,285	232,447	45%
1991	101,845	222,150	46%
1992	97,200	240,100	41%
1993	N/A	N/A	N/A
1994	N/A	N/A	N/A
1995	N/A	N/A	N/A
1996	N/A	N/A	N/A
1997	117,400	208,700	56%
Mexico, 1994:			
1994	59,178	139,772	42%
United States, 1995–1996:			
1995	534,000	1,244,000	43%
1996	581,000	1,295,000	45%

Sources: For Canada, Statistics Canada; for Mexico, Tuman
1995; for United States, U.S. Bureau of Labor Statistics.

employed. The main U.S. union in the auto industry is the
United Auto Workers (UAW).

The degree of unionization in Canada was not calculated for
a number of years and the figure for 1997 was obtained in a tele-
phone conversation with an official of Statistics Canada. The
estimate for union membership in Canada's automotive industry, based on monthly data for the first 11 months of 1997, is
117,400, or 56 percent of the estimated total employment in the
industry. Total unionization in Canada in 1992, the most recent
year for which complete industrial and agricultural unionization

data are available, was 35 percent (Statistics Canada). The main union in the automotive sector in Canada is the Canadian Auto Workers.

In Mexico, union-management negotiation takes place at the plant or sometimes at the enterprise level, whereas the main wage and hour negotiation in the other two countries is either industrywide or pattern bargaining to secure some homogeneity of results. The main Mexican labor confederation, the Confederación de Trabajadores de México (CTM), has been highly politicized for decades, forming one of the three legs of the corporatist stool of the Institutional Revolutionary Party (PRI). Unions affiliated with the CTM also are dominant in the automotive industry. The role of the CTM is now changing following the growth of political opposition in Mexico, coupled with the death in 1997 of Fidel Velázquez, who merited the sobriquet of labor "czar." Despite the growing integration of the automotive industry from the viewpoint of production and marketing, there is no comparable union solidarity across North America (Tuman 1995).

One recent sign of changing unionization patterns was the decision by the Mexican government to recognize an independent (non-CTM) union in a Korean-owned auto parts *maquiladora* in Tijuana in December 1997 (Associated Press, December 17, 1997). The sequence of events was the refusal of the state governor (of Baja California Norte) to recognize the results of an election held in October, dismissal of some workers for union activity, protests from U.S. lawmakers and others over this decision, direct intervention by U.S. vice president Al Gore with Mexican president Ernesto Zedillo, a second union election on December 16, and then formal recognition of the independent union. About 6.5 percent of employees in *maquiladora* plants are either not unionized or in nonaffiliated company unions

Table 6.8 gives data on salaries and table 6.9 on total compensation in this industry in the three countries. Mexican wages and benefits generally suffered in real terms over the past two decades from stabilization programs following economic declines and resurgence of inflation after 1982 and then in 1995. The biggest "hit" in dealing with inflation control was taken by workers. Table 6.10 provides a comparison of wage developments in the three countries in North America for production workers generally. The relative decline of manufacturing compensation in Mexico following the economic crash of 1982 and then again in 1995 jumps out from the table.

Table 6.8
Average Hourly Wages of
Production or Nonsupervisory Workers in the
Motor Vehicle and Equipment Industry, 1991–1996
($)

	Canada		Mexico*		United States	
Year	Vehicles	Parts	Vehicles	Parts and Accessories	Vehicles	Parts and Accessories
1991	17.71	13.96	5.22	3.57	18.34	13.62
1992	17.62	13.48	7.01	4.31	18.32	14.22
1993	17.52	13.10	7.93	5.18	19.44	14.74
1994	17.64	12.96	8.26	5.26	20.71	15.56
1995	18.14	12.89	5.24	3.32	20.57	16.18
1996	18.33	13.05	N/A	N/A	N/A	N/A

Sources: Statistics Canada (unpublished); INEGI; U.S. Bureau of Labor Statistics.

* Mexican figures include wages and benefits. Average weighted by employment in different parts production subcategories. The figures for Mexico in this table were constructed from much more detailed data provided by Raymond Robertson, Department of Economics, Syracuse University. The original data come from INEGI and are not always consistent with the remuneration data from the U.S. Bureau of Labor Statistics in table 6.9.

In dollar terms, the compensation cost for production workers in manufacturing in the United States was $17.74 an hour in 1996 and in Mexico it was $1.50. This hourly cost for manufacturing workers generally is lower than in the vehicle sector in the United States, but approximately equal to that in the parts sector. Wages in the vehicle sector are higher than in the parts sector in Canada as well, as they are in Mexico. There is evidence of a disconnect in Mexico between increases in productivity in the automotive sector and real wage and benefit increases; the evidence is quite strong at the firm level in the terminal sector (Tuman 1998). This outcome might change in the future as independent unions grow in importance because they have a more solid record in wage bargaining than do CTM unions. Unions in *maquiladora* plants in some regions bargain aggressively now (e.g., in Matamoros), but by no means throughout the *maquiladora* sector.

**Table 6.9
Hourly Cost of Remuneration (Wages plus Benefits)
for Production Workers in the Motor Vehicle and
Equipment Industry, 1985–1994**
($)

Year	Canada	Mexico	United States
1985	12.99	2.33	19.71
1986	13.35	1.93	20.09
1987	14.49	1.61	20.40
1988	16.41	1.96	20.80
1989	17.88	2.03	21.39
1990	19.09	2.50	22.48
1991	21.06	2.90	24.28
1992	20.95	3.62	24.70
1993	20.72	3.98	25.52
1994	20.72	4.05	26.56

Source: U.S. Bureau of Labor Statistics, June 1997.

**Table 6.10
Indexes of Hourly Compensation Costs for
Production Workers in Manufacturing in Selected Years**
(U.S.=100)

	1980	1985	1990	1995	1996
United States	100	100	100	100	100
Canada	88	84	106	93	94
Mexico	22	12	11	9	8

Source: Bureau of Labor Statistics 1997.

Some Conclusions

It is evident that a North American auto industry exists for production and that this tri-country integration is likely to deepen
over time. The Canada-U.S. integration has been building for
more than 30 years, while the Mexican connection is much
younger. Over time, the latter should take on increased signifi-

cance. Mexico already is a major player in parts production, for which it rivals Canada. The bulwark of the North American market, however, is still the United States, and in this field the potential for Mexican growth surpasses that of Canada. This, naturally, depends crucially on Mexican economic growth.

Employment in the Mexican parts sector already exceeds that in Canada by 2.5 times and is 45 percent of that in the United States. This implies much lower output per worker in Mexico than in the other two countries for parts production, due largely to lower levels of capitalization and automation in Mexico. Mexican competitiveness in parts production, therefore, seems to depend heavily on a depreciated peso and low worker compensation, and this is not a solid basis for the long term.

The North American labor market is integrated in the sense that just-in-time inventory techniques for production permit the use of Mexican or Canadian labor in locations close to the United States. The three labor markets are not integrated, however, when it comes to wage-and-hour bargaining, at least as between Mexico on the one hand and the United States and Canada on the other. The compensation paid to Mexican workers generally has deteriorated as a consequence of two economic crises 13 years apart and the sharp depreciation of the Mexican currency each time. This has made Mexican labor cheap in dollar terms and surely has stimulated the growth of *maquiladora* plants for the production of auto parts for the integrated market. The Mexican terminal industry has also attracted much new investment, undoubtedly based in part on lower wages but also the promise of the market potential. Mexican output per worker in the terminal sector, based on plant data, is apparently much higher than in the parts sector.

Workers in parts production earn less in all three countries than those in the terminal sector. The evidence in Mexico is that workers in parts production earn compensation comparable to that of production workers in manufacturing generally, whereas the compensation is higher in the terminal sector than in manufacturing generally. This is the pattern in the North American auto industry generally. The reason to single out Mexico in this discussion is that the buying power of worker compensation there has deteriorated sharply in comparison with compensation in the United States and Canada.

The evidence in Mexico, based on analysis of particular plants, is that productivity increases do not lead to comparable wage increases. This undoubtedly is true in the *maquiladora* sector, where producer savings from a depreciated peso were not passed along to workers until the last year or two. This disconnect between productivity and wage increases may diminish as nonpolitical unions become stronger at the expense of the CTM. It is hard to be precise about the situation in the auto industry generally, as opposed to particular plants that have been studied, because the information is sketchy with respect to both productivity and worker compensation, certainly as compared with Canada and the United States.

The auto sector is highly unionized in each of the three NAFTA countries, but the pattern in Mexico differs from the other two. Bargaining in Canada and the United States tends to be industrywide, or based on choosing a lead company with which to bargain in order to establish a pattern for the others. Union bargaining in Mexico is at the plant level, which permits the kinds of differences in compensation packages that have emerged.

There are a number of challenges for the future. One is informational—we simply do not know enough about key indicators in Mexico, particularly productivity and its relationship to wage rates. Over the long term, the more important substantive issue is the health of the Mexican economy and the welfare of the average Mexican. The potential of the market depends on this, as do levels of compensation. The decline in compensation that has beset Mexican workers is the result of two economic crashes, accompanied by high inflation and currency depreciation; and the burden of the stabilization programs that followed was borne primarily by workers in Mexico.

There is a political dimension to the Mexican challenge as well. As the political structure becomes more democratic—which is happening—so too will the union structure become more open—which also is happening. This may change internal worker-management relations and also relative rates of compensation in Mexico compared with the other two NAFTA countries.

The biggest challenge of all, one not taken up in this chapter, is the future competitiveness of the North American automotive industry in relation with the industry in other countries. The rationale of NAFTA is to augment this competitiveness by removing barriers to trade and investment in the North American region. It is still too early to know whether this integration will achieve its objective.

Notes

The information for the tables in this chapter was gathered by Mason Barlow, an intern at the Center for Strategic and International Studies, Washington, D.C., who also prepared the tables.

1. *Automotive News*, January 26, 1998. As a matter of background, the rank order of companies was General Motors, Ford, Nissan, Volkswagen, Chrysler, and then various others, each with a small number of vehicle sales.
2. The Kumar-Holmes data are for vehicles and parts.
3. Both Statistics Canada and the U.S. Bureau of Labor Statistics (BLS) have developed sophisticated multifactor productivity measures, but these will not be discussed here due to problems of comparability.
4. The employment data, unfortunately, do not segregate production from other workers.
5. The American Automobile Manufacturers Association gives total employment in the U.S. industry as 1,145,500 in 1995, about 175,000 more than the BLS figure, and broken down 35 percent for motor vehicle production and 65 percent for automotive parts.

Bibliography

Automotive News 1998 Market Data Book. 1998. Detroit, Mich.: Crain Communications, Inc.

Bancomer. 1997. Industria Automotriz (Automotive Industry). *Informe Económico* (November-December):49-64.

Bureau of Labor Statistics (BLS), U.S. 1997. International Comparisons of Hourly Compensation Costs for Productive Workers in Manufacturing. June.

Card, Andrew H., president and CEO, American Automobile Manufacturers Association. 1997. Statement before the U.S. International Trade Commission. May.

de Jong, Gjalt. 1996. Canada's Post-War Manufacturing Performance: A Comparison with the United States. Netherlands: University of Groningen, Groningen Growth and Development Center.

Harbour and Associates. 1994. Harbour Report 1994. Ellensburg, Wash.: Central Washington University.

Salgado, Ranil. 1997. Productivity Growth in Canada and the United States. *Finance & Development* 34, no. 4 (December):26-29.

Statistics Canada. 1994. Aggregate Productivity Measures. Input-Output Division.

Tuman, John P. 1995. Union Democracy and Industrial Relations in the Mexican Automobile Industry: A Comparative Analysis. Paper prepared for National Administrative Office, U.S. Department of Labor.

———. 1998. The Political Economy of Restructuring in Mexico's 'Brownfield' Plants: A Comparative Analysis. In *Transforming the Latin American Automobile Industry: Workers and the Politics of Restructuring*, edited by John P. Tuman and John T. Morris, 148-215. Armonk, N.Y.: M. E. Sharpe.

7

The North American Auto Industry: Where Do We Go from Here?

Sidney Weintraub and Christopher Sands

The preceding chapters have begun to answer some important questions about how the auto industry has adjusted to NAFTA, one of the most significant recent changes to the policies of the three NAFTA countries toward this key industry. For reasons particular to the circumstances of each, and owing to the strong U.S. economic performance since 1994, the auto sector has performed well in the United States, Mexico, and Canada since NAFTA came into effect. This broad conclusion is sustained by the authors in this volume whether based on measures of employment, incomes, investment, productivity, or amelioration of the environmental impact of automotive manufacturing.

Just as important, the analysis suggests that the industry is adapting its strategies, in part through the continental specialization of production and improvements in productivity, to become more competitive within the global marketplace. This is a hopeful sign of future good times for North American automakers, for their suppliers, and for the health and vitality of the three economies. In other words, the strong performance of the auto industry in North America since NAFTA is good news for all North Americans.

So far, so good. But where will the industry go from here?

The chapters in this volume raise a number of questions in our minds about the future of the industry under NAFTA and the challenge of making policies to influence decisions and outcomes in a sector that operates in a highly integrated fashion across national boundaries. Rather than speculate here, it may be more useful to conclude this volume by outlining some of the most pressing researchable questions that arose during the preparation of this book. For the reader, these questions may indicate the nature and scope of the changes now under way in the industry. For us, the following discussion charts the course we hope to pursue in the next phase of our research.

Organized Labor

The competitive position of the auto industry in North America is tied to the competitiveness of its skilled workforce, most of which belongs to a union. The traditional structures of manufacturing work are changing. In Canada and the United States, labor and management together face the challenging task of adapting past practices to the current competitive environment. But what is the role of organized labor in the Mexican segment of the industry? How do rates of unionization in assembly and parts plants in Mexico compare with those in Canada and the United States? What can the UAW and CAW do to foster the growth of strong unions in Mexico? Will more independent unions in Mexico reduce the opposition of the American Federation of Labor-Congress of Industrial Organizations to NAFTA?

Economic Contribution of the Auto Industry

Once, it was simpler to account for the economic activity related to an auto industry in North America that was made up of just a few large, vertically integrated manufacturers located within a short distance of Detroit. Today the process of designing and building cars and trucks draws on companies of all sizes in communities around the continent. As a result, it is more difficult to identify precisely the linkages between the competitive strength and prosperity of the auto industry and that of the rest of the economy.

In light of the profound changes that have taken place in the structure of the auto industry in North America, what is the nature and scope of the contribution that it makes to the economies of the three countries? This question should be answered in the context of a broad, statistical inventory inclusive of assemblers and suppliers and the related activities of research and development, marketing, and so forth. Is it possible to create a "Gross Sectoral Product" figure?

Standards

NAFTA removed many barriers to trade, but with tariff levels low and diminishing, standards of various kinds often represent the most significant remaining hindrance to trade. Negotiators established a framework for future discussion of standards harmonization within NAFTA, but its use to date has been limited.

Separately, many countries have begun moving toward the full adoption of European industrial design and product safety standards that were developed through dialogue among members of the European Union.

What are the potential gains from the harmonization of industrial, product design, and consumer safety standards across North America? Can the three countries agree on accession to the European Working Party 29 standards, and if so what might the costs and benefits be?[1] To what extent can the NAFTA countries accept mutual recognition of automotive standards and testing results in order to facilitate greater trade and investment? What role might the NAFTA mechanism for the discussion of standards harmonizations have in moving toward a common standards regime?

Currency Risk

As Ramírez de la O points out in his chapter in this volume, the 1995 devaluation of the Mexican peso had the effect of slowing the growth of the Mexican economy that increased trade had accelerated following NAFTA's implementation. In response to Mexico's economic crisis, the United States provided key leadership and financial assistance to restore international confidence in Mexico's currency and macroeconomic stability. Canada also made a contribution; and although it was perhaps more important symbolically than financially, it was an unprecedented Canadian commitment to a Latin American country and underscored the degree to which NAFTA fostered linkages that tied Canada's national interests to the future of Mexico.

Since the 1995 peso crisis, integration in the auto sector has moved ahead, tightening the web of interdependence that binds the three countries together. In light of this trend, what are the risks should Mexico devalue the peso once more? How have companies in the industry responded to the 1995 devaluation to protect themselves in a future currency crisis? What pressures on commerce are created by operation with three separate currencies in a highly integrated industry such as autos, and what are the potential risks and benefits associated with Mexican adoption of the U.S. dollar (or fixing the value of the peso to the dollar, as in Argentina)? What consequences might follow a peso crash in 2000 or thereafter? And in the wake of similar currency crises in Asia that had a larger impact on the Canadian currency than many had anticipated, what is the effect of the undervalued

Canadian dollar on the current pattern of automotive industry trade and investment?

Common Automotive Tariffs and Border Barriers

NAFTA negotiators were not authorized to attempt the creation of a full customs union in North America, which would have resulted in a common set of external tariffs shared by the three countries. Three diverse economies with important sovereignty reservations and linked by an uneven pattern of economic integration may perhaps have found such an objective too difficult to implement. The case, however, for a common external tariff is stronger in some sectors than others, and particularly in the highly integrated auto sector.

A recent Canadian decision to unilaterally eliminate the country's external tariff on certain auto parts demonstrated the way in which separate external tariffs could be manipulated to create local comparative advantages within the region. How did the Canadian tariff cut affect trade and investment, and how did this action affect suppliers of these components in Mexico and the United States? How would a proposal to eliminate the Canadian external tariff on finished vehicles affect the industry? What are the operational costs and benefits for the industry of the current system of three separate external tariff schedules, and what are the merits of moving toward a North American common external tariff in the automotive sector? In particular, if the three countries move to a common tariff for products in auto-related categories, are automotive rules of origin still needed to foster North American content?

North America As a Competitive Global Export Platform

The growth potential of auto sales in mature markets like Canada and the United States is limited. As incomes improve in Mexico, there is the prospect that a market for new vehicles larger than Canada's may develop over time. Yet policies designed to foster the competitiveness of North America as a place to design and build cars and trucks, relative to the rest of the world, also raise the possibility that North America will supply other markets around the world through trade.

What potential is there for North America to supply international automotive markets, serving as a manufacturing and export platform for an increasingly concentrated global auto industry? What opportunities and challenges are created for suppliers and assemblers with the development of multimarket—and even global—vehicles? How can suppliers take advantage of greater economies of scale through export, rather than risk capital investment in an increasing number of markets where local assembly is deemed to be advantageous? How will North America fare if the number of global assemblers and Tier One suppliers is reduced through consolidation and attrition? How are European and Asian assemblers and suppliers positioning themselves for manufacturing in North America? What areas of public policy most contribute to the competitiveness of the North American segment of the global industry? How do company policies and trade policies interact in this area?

Divided Jurisdictions

Each of the NAFTA countries is organized as a federation. Where regulatory jurisdiction is divided between federal and state/provincial authorities in the United States and Canada, how can the needs of the larger North American market be balanced against the need to respect local authority as constitutionally established? How will pressures for the decentralization of power within Mexico affect the regulatory environment for auto manufacturing? Does the experience of Canada or the United States provide any valuable comparisons for Mexican policymakers working in this area? Are there any areas where Mexican states are empowered to regulate industry activity, and to what extent have these powers been exercised in the past? What are the costs and benefits of state environmental mandates versus federal standards? In each country, which level of government can more efficiently obtain compliance and/or positive results through regulation? What are the most problematic areas of divided jurisdiction, and are there areas where cooperation has worked well?

Social Policy and Competitiveness

Each NAFTA member country operates a system of social policies, managing education, health care, retirement, and unemployment benefit programs that allocate benefits and costs to taxpayers differently. Where the public sector has not undertaken to provide certain benefits for all workers, such as health care in the United States, companies often turn to the private sector to respond to contract demands from their employees.

How do the social policy regimes of the United States, Canada, and Mexico contribute to costs in the auto industry? Addressing specifically education, retirement/pension, and health care systems, how do the three countries compare in terms of the quality of benefits provided and their relative cost? What are the implications of North American economic integration for levels of taxation, and what does this imply about the resources available for social policy in each country?

Incomes and Productivity

In the previous chapter, Weintraub offered a preliminary assessment of the trends in productivity and income growth within the industry. The tentative conclusion that was drawn from the limited and preliminary data available was that the industry is seeing growth in both areas in all three countries, but that the relationship between productivity growth and income levels remains inconsistent. In chapter 3, Ramírez de la O argues that productivity growth is rising appreciably faster than incomes in Mexico, although the gap may be narrowing somewhat.

How is productivity taken into account in wage settlements in the North American auto industry? Have auto companies invoked NAFTA to pressure U.S. workers into moderating their demands in labor negotiations? How does auto sector productivity compare in the three countries? Is there a stronger relationship between wage settlements and productivity in unionized as opposed to non-union facilities, or in the facilities of the assemblers versus those of the suppliers? Is Mexico "catching up" to Canada and the United States in terms of incomes?

As Kumar and Holmes point out in chapter 4 in this volume, Canada boasts some of the most productive assembly plants in North America. But some economists have expressed concern that productivity improvement has been slower in Canada than in the United States because of a variety of factors, including the level of investment in research and development and new manufacturing technologies, weaknesses in Canadian math and science education, and rising costs in Canada's social programs (passed on in many areas through the tax system). Does Canada suffer from a "productivity gap" in this sector?

Environmental Impact

In chapter 5 in this volume, Kirton argues on the basis of a thorough review of regulatory policies affecting the industry in each of the three countries that the "race to the bottom"—a reduction of environmental standards to the lowest level in force within North America due to the mobility of capital investment and the competitive pressures driving costs down within the industry—has not happened. Instead, policymakers are adopting higher standards, and these are converging upward in a number of areas directly affecting the auto industry.

The standards may be higher, but are they working? How well have public policies designed to minimize the negative environmental impact associated with motor vehicle manufacturing and use worked to date? How can public policy promote engineering and scientific innovation? How are costs (to consumers, to producers, to the other NAFTA countries, to associated industries such as energy and waste management) weighed and distributed in the formation of public policy in this area? How much are environmental regulations being harmonized in the three countries?

Location and Specialization of Production

The recession of the early 1980s saw aggressive competition among local governments for jobs and investment, and this trend was repeated in the early 1990s. Policymakers sought to entice corporations to provide the economic development benefits that public investment in infrastructure and training alone had often failed to engender. Yet what accounts for the geographic distribution of manufacturing capacity within the North American auto industry and among the three countries? How important are various factors (e.g., tax rates and/or incentives, labor costs and/or availability, proximity to customers or suppliers) in the investment decisions of companies in this sector? Do national borders matter in the decision to award work to a particular plant?

The integration of the industry and its post-NAFTA rationalization should allow for certain areas to become loci of comparative advantage. In his chapter, Doh argues that there is preliminary evidence that such specialization may be taking place as measured by the composition of trade in automotive products among the NAFTA countries. To what extent is specialization in the design, engineering, production, and marketing of parts and finished vehicles evident to date among the three countries? How do company policies and trade policies interact in this area?

NAFTA Operation

As with any complex agreement, important questions remain about how well certain provisions are working. These may lead to improvements in the present arrangement or to lessons for future negotiators.

How is the NAFTA rule of origin working in the auto industry? What problems, if any, have emerged in the calculation and verification of origin? What measurable effect has the rule of origin had on investment and sourcing decisions in this sector (considering in particular the non-North American assemblers and suppliers)? What lessons can be drawn from the NAFTA rule of origin that can benefit negotiators working toward NAFTA expansion and/or other trade agreements?

Do delays at the border due to customs procedures have a significant impact, given just-in-time inventory management? In 1997, the U.S. Congress mandated that the Immigration and Naturalization Service implement a system to document the entry of individuals into the United States, raising fears of long delays at the border. How might this affect logistics within the industry? Does the potential for border delays affect the decision to source components from facilities on the opposite side of the border?

How have the trade dispute resolution mechanisms of CUFTA and NAFTA worked on auto industry-related cases? Does NAFTA dispute resolution provide enough options to resolve most industry concerns?

Where Do We Go from Here?

The long list of questions that we have raised in this concluding chapter suggest to us that the North American auto industry, so ubiquitous in our daily lives as Americans, Canadians, and Mexicans, holds the key to understanding how NAFTA is working and what sort of economy we are building together as a legacy for future generations. As such, it deserves far more attention from the scholarly community than it has received over the years. What we might learn from serious study of the North

American auto industry experience under NAFTA will matter not just to corporate decisionmakers, industry workers, and policymakers in the United States, Canada, and Mexico, but more importantly to those who will live in the North America of the next millennium.

Note

1. The United Nations Economic Commission for Europe (UN-ECE) established Working Party 29 as the principal working party on road transport and the construction of vehicles within a broad initiative to develop common technical standards in a wide range of sectors. UN-ECE Working Party 29 standards took effect for European motor vehicles in 1995.

Index

About the Editors and Contributors

Jonathan P. Doh is the academic director of the International Business and Trade Semester at The American University. He is also an adjunct professor at the Walsh School of Foreign Service at Georgetown University, an adjunct fellow at the Center for Strategic and International Studies, and a consultant to government and business on trade, investment, and privatization. Previously, he was a trade official with the U.S. government, serving as director of the Canada Trade Policy Division and, later, as director of the NAFTA Affairs Division, both at the U.S. Department of Commerce.

John Holmes is professor of geography and head of the department of geography at Queen's University in Kingston, Ontario. He is also a faculty associate at the university's School of Industrial Relations. His teaching and research center on the geographical aspects of contemporary economic and social change in North America. The author of numerous journal articles and chapters on the restructuring of the automobile industry, he recently has also written on the pulp and paper industry. Dr. Holmes received his Ph.D. in geography at Ohio State University.

John Kirton is associate professor of political science, research associate of the Center for International Studies, and director of the G-8 Research Group and the Trade, Environment, and Competitiveness Program at the University of Toronto. Dr. Kirton has served as chair of the North American Environmental Standards Working Group, as team leader of the Commission on Environmental Cooperation's Project on NAFTA's Environmental Effects, and as a member of the Canadian government's International Trade Advisory Committee and of the Foreign Policy Committee of the National Roundtable on the Environment and the Economy. He received his Ph.D. from The Johns Hopkins University School of Advanced International Studies and his

M.A. from the School of International Affairs at Carleton University. He is co-author of *Environmental Regulations and Corporate Competitiveness: A NAFTA Perspective* (Oxford University Press, forthcoming 1999).

Pradeep Kumar is professor of industrial relations at Queen's University, Kingston, Ontario. He received his M.A. and Ph.D. in economics from Queen's University and is author of a number of books and articles on unions and collective bargaining in North America. His current research focuses on changes in labor relations human resource strategies and approaches in the Canadian automotive industry in the context of NAFTA and the North American economic integration.

Rogelio Ramírez de la O is a Mexican economist with a Ph.D. in economics from Cambridge University and a bachelor's degree, also in economics, from the National Autonomous University of Mexico. He is president of Ecanal S.A. in Mexico City, where he is frequently consulted by multinational firms with operations in Mexico on economic prospects and risks as well as corporate strategies. He is also an adviser to Citibank's Latin American Libra2000 Fund, a member of the supervisory board of ABN-AMRO Bank Mexico, and a director of Cerveceria Modelo SA de CV. He works closely with the senior management of several multinational firms and is a regular speaker at international economic conferences.

Christopher Sands is a fellow in the Americas Program at the Center for Strategic and International Studies and director of the program's Canada Project. He served as project coordinator for the present study of the North American auto industry. He is the chairman of the CSIS Canada Briefing series. He also co-chairs the CSIS North American Congressional Staff Forum and organizes meetings of the CSIS Congressional Study Group on Canada. He has lectured at Georgetown University, George Mason University, and the U.S. National Defense University. Mr. Sands received an M.A. from The Johns Hopkins University School of Advanced International Studies and a B.A. from Macalester College.

Sidney Weintraub holds the William E. Simon Chair in Political Economy at the Center for Strategic and International Studies. He is also professor emeritus at the Lyndon B. Johnson School of

Public Affairs of the University of Texas at Austin, where he has been a member of the faculty since 1976. A member of the U.S. Foreign Service from 1949 to 1975, Dr. Weintraub held the post of deputy assistant secretary of state for international finance and development from 1969 to 1974 and assistant administrator of the U.S. Agency for International Development in 1975. He was also a senior fellow at the Brookings Institution. He received his Ph.D. in economics from The American University.